Iron Cross, Iron Curtain, Iron Will

Christopher J. Falvai

Iron Cross, Iron Curtain, Iron Will.

Copyright © 2012 Christopher J. Falvai

All rights reserved. Published in the United States of America. No part of this book may be used or reproduced in any manner whatsoever without written permission except in the case of brief quotations embodied in critical articles and reviews.

ISBN: 1479295388
ISBN-13: 978-1479295388

DEDICATION

For dad, who we lost Father's Day, 2012.

Table of Contents

1. Life among the Cross 1
2. Desperation 26
3. Andreas and Frances 80
4. The Curtain Draws 105
5. Transition 117
6. Passage 134
7. Descent 152
8. Away 174
9. Risks 218
10. The Will 253

PREFACE

Iron Cross, Iron Curtain, Iron Will is my first novel. Having wished to chronicle my father's early years, I finally began the journey of penning his experiences some four years before publication. As a result of the research for the book's background, not only did I learn a lot about my father, his family and their past, but of the politics, geography, and peoples of the region as well.

For years people had urged my father to put his story to the written word, but he just never seemed to find the time. Given his incredible journey through the turmoil of mid-twentieth century eastern Europe, and his eventual flight to the United States, I decided to chronicle his early life as my first novel. His experiences certainly provided ample material to weave an amazing story.

The story was born from a combination of a recording my father made late in life that described his tumultuous early days, together with anecdotes and experiences not included in the recording. These were related to me as I was growing up, mostly when we spent long periods of time together working on home improvement projects.

The appendices contain some interesting background about Hungary and Miklós' family meant to enhance the reader's experience.

1 Life among the Cross

Miklós stared down at the ball, concentrating. "Gyerünk, rúgja!" "*Come on, kick!*" yelled Tibi as he guarded the makeshift goal. It was Miklós' last shot before having to trade positions with his cousin, who, being two years older, usually bested him. Taking two steps in he kicked without looking up, sailing the ball through. "Igen!" "*Yes!*" Miklós shouted, throwing his hands in the air. His elation, however, was short lived, realizing Tibi had made no effort to defend, instead gazing skyward past him. The faint drone of aircraft engines caused Miklós' to turn in the direction of his cousin's gaze. Recognizing the cross-shaped silhouettes, Tibi cried out "They're heading our way" as he scampered across the road into the fallow wheat field, Miklós quickly following. Down the slope they dashed to the rock outcrop they had played on so many times, their favorite vantage point, the boys climbing it more often of late, the aerial missions occurring with greater frequency.

Reaching the base they paused to catch their breath, labored from the run across the field. Their attention turned toward the din filling the air, the hum of engines having silenced summer's familiar birdsong, its absence now more obvious than its presence had been. The planes would pass close this time. Miklós and Tibi exchanged glances then turned to scramble up the rocks. At the crown lay an area rimmed with boulders. There they would huddle and watch, leaning forward against a granite face just low enough to peer over, craning their necks to catch a glimpse.

Russian bombers were approaching from the east. What appeared to be a dozen multi-engine aircraft were visible, flying lower than usual. Miklós noticed more engines buzzing from the southwest. Coming in fast were German interceptors. Pointing, he shouted "Figyusz, figyusz!" "*Look, look!*" Suddenly more aircraft, until then unseen, came screaming from above the bombers on an intercept course, Russian fighter escorts prowling from overhead. The German pilots split left and right into two groups. The escorts gave chase but seemed outnumbered. A mixture of excitement and fear gripped the boys as the blare of engines hammered in their ears. They had witnessed dogfights before, but none this close.

The German interceptors that had broken left were now banking hard right to take the bombers head on. The second group tried drawing off the escorts by diving steeply and then attacking from below. The rapport of automatic gun fire rang out, puffs of smoke streaming behind the planes. Awestruck, the boys continued watching the scene unfold. One bomber banked into a dive, breaking formation. The whine of the engines grew louder and higher as the pilot pitched the plane forward. A German fighter had taken up pursuit, machine guns blazing. Bullets streamed into the ground, spurts of dust rising from the impacts, the thump-thump-thump of rounds heard penetrating the earth. Moments later, smoke began billowing from one of the bomber's engines.

From seemingly out of nowhere a Russian fighter took chase causing the German interceptor to break pursuit and pull straight up. The escort attempted to follow but overshot, breaking right, passing low over town. The bomber, still accelerating in its dive, began leveling out. No more than a hundred feet off the ground it appeared to be heading straight for the boys. "Levesz!", "*Get down!*" yelled Tibi. They slid to the ground, backs to the boulder, watching the bomber whiz overhead. The smell of burning oil filled the air as smoke from the damaged engine drifted down over them. Barely clearing the trees the plane began climbing again, sputtering under the strain of the crippled motor. Banking left it turned back east, unable to complete its mission. The remaining aircraft continued battling toward the west.

For a few minutes they sat speechless, glancing back and forth between each other and the direction they last saw the crippled bomber. No sound of a crash, no column of smoke, appearing as though the crew may live to fly another day. Soon the planes faded from sight, their existence revealed by only an ebbing hum in the distance.

From up the slope, in the direction the boys had come,

voices were heard near the village edge. People had emerged from hiding, discussing the scene that had just unfolded, searching for loved ones, friends and neighbors. A woman's voice called "Miklós, Miklós, where are you!?" The boys looked at each other, realizing they had better head back. Scrambling down the rocks they went running back through the field. Half way across Miklós began yelling to his mother "Itt én vagyok mama." "*Mama, I'm here*. Here we come!" "Who's with you?" she yelled, descending the slope toward them. "Én vagyok az" "*It's me*" responded Tibi, waving. Miklós' mother, Margit, turned and called back up the hill "Klara, Tibi's here. He's with Miklós." Tibi's mother Klara, Margit's sister in law, came quickly striding down the hill, joining Margit.

Standing there, hair splayed across their faces, the women held their billowing skirts in the late summer breeze. Upon reaching their mothers the boys hugged them tight about the waist, talking excitedly about what had just transpired. They were, however, admonished for leaving the safety of the village. "You two need to run home, not away! We were worried sick not knowing where you were. It's dangerous!" Of course, that was their way of thinking. If a plane crashed into the village, how much safer was it really than the shelter of the rocks? Miklós looked up at his mother. "I'm sorry mama." "Alright Miklós" she responded looking into his eyes, brushing her hand through his hair as he clung to her. "Now hurry home to the coop and gather all the eggs you can find" Margit instructed. "It's almost lunch. And wash up before you come in the house!" "Alright, but can Tibi come over? We want to talk about the airplanes!" Tilting her head sideways

Margit frowned at Klara in a gesture of permission. Klara couldn't help but return the smile and begrudgingly nod approval. "Yes, you crazy boys have a lot to chat about I'm sure. And Tibi, you help Miklós gather eggs and then wash up too. When you're done you need to come home and finish your chores – and mind your manners!"

The cousins took off running toward the village, holding their arms straight out, making engine sounds, mimicking airplanes, still excited over the aerial duel. Their mothers, however, did not share in their sons' naïve enthusiasm. This conflict had dragged on for years; governments shifting policies and alliances, young men forced into military conscriptions. Residing in a rural village, they were mostly detached from the political struggles. What lay ahead was anyone's guess. Everyone just wanted the war over, sharing a common desire to get back to the way things had been.

As the boys darted up the hill in mock flight Miklós noticed something shiny, stopping to pick it up. He turned it over in his hands then held it up against the sky. A shell casing from a large caliber machine gun, discharged during the dogfight. "Hey Tibi, look what I found" yelled Miklós, running to catch up. Tibi, oblivious to the fact Miklós was no longer right behind him continued zigzagging up the hill with his arms outstretched imitating an airplane.

It was late summer, 1944.

Spending a great deal of time in each other's company the cousins had developed a close bond, becoming more like playmates. Klara was married to Pál,

Margit's brother, and Tibi, like Miklós, was an only child.

After gathering eggs from the chicken coop the boys washed up at the well pump and headed to the house. Miklós recalled leaving his ball out front, next to the road. "Tibi, let's get my ball first." His cousin brought it through the gate as Miklós carried the basket of eggs. Climbing the porch steps the boys lowered their voices, a practice they had become accustomed to of late. Just then two German officers residing in the house stepped out the front door dressed in field uniforms, involved in conversation. The boys recognized a few words, having recently been required to learn some German as a result of the occupation, a mandatory part of the school's curriculum that previous academic year. Turning toward the steps the officers came upon the boys. "Ah Miklós, was ist das haben Sie es in den Warenkorb legen?" "*What is it you have there in the basket?*" the ranking officer questioned, smiling. "Tojás", "*Eggs*", Miklós responded in Hungarian, then quickly corrected himself, responding "Eier" in German. "Ah, sehr gut. Genießen Sie Ihre Mittagspause. Und speichern Sie einige Eier für uns, ja?!" "*Ah, very good. Enjoy your lunch. And save some eggs for us, will you?!*" The men chuckled and went toward the road. The boys turned to watch them walk out the front gate, then looked at each other and shrugged neither really understanding most of what the man had said.

Rumbling down the dirt road, trailing dust, were a staff car and halftrack to meet the officers. The halftrack carried a dozen German regulars seated in back, with a large caliber machine gun mounted over the cab attended by another. The vehicles were painted camouflage with large crosses emblazoned across the hood and doors. The boys watched as the officers met the approaching vehicles then turned to run up the remaining steps and in through the open door. Margit was in the kitchen and heard the clop-clop of their running footsteps on the wooden floor. "Légy óvatos minden fiú!" "*Careful, boys!* If you fall with those eggs you'll have a long wait until supper." They were too young to appreciate their good fortune at having eggs, the war making them an otherwise scarce commodity.

Food shortages occurred with regularity, especially during winter. Early on the Hungarian army required quotas from farming villages to feed its soldiers. With the occupation, production had shifted to the German military. Miklós' family had a large garden, chickens, and a few goats, but still had to purchase other essentials in the market when available. Even the market had become relatively sparse of late.

Early in the conflict the Hungarian government participated in on-again, off-again collaboration with Berlin as part of an agreement to regain territory ceded after World War I, attempting to benefit from membership in the Axis Powers. Later, as Russia's counter offensive began to successfully repel the *Wehrmacht*, the administration secretly attempted to enter an armistice with the Allies, only to have the plan divulged. Germany subsequently forced its occupation on Hungary as its premier fled the country. A puppet government was seated, and with consent of German authority the Arrow Cross (a national socialist party modeled after the German Nazi party) eventually seized control of the capitol.

As a result, villagers where German soldiers were stationed often had their homes occupied as shared living quarters. Miklós' family lived in a relatively comfortable home on the outskirts of town, having a small vineyard, a barn, and a cellar. A few officers had chosen to take up quarters there. Miklós and his parents were forced to live in one room, with the officers occupying the rest. The family was allowed to come and go freely during daylight hours and use the kitchen and dining area as needed, but for the most part remained confined to one bedroom when officers were present. Nighttime curfews were sometimes imposed when the military felt it necessary.

The staff car and half-track rumbled away, their sounds soon fading into the distance. Miklós and Tibi began setting the table for lunch. With the officers absent they relaxed, speaking openly. "Someday I'm going to fly airplanes!" exclaimed Miklós, innocently admiring the objects sparking his fascination, not fully appreciating their destructive purpose. "I'll fly over mountains and across the ocean. I could take you with me Mama. Wouldn't that be fun?" "Oh, Miklós, that would be quite the adventure" she responded smiling. Tibi chimed in "And I'll be your copilot. That way we can go as long as we want. We can take turns flying and taking naps so that we never have to stop." Margit smiled, rolling her eyes and shaking her head. She began making lunch for the three of them and had already started dinner for that night, having to cook for the soldiers as well. They would bring her food to prepare, occasionally providing an opportunity to put some leftovers aside for the family.

They sat down to a lunch of freshly gathered eggs - scrambled - with wild mushrooms picked from the forest and sautéed in animal fat (no butter - or cow's milk - available lately), dark bread, and some figs from their tree in the yard. After eating the boys helped Margit clear the table. "Miklós" his mother said "you need to finish your chores now. Then you can go and play. And if any more planes come around, you come inside. You hear?" Miklós responded with a less than enthusiastic "Igen mama", "*Yes mama*". His cousin said "I need to go finish my chores too before my mama comes looking for me." Out the door the boys went, Tibi waving bye to Miklós as he ran toward home.

Daily chores included cleaning the barn and the chicken coop, feeding and watering the goats, pumping water for household use, and bringing firewood or coal in the house for the stove and fireplace. A lot to do for a boy his age, but with his father away so much his mother couldn't do it all.

József, worked for the local coal mining operation south of the village. This mine was subterranean, not an open pit. A foreman for the machine shop, he was responsible for moving machinery in need of repair out of the mine, and replacements back in. There in the shop machinists would restore equipment, build various apparatus as needed, and perform regular maintenance.

Coal was a vital ingredient in fueling the war effort, with power plants and steam locomotives the major consumers. However, with so many men of age conscripted into service, the labor pool had become insufficient to keep the operation running smoothly.

Manufacturing of replacement equipment had all but ceased with industrial resources shifted to the manufacture of military hardware. As a result József put in long hours, often not making it home in the evening, sleeping on a cot in his office. Just as well, since it was a hassle explaining his situation when stopped by a German patrol during curfew.

Finishing his chores, Miklós went inside to wash up. Passing the officer's bedroom he took notice of the open door, usually locked in their absence. Approaching, he peered through the doorway, examining the room's contents. Something caught his eye. A model airplane reminiscent of those involved in the morning's dogfight sat on the desk. Curiosity getting the best of him he entered, walking over to it slowly, desiring a closer look. It was beautiful, made to scale and very detailed, a Messerschmitt Me109, the make and model lost on Miklós. He stared at it in admiration, the memory of the skirmish still fresh in his mind. He reached out to touch the propeller, and to his surprise it spun! Miklós had never seen anything like it, a miniature produced with such detail.

"He! Was machst du da?!" a man's voice boomed from behind. "*Hey! What are you doing there?!*" Miklós, so startled, almost wet himself. He stepped back, turning toward the voice, placing his hands behind his back. The commanding officer had returned, staring at Miklós from the bedroom doorway. Turning his gaze to the plane, and then back to the officer, Miklós shook his head nervously, trying to communicate he had not meant any harm. The officer, interpreting the gesture, realized that the boy had merely been admiring the model. He grinned and stepped toward Miklós. "I see you like airplanes. It was quite a show today, wasn't it?" Miklós stared up into the man's face, frightened, grasping very little of what he said. "I have a son about your age back home" the officer continued wistfully. "You remind me of him. I miss him and his mother very much, having been away a while now." He looked down at Miklós for a moment and sighed. "Wir sind nicht alle schlecht, Sie wissen." "*We're not all bad, you know.* Many of us did not want this war. But I took an oath to my country, for better or for worse." The officer seemed to be making confession with a six year old, feeling a need to get things off his chest, as though the admission might somehow lift his burden. He picked up the model, about a foot long, turning it in his hands to examine its detail, and then offered it to Miklós. "Here, take it. It's yours" he said, holding it in his outstretched hand. Miklós was unsure of the gesture. "Go on, take it. I'm offering it to you. It's yours!" Miklós reached out tentatively then grasped it gingerly. The officer nodded in encouragement upon seeing Miklós hesitation. The boy stared at it in his hands, then looked up into the man's eyes and smiled, the officer smiling back. "Danke, danke!" "*Thank you, thank you!*" This much Miklós knew how to say. "Now go on" the officer said gesturing toward the door with a stern look. "And don't let me catch you in here again!" Miklós exited the room smiling, admiring what was now his most treasured possession. The officer grabbed some papers and a map off the desk, locked the door, and quickly stepped to his waiting vehicle.

After washing up Miklós went to sit on the porch. He

looked into the sky daydreaming about the great flying machines, holding his model airplane up toward the setting sun, silhouetted against the evening sky. Today's flyover had captured his imagination more than ever. That was the closest he had ever been to actual aircraft. He recalled feeling the rumble of motors in his chest as the wounded bomber passed overhead, the experience having been the most intense of his young life.

Glimpsing something from the corner of his eye he turned to see a trail of dust coming down the road. When closer, he could see it was a truck. Miklós stood and walked to the gate. The truck slowed and then stopped in front of the house. The passenger door opened and a man stepped down from the cab. "Papa" yelled Miklós as he ran to his father. He hadn't been home in days, longer than usual. József said something to the driver, closed the door, and waved. The driver put the truck in gear and continued on, waving back. Normally that time of year, with the mild weather, József would have preferred to commute on his motorcycle. It was rare to even ride the old two-stroke around the neighborhood since the imposition of gasoline and oil rationing. When Miklós reached his father he grabbed him in a big hug, receiving one back equally as enthusiastic. "Miklós, such a greeting! It's good to be home finally." József lifted Miklós into his arms, hugged him again then placed him up on his shoulders, carrying him to the front porch. All the while Miklós giggled and laughed. "Mama, mama. Papa's home!" Miklós yelled toward the house. Margit came out onto the porch smiling. A moment later she placed her hand to her mouth, a sudden look of concern showing on her face.

Miklós' father put him down and stepped onto the porch to greet her. She could tell by looking at him that something dreadful must have happened at the mine, for József never came home looking this way, disheveled and still fairly coated in coal dust, save for his face and hands. Recognizing her distraught look he began recounting the unfortunate events.

"There was a cave-in the day before yesterday. Two men, István and János, were trapped. You know István and his wife from church. It took us a while to reach them. We lost János. He was buried in the cave-in and didn't make it. We were unsure of István until reaching him this afternoon. He's alive, but not doing well at the moment. Trapped in an air pocket, he was unconscious when the men found him. We managed to revive him, but after a couple of days without food or water, and low on air, he's hurting. After cleaning up I need to go inform his family." István's family resided close by in the same village. Margit hugged him and they walked inside arm in arm. Miklós' father felt fortunate not having to deliver the dreadful news to the family of the deceased. That was the duty of the mine superintendent, who normally would have broken the news to István's family as well, but József had volunteered instead, being a friend of the family (István is Hungarian for Steven or Stephen).

Once inside Margit instructed "Miklós bring in a couple more arm loads of firewood and some water, please. We need to make your father a warm bath." It was fortunate timing the officers were away, providing an opportunity for some family time. Often the patrols lasted overnight. Perhaps tonight was one of those nights. It would be nice to have the home to themselves, given what József had been through.

After bathing and then enjoying the meal Margit had prepared, József rose from the table to report the news. It would likely be several days before István recovered sufficiently to leave the mine's infirmary. Besides, István was better off remaining to recuperate since he would get paid while there, for up to a week, as per the mine's policy regarding a worker severely injured on the job. Recuperating at home would be considered unpaid leave. Elena would be unaware of the situation, for lately it was not at all unusual for the men to be away at the mine for days at a time. Telephones were practically nonexistent. József thought it best to break the news that night. She needed to know what had happened to her husband.

József walked toward the door, grabbing his hat off the hook. Miklós, following, said "Papa, I want to go with you." József paused for a moment, contemplating his son's request. "All right, but it may be sad with lots of crying." Miklós nodded. József said "Come, take my hand" and they set off to see Elena, her home about a kilometer's walk toward the center of town.

* * *

Arriving at the home of István and Elena, the pair encountered off-duty German regulars sitting on the front porch in the dark smoking cigarettes and drinking wine. As József and Miklós approached a voice called out in German "Wer ist es?" "*Who's there?*" Understanding the question, József stopped and replied in his best broken German "It's Falvai József and my son Miklós. I bring news regarding Elena's husband István." "What sort of news?" responded another. József approached them to keep his message from being overheard by anyone else. "There's been an accident at the mine, a cave-in. István is hurt and in the infirmary. I've come to tell Elena." The soldier responded in broken Hungarian "Igen, igen." "*Yes, yes.*" "Tell her. Inside she is." The two stepped onto the porch and József removed his hat, nodding in greeting toward the men. Miklós held his father's hand, staring quietly at the soldiers as the pair walked into the house.

Inside, Elena was drying and putting away the dinner dishes by lantern light. "Elena" József called out. "It's József and Miklós." "Oh! Hello. I'm in the kitchen. Are you hungry?" The two walked back joining her. The children, ages three and five, were already upstairs getting ready for bed. "No, we just ate supper ourselves" responded József. "Well I'm glad *you* got to come home for a nice meal with the family" she said chuckling, believing her husband hadn't come home because he was working an extra shift. She turned from the cupboards to face them. József's somber expression revealed this was no social call. She began shaking her head, "No, no!" and fearing the worst was on the verge of tears when József said "Elena, wait. István's been hurt. We had a cave-in but he's alive and seems fine." She broke down anyway, partly from fear, but mostly from relief at the news. "Miklós bring her a chair" he said pointing. Turning back to her "Elena, he's going to be all right. He was fortunate. But, we lost János. He was deeper in and didn't make it." Miklós brought the chair to Elena, and József helped her into it, continuing "When the cave-in happened we lost power to the tunnel they were in. It was completely dark and the lift wouldn't descend because of debris partially blocking the shaft. It happened during crew rotation and János and István were the only ones still in the passage, finishing up some work before the next shift came on. No one could assess the situation for a while. The dust was so heavy breathing was difficult and visibility limited. Finally, we managed to lower some men down by rope in baskets, carrying hand tools. With the ventilators inoperative they began digging in short shifts."

"Finally when they got to the main tunnel they were able to chip away enough to move some large rocks. The braver and stronger among them managed to squeeze in and creep through a small opening they had made, about 6 meters long, intersecting the main passage way. Conditions were still unstable and we feared losing some of the rescuers." József refrained from going into great detail, fearing it would only serve to upset Elena further. "They found István first – not conscious – but breathing. He was in a small chamber that had caved in on two sides, becoming trapped between."

Cave-ins are chaotic. Assessing the situation takes time, something trapped miners have little to spare. Once the mine floor became accessible preparations for a rescue began in earnest. Tools and supplies were lowered down the shaft to aid the effort. Smaller escape passages that miners could crawl through, in the event of a main shaft or tunnel cave in, were present at strategic points throughout the mine as a means of escape. Unfortunately, the event had left the men stranded between segments, their survival dependent on the other miners digging to them.

Before the rescuers edged into the small tunnel they were excavating, ropes were tied about their waists and ankles to facilitate being pulled out in the event of further collapses. These lifelines also enabled moving tools and supplies back and forth once they broke through. Burrowing this way was dark, dangerous work, the men taking only ten minutes at a turn. A lack of operational ventilators kept the air thick with coal dust. The only light in the tight tunnel was from the miner's own helmet, and whatever could be shone from behind by lanterns. Using small shovels and pick-axes the miners would dig as far as they could, put the loose earth into a sack tied to another rope, and then back out of the tunnel so that the debris could be removed, allowing the next man to continue. Ever so often a small cave in occurred, usually minor, but sometimes sufficient to bury a man and warrant pulling him out by his lifeline. Once extricated, the tunnel would be cleared and work continued. Anyone getting covered was rinsed and sent topside to recuperate.

As someone was digging others hastily nailed together wooden bracing to help shore up the walls and ceiling of the freshly dug sections. As each man went in someone else would crawl behind to set some bracing. Crude and questionable in effectiveness, it was all that could be done under the circumstances. Everyone worked with both a sense of urgency and empathy, each feeling that if it was one of them trapped on the other side they could count on their comrades for rescue.

Finally, someone broke through into a small pocket, locating István. Still breathing, the miner called down the tunnel for assistance. Immediately the next in line fastened ropes about his body and wriggled through with water and a large burlap sack. Wrapping István in the burlap they tied one of the ropes to István's ankles and another around his wrists. The men at the opening pulled István through feet first. After being unwrapped he was rushed up the shaft. The rope removed from his ankles was then tied through some food and water containers, with the untied end remaining at the opening of the small passage. The rope from István's wrists was used by rescuers at the other end of the tunnel to pull supplies through so the search for János could continue. Exiting the tunnel would require backing out in the event of collapse. If need be it was safer and easier to be pulled out feet first.

József continued with his story: "Finally, toward the end of the day the tunnel was cleared enough to bring in some larger equipment and we started making real progress. When we found János he had been buried alive. He probably died instantly. Our superintendent was going to inform his family tonight of their loss."

"István should recover. He's in the infirmary, and will be paid while there. Besides, I don't think his injuries would permit moving him. You're welcome to ride to the mine with us tomorrow morning if you wish. I know you're anxious to see him now, tonight, but that won't be possible. The children can stay with Margit while

you're gone. We'll return by evening tomorrow."
József sat looking at Elena for a while, wondering if she was going to say anything. Miklós had been sitting on the floor in the living area cross-legged, listening to the story. Elena was wiping away tears with József's handkerchief. Finally, through her crying she said "Thank you for coming József. I think I will take you up on the offer. If I try to get my mother to watch the children, or István's for that matter, they'll want to come along as well. It would be better if we kept this to ourselves for a day or two. At least until I can see him for myself. Then I'll let everyone know how he is. I don't think I'll even tell the children until I get back." József agreed. "That would be wise, Elena. I don't think any of the other men will tell anyone except their wives. That should keep it secret at least until morning. Bring the children so we can take you in the truck from my house without anyone noticing." Elena nodded. "I will József. And thank you again." József walked over to Miklós and took his hand. "Come on, Miklós. Let's go home. It's getting to be bed time. Good night Elena." They all hugged, and with that the two walked home.

As Miklós walked with his father, he began wondering what it was like to work in the mines. It had to be a dreadful place; dark, dusty, and loud. His father lit one of his hand-rolled cigarettes along the way, still holding Miklós' hand, but alone in his thoughts. They walked together in silence looking at the stars, listening to the crickets. As they got to their front porch József said "Miklós sit here on the step with me. I need to talk to you." József lit another cigarette and continued "I may not be around much for a while. They want us to increase production at the mine. You're going to have to take on more responsibility around here. Be the man of the house when I'm away." Miklós tried to absorb his father's words, understanding the gist of the message. Suddenly it occurred to him "Papa, does that mean I get to chop firewood?" With a chuckle and a smile József said "I suppose it might. We just need to make sure you don't chop your foot off. Your mother would be awfully upset with the both of us, especially me!" Miklós smiled, though not finding the humor in chopping one's foot off. "I won't Papa. I'm big now. I can do it." "Well then, I'll have to find the axe that fits you best. Remind me to get one from the barn in the morning. We'll have you practice supervised until you can do it on your own. Come on, let's go in. Mama is probably wondering if we fell in the well or something."

* * *

In the morning József went to the barn as promised. He chose the smallest axe he could find and one of his sharpening stones, along with a small and a medium size wedge. József had shown Miklós how to sharpen a blade on previous occasions. He set the items inside the barn door and returned to the house.

Miklós was eating breakfast when his father walked in. The sun was just coming up, peeking through the windows. József sat down to a breakfast of dark rye bread and goat cheese. Thankfully the officers had remained on patrol overnight, allowing for a rare evening of quality family time. "Miklós" Margit reminded him, "Elena is bringing the children over to spend the day with us, remember?" "Oh, yes" he recalled. József got up from the table and put his plate on the counter. "Well, I'm off. I'm going to meet Jani at the truck. Elena should be over with the children any time now. We'll be back to pick her up. She'll return this evening, whether or not I do. And remember, she wants this kept secret until she's ready to tell her family." He gave Margit a big hug and a couple of long kisses. József put his hat on and Miklós followed him out onto the porch. József picked him up. "Now help your mother out around here. Remember, you're the man of the house while I'm gone!" "I will" responded Miklós, giving his father a big hug around the neck. His father put him down and rustled his hair with a smile and a wink. Others were coming out of their homes as well, beginning the day's activities, whatever they might be.

Suddenly Miklós remembered the axe. He ran to the barn for a look. With the morning sun still low he carried the tool outside into the light. The sharpened edge glistened in the morning sun. Just then Miklós heard voices coming from the house. *Mrs. Elena must be here*, he thought. Tamás, her son, and Elsebeth accompanied her. Tamás and Miklós had played together at family gatherings. Returning the axe where found, he closed the barn door. Starting back toward the house he noticed a large rhinoceros beetle inching across the yard, the sort he and his friends liked to catch. Apparently it was tardy getting out of the sun this morning. These beetles were shiny, black, and about five centimeters (two inches) long, slow moving, yet strong for their size. Miklós picked it up and placed it in an empty egg basket next to the chicken coop. He wouldn't dare bring it in the house. *Mama would have a fit!*

Running to the house he heard the rumble and squeaks of a truck bouncing down the dirt road. As he rounded the corner he could see it kicking up a trail of dust. Elena walked out the front door with Margit and the children, holding their hands. She knelt down and gave each one a hug and a kiss "Now you listen to Mrs. Margit and do as she says. I want you both to be on your best behavior. I have to go visit someone today and Mr. József is kind enough to offer me a ride. I'll be back tonight." "Yes mama" the children replied. Elena gave them each another kiss on the forehead just as the truck pulled up. "Thank you so much Margit. I hope they won't be too much trouble." "Oh nonsense, Elena. Tamás has played over here with the boys all day before, and Elsebeth is a sweetheart (Thomas and Elizabeth in Western languages). Don't worry, we'll be fine, won't we kids" she said smiling. "You go on now. We'll be here when you get back." Elena walked around to the passenger side of the truck. József had already stepped out, standing in front of the flatbed waiting to help her up into the cab. Jani was driving. When the others were situated he put the truck in gear. They all waved goodbye, Margit and the children watching for a moment as the truck rolled away.

"Did you two eat breakfast yet?" asked Margit. "Yes ma'am, we did, thank you" said Tamás. "Come on Tamás, let's go play with the beetle I caught this morning" Miklós offered. "Okay" and they took off running for the backyard. "Oh Miklós, how can you play with those things. Yuck!" said Margit. "Eewww, I don't like bugs" said Elsebeth. "Good" responded Margit. "Let's go inside and do some girl stuff, yes?" Elsebeth smiled and nodded. Margit took Elsebeth's hand, leading her into the house.

Meanwhile, the boys were back at the chicken coop peering into the egg basket. *Good, the beetle was still there*. Miklós reached in to pluck it out. "Wow, that's the biggest one I've ever seen" exclaimed Tamás. "Did I ever show you my beetle pull-toys?" asked Miklós. "My dad and I made them. He showed me how he used to make them with my grandpapa when he was a boy." Tamás gave a quizzical look and asked "Pull toys?" Miklós put the beetle back in the basket. "Come on, I'll show you." He ran to the barn door with Tamás following, back to a shelf where the toys were kept. Miklós took one down that resembled a little horse drawn cart. A thin piece of wood with four empty thread spools for wheels. A piece of tin wire looped through the front served as a harness. Tamás thought it one of the best toys he had ever seen. "Wow, can you show me how to make one?" Miklós nodded "Ok, but let's see how strong the beetle is." They returned to the basket, and luckily hadn't stayed away longer, for the beetle was on the verge of escaping, just struggling over the basket's lip.

Miklós put down the toy and grabbed the insect. Taking the wire harness's leading end, which was wound into a loop, he attempted to slip the beetle through it. This beetle was bigger than the last one apparently. He adjusted the loop and tried again. This time it went over the front of beetle's body so that his front legs were sticking out. Sure enough, the beetle started crawling away with the cart. "Wow, let's see if we can load up the cart" said Tamás. He gathered up pebbles, placing them on the little cart one by one to

see how many the beetle could pull. After a couple
dozen or so, it was apparent this was one strong bug.
"I think it's stronger than an ox!" exclaimed Tamás
giggling. "And he kind of looks like one pulling that cart."
They both laughed and continued watching for a while.
Every time the beetle pulled the cart over some small
obstruction a pebble or two would roll off. After a few
more minutes Miklós detached the cart and placed the
beetle back in the basket. This time he secured the lid
to prevent the beetle from escaping. "Come on Tamás.
Let's go see if we can make a pull-toy for you."

Meanwhile, the girls gathered ingredients to bake
bread. Margit had Elsebeth standing on a wooden
chair so she could reach the butcher block counter top.
Measuring out the ingredients, she handed each one to
Elsebeth to pour into a large ceramic mixing bowl.
Elsebeth had watched her mother make bread before,
but being only three she had never been given the
opportunity to actually participate. She was thoroughly
enjoying herself, though clumsy with the utensils.
Making a little mess was part of the enjoyment. Margit
was enjoying herself as well, not having a daughter to
share this sort of experience with. Miklós had no
interest whatsoever in baking or cooking. "Uh-oh" said
Elsebeth in her little girl voice. She had stopped
cranking the flour sifter, realizing she had been missing
the bowl almost completely. Children that age tend to
focus on what their hands are doing rather than the
task they are meant to perform. Margit smiled.
"That's all right. Here use this" showing Elsebeth how
to put the flour in the bowl using a spatula to scrape it
off the counter. Eventually the "missing" ingredient
made it into the bowl. Elsebeth tried helping mix as

best she could but her little arms and hands just didn't have the strength.

Once the dough was mixed Margit showed Elsebeth how to knead, sprinkling flour onto the counter to keep the dough from sticking. Elsebeth liked this part. "It feels squishy!" They kneaded and folded until the dough was ready. "Now we need to let it rise" said Margit. "What's rise?" asked Elsebeth. "Well, the yeast will make the dough grow bigger and get tiny air bubbles in it. That's the rising part. Then it will bake bigger and fluffier, instead of flat and hard." "Oh" responded Elsebeth, not really understanding why, just thinking it some mystical process by which dough became bread. Margit placed the dough on a baking pan, loosely wrapping it with a moist cloth. "We need this to prevent it from drying out before baking" she explained. "It wouldn't bake very well left in the air." They cleaned up while waiting for the dough to rise. When finished Margit said "Let's go see what the boys are up to."

2 Desperation

Miklos was born in May of 1937, the first child of Falvai József (Joseph, pronounced Yozsef, the **zs** pronounced like the s-sound of mea**s**ure) and Falvai Margit (Margaret). In Hungarian (or Magyarok, as called in their native tongue) the surname comes first, followed by the given name. Middle names are rarely given. The people refer to themselves as Magyar. The Western translation of Miklós is Nicholas (sometimes Nickolas). He was born and raised in the village of Csékút (pronounced Chey-koot). Miklós' father, József, had taken the name of his father, Farpek József.

During the occupation families of German descent feared forced repatriation to Germany. Given their family name they faced the possibility of losing their home and life in Csékút. József's ancestors had been in Hungary for several generations, all ties to Germany having faded over time. To avoid discovery the family name was discreetly changed to Falvai, one of

Hungarian origin.

Zsvéndley Margit's family possessed two large farms on the outskirts of town. They lived a relatively good life, having productive farming land in an area considered part of the Hungarian breadbasket.

They all attended Roman Catholic Church together on Sundays, the social center of town for most residents. Margit's parents would arrive early by horse drawn cart to pick up Miklós, their little ray of sunshine, making a day of it, spending time with him and his family on Sundays. József and Margit would pick up József's parents on their way and then meet Klara, Pál, and Tibi. The boys, as close as they were, always sat next to each other during mass.

After service they would gather back at Margit and Pál's parent's house for the big Sunday meal. While the women prepared supper, the men went into the living room. There lied a large rug in the middle that Miklós liked to wrestle on. He and József would move the coffee table and have a mock wrestling match, consisting mostly of Miklós trying to knock his father over or jump on his back. Like most boys his age he could do this for hours. Margit's father would watch and chuckle, coaching Miklós on how to best his father. The three together created infectious laughter with their rolling and growling. Of course József occasionally feigned being bested, drawing giggles from Miklós and applause from grandpapa.

"Vacsora van felkészül!" "*Dinner's ready!*" came the call from the dining room. Discussions around the table were always lively, and on this particular Sunday Miklós couldn't wait to tell his grandparents about the exciting flying machine encounter he and Tibi had earlier in the week.

The boys were always seated on either side of their grandfather at the head of the table. "Grandpapa, you should have seen it. The planes came roaring out of the skies, zooming and turning. So close, we actually saw the men flying the planes through their windows!" Miklós exclaimed as he illustrated the plane's maneuvers using back and forth hand gestures. "Well, well" said grandpapa, who stopped buttering his bread to lean over to Miklós. "Did the Russians take care of those pain-in-the-ass Germans!" "Grandpapa, you shouldn't use such language around the boys!" chimed in his wife. Grandpapa often displayed his dislike for their "guests" openly. "Well, they are!" he retorted shaking his head. Their home had been passed over for occupation, their ability to attend to soldiers limited by the obligations of the farm. At liberty to speak his mind indoors, he usually did so. Miklós looked back and forth between his grandparents, giggled, and then continued his tale. "I don't know grandpapa, we didn't see. But the big plane had smoke coming out of it as it flew over us." Margit chimed in "Oh, he's been talking about this all week; can't seem to get it out of his head. The whole thing scared me half to death!" And so the afternoon went, with story telling and political discussions, continuing well into the evening. The boys kept themselves occupied while the grown ups talked, playing in the yard on a tire swing, or with toys from the large wooden chest, passed down through the generations.

Margit and József provided the wine with supper. They cultivated a small vineyard on their property, every autumn harvesting the grapes as the weather cooled. Most years the harvest was sufficient to produce a few good barrels. Everyone was partial to the reds, so that was what József concentrated on. Growing a type of red grape, the Juhfark, suited to the soil and climate of the region, the couple produced a hearty version of Egri Bikavér, or "Bull's Blood", a full-bodied red wine. Having just enough land, their fondness for both wine and gardening had led them to become amateur vintners.

Hungary contains some of the most productive farmland in Europe. The ancient volcanic soil, combined with the climate, create an ideal combination for growing crops. Cool damp falls, short yet cold winters, and hot, dry summers mix with the rich soil to produce a variety of high yield crops. Large expanses of grain, and a productive wine region, make for a rich agrarian landscape.

Pál, the local butcher, supplied the meat for Sunday meals. Almost nothing went to waste. Regular cuts along with organ meats, such as liver and tongue, were sold on their own. Lower quality cuts and fat were ground up for things like sausage. Bone and hoof were used for gelatin or glue. Blood was cooked into the sausage or used for sauces and gravies. Through the years Tibi and Miklós had helped Pál by performing age appropriate tasks. Growing up around the shop the boys were accustomed to handling animal parts and blood in relation to livestock slaughter and butchering. They sometimes competed for the calf brains at Sunday meals.

The adults enjoyed finishing the meal with a nightcap. The drink of choice was Tokaji-Aszú, or just simply Tokaji. Tokaji is considered one of the original whites, a dessert wine, fermented long before wines were ever produced in Western Europe. The botrytised (aszú) grapes are harvested late in the season to encourage the "noble rot", enhancing the sweetness desired for dessert wines. The process occurs under conditions requiring a cycle of damp, misty mornings followed by warm, sunny afternoons. Hopefully one is left with shriveled, dehydrated grapes, rich in sugar. Tokaj is named for the region in which it is primarily made, around the town of Tokay, which Hungarians call *Tokaj*. It was christened the "Wine of Kings, the King of Wines" by Louis XIV of France.

After a couple of drinks the conversation often shifted to town gossip; what was going on with various families, who was expecting, who they thought would get married, and so forth. One evening the talk eventually led back to the families of the Kokhner's and Szabo's, young Jewish families from Budapest. Tibi's mother had a sister residing there, and during visits Klara and Pál had befriended the families. It was through this friendship that they had become acquaintances of the Falvai's during visits to Csékút.

* * *

During the 1930's, at the outbreak of World War II, in a pact with Germany prior to the occupation, the Hungarian government collaborated in the forced expatriation of Jewish citizens. Rumors of incidents circulated, but at the time accurate information was difficult to corroborate living in an isolated rural village.

Iron Cross, Iron Curtain, Iron Will

Having been friends for some time, the couples discussed events unfolding during visits to the village. Residents of Jewish neighborhoods in Budapest were growing increasingly nervous. The government's motives were becoming clear, with recently passed anti-Semitic laws appearing senseless and confusing. As with most of the world at the time substantive news of The Holocaust had not reached the village, but there were signs. Propaganda was intensifying, though the government had been waffling of late over their agreements with Germany, including the policies regarding Jews.

And so it happened. One spring day, while working at his tailor shop in Budapest, Jakab Szabo overheard of a sweep making its way through the city. Rumors were rampant of a mass exodus toward Yugoslavia. He waited as long as he dare, so as to not attract attention, then closed up, slipping out the back unnoticed. He hadn't really needed to wait. Families were already making there way through the streets carrying what they could, on their way to points unknown. Jakab got on his bicycle, pedaling home at a brisk pace to gather his family, dodging the ever growing pedestrian traffic as he made his way. Arriving home he hopped off his bike and ran up the steps to the landing of their home, hurrying through the door. "Helena!" yelled Jakab. "Jakab, is that you?" she called back. "Quickly, get Petronÿa ready. We must leave now!" Helena appeared from out of a bedroom doorway, staring down the hall at Jakab with a look of both confusion and fear on her face. "They are coming. We must leave" he reiterated, staring her straight in the eye. She nodded and went back into the room to fetch their daughter. They packed a few items of clothing then grabbed a couple of keepsakes and photographs, placing them in their pockets. Leaving through the back door to the small barn in their courtyard Jakab hitched their horse to the wagon.

Jakab sent Helena and Petronÿa ahead to meet at the fountain a couple of blocks away. Helena guided the cart through the alley leading to the street, heading for the rendezvous point. Once safely on their way Jakab walked out front to his bicycle. Thankfully it was still there. Given the panicked flight it was a wonder nobody had grabbed it making a hasty escape. He began pedaling toward the Kokhner's to alert them. With the streets filling up Jakab began fearing for his family's safety, worrying that travel might slow sufficiently to delay their departure. *The authorities could begin rounding people up in the streets, wanting to act quickly. If the girls get caught up in traffic they would be easily apprehended.* He shook his head trying to clear his mind. No time for such thoughts. Time to stay focused. Helena was resourceful. She would manage.

Once at the Kokhner's he hurriedly walked up the front steps, looked around, and knocked. Answering, Ilona could read the look on Jakab's face. Something was wrong. The Jewish population in this neighborhood was not as large as in Jakab's. There was not the same activity in the streets that would have otherwise alerted her. She let him in and shut the door. "They are coming" he said. "I received word at the shop as people began filling the streets. I've closed up and sent Helena and the children ahead to meet us. Hurry, we must leave, now!" "What about Mihály? He's not home yet!" she exclaimed. She couldn't leave without her husband. "There's no time. The situation is becoming chaotic. If we don't move we may miss our opportunity." She nodded in agreement, though with trepidation. "Leave him a note" Jakab told her. She seemed bewildered. Jakab grabbed her firmly by the shoulders. "Mihály will make it. I know he will." She nodded again, tears beginning to form then turned to gather the children and what ever last minute belongings they could carry. "We're meeting at the fountain before heading on to Csékút" he said, helping her pack. Just before leaving she placed a cryptic note in the foyer explaining their plan to Mihály, hopeful that he would soon follow. Taking both her children by the hand, they proceeded on foot to the meeting place.

Helena and Petronÿa arrived at the fountain within minutes. People stopped to request a ride, wondering where the girls might be headed, asking which way to go after being politely turned down. Helena felt terrible. The look of bewilderment in people's faces knotted her stomach. Women with children, their husbands not yet home, and elderly couples with no one to help them.

Helena was becoming anxious. None of them had accounted for the situation unfolding. She stood in the wagon, craning her neck over the crowd flowing through the street, looking for any sign of Jakab. With the throngs of people it was taking longer than anticipated to reach the meeting place. Finally, spotting her husband walking alongside Ilona and the children, she felt relief. *There they are. I see them*. Helena yelled "Over here, over here", waving her arms over her head.

Jakab threw his bicycle in the wagon then waited by the horse, steadying the animal should something in the crowd spook it. Helena climbed down to assist Ilona with the children. "Oh, I had no idea it was going to be like this. When Jakab came to the house there was barely anyone on the streets. Now look at it!" "Yes and its worse than you know. People are confused about where to go. It's going to get bad I have a feeling. We need to get out of here quickly!"

They loaded the children and climbed in. "Oh I pray Mihály makes it. I don't think I could go on without him." Helena looked at her with sudden realization. Having been so caught up in events it hadn't dawned on her until that moment they may have to leave someone behind.

They set forth to Csékút. It would be getting dark when they arrived, working to their advantage. Jakab put the wagon in motion. Their escape was slowed by the burgeoning crowd, restricting movement through the streets. Helena tended to the children as Ilona became preoccupied with what might become of Mihály.

* * *

Hours later, near twilight, they arrived at the outskirts of Csékút, pulling around to Klara and Pál's barn just as the family was sitting down to dinner. The couple exchanged confused expressions at the sound of horse's hoofs coming from the backyard. Pál went to the rear window and peeked through the curtains, recognizing the group at once. Opening the door he waved, letting them know he had taken note of their arrival, then hurried back to alert his family. Something was amiss for them to be there unannounced. "Jakab is here with his family. There must be trouble for them to be coming now." Klara and Tibi hurried from the table, following Pál.

"They're rounding up people in Budapest" Jakab said. "The streets filled with people trying to get out. We didn't know where else to go." "Quick, let's get the rig into the barn" Pál replied. "Klara, get everyone into the house." The women and children disappeared as the men concealed the horse and wagon.

Klara offered everyone dinner but they were far too distracted to eat. She immediately began wondering what to do. There wasn't room in their tiny three room house to take them in for long. If events were unfolding in Budapest as described the authorities would soon find their way to Csékút.

The backdoor swung open, startling Klara. "Stay put for now," Pál was saying to Jakab, "until we figure out what to do. I'll run over to Margit's to see if she and József might help." With Pál gone Klara insisted everyone eat, gathering them around the table. "Klara, we can't stay here long" Jakab said. "Someone will find out about us. It's only a matter of time. The two of you would be implicated, putting us all in jeopardy." "We'll think of something" Klara replied. "It's too dark for you to leave now, and risky to go anywhere without a plan. We have to find out where the authorities will be looking."

Pál arrived at Margit's, rapping loudly on the door. Margit answered, thinking Pál had come to borrow something. "Well hello, brother. What do I owe this visit to?" Pál slipped in and closed the door. "Sorry, it's not a social call. Jakab, Helena, and Ilona have come with the children. The authorities are rounding up Jews in Budapest. Fortunately they received word and made a quick escape, caught up in the exodus out of the city." Margit listened intently as Pál spoke, the wheels in her head beginning to turn. "Where's Mihály?" "They don't know. He was at work and they couldn't wait. They left him a note, hoping for the best."

Margit mulled the situation over. Finally, after a long pause "Pál, they can't stay with you. There's not enough room." "Well, we can't just turn them out. They have no provisions and there's no telling where it's safe." "Bring them here." "What?" Pál responded, confused. "Your place is bigger, but I don't think it would be any safer." "We'll use the attic."

Margit's home had an attic with hidden access, an open room constructed of wooden planks, lacking interior walls. There were no dormers or windows, minimizing the chance of detection. A ceiling panel, identical to the rest, concealed an opening through which a ladder was raised and lowered. This particular panel, located in a corner of the rear foyer off the kitchen, blended seamlessly with the rest, appearing indistinguishable amongst the others when in place.

Margit and Pál hastily made plans. The greatest challenge would be supplying food and water, and removing waste. Key necessities would be placed in the attic first to expedite the transition into hiding.

Smaller items were to be hoisted up with rope tied to baskets and buckets. Larger items could be brought up simply by ladder and handed through the opening.

***

Helena and her children would walk ahead first. Ilona and Petronÿa would follow, after which Jakab would come by bicycle. When Margit heard Helena coming up the porch with the children she opened the front door, greeting them as though it were any other casual encounter, masking her tension the best she could. "Come in, come in. Good to see you" she said. The children had already been coached on the plan in terms they could understand. Thankfully they did not appear the least bit out of sorts yet, the situation appearing more an adventure to them.

Once inside, Helena began recounting events to Margit. "Jakab received word at the shop and closed up early, rushing home to send us ahead before heading to Ilona's. Mihály wasn't home yet and the situation was becoming unruly, people panicking in the streets." She paused. "Oh, Margit I'm so scared. What if they find us? What would they do to you?" She was visibly shaken, almost to tears, the tension showing on her face. Margit put her arms around her and said "There, there. Don't worry. Everything is going to be fine. That's why we have the plan, to avoid complications." She had to show strength and calm despite her own anxieties. If not, the situation could quickly unravel.

Margit settled them into the kitchen. She had just finished baking bread and invited everyone to have some. It smelled delightful but Helena was too anxious, though the children gladly partook. "Oh, where is he. He should be here by now" said Helena. Time seemed to be going by faster than it actually was.

Jakab pedaled by Ilona just as she was walking up the steps. Nodding toward her, he continued past, ducking into the yard behind the house, finding Miklós sitting on the wood chopping stump. So engrossed in what he was doing he hadn't taken notice of Jakab. "Miklós you seem to be hard at work there. Has your father given you a chore?" Miklós looked up toward the voice. "Oh no, me and papa make these bug wagons. See?" He held the toy up for Jakab to see in the fading light, hands smeared with paint. "Well, that's certainly a skill every boy should learn. Hey, I'm putting my bicycle in the barn then going in the house. See you inside?" Miklós smiled and nodded, returning his attention to the toy. Jakab grabbed the ladder from the barn on his way out, carrying it to the back door.

Margit answered the knock "Who is it?" "It's Jakab." Margit opened the door and Jakab brought the ladder into the kitchen. Everyone had gathered there to occupy the children while the adults discussed the matter at hand. Jakab mentioned "Miklós is still outside. Should we have him come in?" Margit agreed that would be wise in case somebody happened by and struck up a conversation with him. As innocently as it might come about, best not to tempt fate. She went to the back door and called for him. "Miklós please put away whatever you are doing and bring me some firewood. I need to start preparing dinner. "Igen, mama" "*Yes, mother.*"

* * *

That morning Ilona's husband, Mihály, had been going about his job at the saw mill on the Danube, just outside Budapest. The river was utilized for transporting timbers after harvest, and its current harnessed to power the mill's machinery. On a break, while waiting for replacement of a machine belt, Mihály stepped to an open window and lit a cigarette. Taking a drag he spotted two military trucks pull up, blocking the mill's entrance. A couple dozen soldiers climbed out the back, the drivers remaining at the wheel. What appeared to be an officer walked over to the guardhouse and went in. A moment later he exited with the guard, pointing towards the mill. The officer walked back to his vehicle as the gate was opened. The trucks drove through, most of the soldiers following, a few remaining to man the entrance.

Mihály's heart skipped a beat, suspecting what the military presence meant. He flicked his cigarette out the second floor window and dashed for the stairway. Running outside he hid behind some bushes, wondering if he could make a break for it. *They're all trapped* he thought to himself, Jewish coworkers and friends unaware of events unfolding outside. A feeling of guilt washed over him for not getting warning out, but would have been trapped himself. With soldiers already sweeping the grounds he was fortunate to have gone unnoticed. At each doorway a sentry was posted while others went in. Mihály watched from his concealment as a friend came running out the same door he had. Finding himself staring down the barrel of a rifle he raised his hands. The soldier gestured for the man to get up against the wall. Soon others were rounded up in the same manner, frisked, and marched to the trucks, hands on their heads. Mihály could not tell if anyone was still inside looking for him, deciding to sit tight for the time being.

Minutes later the remaining soldiers departed. With no one looking Mihály ducked and ran off through a stand of trees. After a quarter mile or so he emerged onto a road that passed near the mill entrance. Walking briskly, he kept watch for patrols, a couple of kilometers later coming upon the local market. Needing to get home quickly and warn the others he spied a bike leaning against a light post. Mihály had never stolen anything in his life, but this was an extraordinary circumstance. Seeing no one around he grabbed the handlebar and hopped on, pedaling away at a rapid pace should the owner spot him before he was out of sight.

Coasting up to his row home the street was quiet. Climbing the steps he noticed the living room curtains partially drawn. Being that the sun was still out *that's a signal* he thought. His heart sank and the adrenaline started pumping, his mind racing now. He needed to get inside and make sure. He turned around to see if anyone was watching. The street was empty except for a couple of small groups in the distance. They seemed to be looking in his direction, talking amongst them selves. He resisted the urge to run up the remaining steps. His hands began to tremble. Fumbling with his keys trying to unlock the door he dropped them, the sound causing doves to flutter up and away. Startled, he gasped, darting his head around. *All right, Mihály* he thought to himself. *Just calm down*. He managed to unlock the door and go inside.

Ilona's note was lying on the foyer table. "*We've already left for the visit to our friends out of town. See you there! Love, Ilona.*" After reading he dropped it, rubbing his face to compose himself. Walking through the house he grabbed a few keepsakes. He was scared and angry, his mind racing. *Is everyone on the way?* He wondered. *Surely they must be. Jakab works nearby, and somebody must have come to warn Ilona.* She rarely left the house when Mihály wasn't around. Stepping into the living room he plopped into his favorite chair, something he normally wouldn't do still coated in remnants of the mill. He looked around slowly, taking in everything they had worked for and cherished. He wondered if he would ever see his home again. *Would the nightmare just beginning ever end? Would it be over before his home was in ruin? If and when he could ever return.* His daughter was too young to ever have memories of this place. *What would her first memories be? Living on the run? Surely it would be over soon, wouldn't it?* He wanted to cry, beginning to drift off in thought. The clop-clop of a horse-drawn cart outside shook his mind from its wandering state. Standing, he walked to the back room, washed up, and put on a change of clothes. Finished, he went to the front window, peering out from the shadows. *Good. No one is around.* Those on the street earlier were gone. Casually stepping out he locked the front door and got back on the bike, taking his last ride resembling anything leisurely for a while. His trek would last hours. As he rounded the corner onto the next avenue a half dozen military trucks pulled onto the street behind him, stopping at various points to disperse troops. His neighborhood's sweep was beginning. Mihály continued on, unaware how timely his departure had been.

He headed for the nearby rail yard, travel to Csékút impractical by bicycle. Catching a westbound freight train he would become a stowaway, running alongside and hopping aboard unnoticed. Having made the trip by rail several times he was familiar with the stops and switches. Casually pedaling past the depot he ducked between some stationary freight cars, spying a train being loaded and prepared for departure. Abandoning the bike, he crawled onto a track parallel to the train he intended to board, hiding under a freight car. Ten minutes later the locomotive hissed, blew its horn, and slowly began moving. He peeked out from under his hiding place, and seeing nobody, edged out and started jogging alongside. Spotting a freight car with its door open he hopped in. His first stop would require switching trains for Csékút. In the days that followed, unbeknownst to him, this very freight car would be used to transport others to Poland, rounded up and packed in on their way to Hitler's *final solution*.

* * *

Those gathered in Csékút prepared to move into the attic since there was no way of knowing where authorities might search next. Best to hide even without Mihály. Jakab said "I'll go up first. Fill the basket as I lower it." Climbing the ladder to the ceiling he pushed the panel up and over to climb through, retrieving a large woven basket with rope tied to the corners. He went to the edge of the opening and lowered it. The women began filling it with last minute items. The exercise was repeated several times with additional provisions and personal items.

After a while they hurriedly broke for dinner, not knowing how much time they had. The women prepared the meal as Jakab continued moving things into the attic, the boys helping when needed. Finally, Ilona and Mihály's four month old baby daughter was wrapped in a blanket and lifted by basket. Swaying, she looked up at her mother with a curious grin.

Planks were heard creaking from the front porch. Looking toward the door everyone froze in a moment of indecision. Jakab, realizing he couldn't leave the baby dangling there, resumed retrieving rope at a quickened pace. There was a knock. Margit whispered sharply "Hide the ladder and close the ceiling. I'll see who it is." She walked to the door as the others straightened the room. Jakab set the ceiling panel in place, he and the baby immersed in total darkness. In his excitement he neglected to retrieve the ladder. "Damn!" he exclaimed under his breath. Shaking his head he thought to himself *you've got to stay calm and think, man!* He dare not move now for it might draw attention to their presence in the attic. Helena and Ilona grabbed the ladder, managing to hurriedly bump their way into one of the bedrooms. Margit, satisfied the others were hidden, finally opened the front door, hoping the delay was not obvious.

So relieved to see Mihály she grabbed him by the arm, pulling him in the house. She shut the door and hugged him. "Mihály, you certainly gave us a startle" Margit jokingly scolded him with her finger. "Oh, thank God" said Ilona, hearing the conversation from the back.

Running out she jumped into his arms. "We were wondering if you'd get here. I was so scared." Mihály hugged and kissed her. "When I got to Pál and Klara's nobody was home. I figured this was the only other place you could be. We'll be alright now that we're all together." Helena came over to deliver Mihály a hug as well. Only József was missing. No one could know when he might arrive, often stuck at the mine for days at a time. "Where are Petronÿa and Jakab?" Mihály asked with a quizzical look on his face. "Oh my!" exclaimed Ilona. "They were just going up into the attic as you knocked. They're closed up in there right now!" "Where?" Mihály inquired. The women scurried to the bedroom retrieving the ladder. "There, that one" Margit pointed. Mihály set the ladder and climbed to the ceiling, tapping to announce his presence. "Jakab, it's me, Mihály." Jakab opened the panel, setting it aside. Looking down Jakab shook Mihály's hand exclaiming "Hey, you crazy son of a bitch, you scared the hell out of us!" They both had a good chuckle as Mihály finished climbing up. "Let's get some light" Jakab mumbled "before we do anything else. It's total darkness in here with that panel in place." Mihály knelt to look at his daughter. As his eyes adjusted to the darkness he could see her wide-eyed expression, unsure of her surroundings, turning her head this way and that. As the lantern's glow came up she recognized the figure kneeling as that of her father, then smiled and started kicking. She let out an enthusiastic squeal. "Hello. How's daddy's little girl, hmmm?" He bent over and kissed her forehead. She let out another happy squeal, kicking faster.

With the reunion over, it was time to focus. He moved Petronÿa to another part of the attic. Jakab went down to bring up any remaining items, and to assist the wives and children with the climb. Mihály grabbed a quick bite to eat while all this was happening. It would be up to Margit and company to set things back in place down below. Jakab coaxed the children up the ladder one at a time, remaining close, then Ilona and Helena, followed by Mihály. When everyone else was safely in the attic Jakab turned to Margit. "Margit, we can't thank you and József enough. We're all so grateful for friends like you." They hugged and she said smiling "Now get up there, and don't forget to bring the ladder up this time!" "Alright, alright, yes ma'am, I'm going. I'm going" he teased as he climbed. Once up, and the panel secured, Margit thought *and József doesn't even know yet*. During daylight hours the opening would remain uncovered unless those in the attic were alerted otherwise, simplifying communications. However, they would have to remain vigilant, closing up at night to sleep, should surprise visitors happen by.

Margit decided to keep their guest's presence secret upon József's return in order to gauge their concealment. "Mama, how long do they have to stay up there?" Miklós asked. "It's hard to say, dear. Hopefully not long", dreading what the truth might be. "Remember, you are not to speak of this to anyone, understand?" Miklós nodded. "Mama, when's Papa coming home?" "Soon I hope. I miss him too. Won't he be surprised to see everyone? We'll keep it a secret from him for a little while, just to see if he notices. What do you think?" Miklós nodded with a smile. "That sounds fun. We'll surprise him, won't we?" Margit forced a smile, nodding back. "Now go get ready for bed. It's been a long day, and I'll need your help tomorrow so I want you well rested." Miklós hugged her and headed for his room to change for bed. "I'll tuck you in as soon as I finish folding this laundry" she called after him.

She realized her peaceful evenings had ended. Life would be anything but routine for the foreseeable future. She would have to be diligent in attending to her guests, remaining alert for authorities. In a small town everyone knew each other for the most part, making it easier to spot strangers. There could be spies, soldiers, or government agents looking to round up Jewish residents. A sweep was likely coming, or so the events unfolding in Budapest indicated. The matter required patient attention, keeping watch for potential threats.

Margit gathered the rest of the laundry from the line in the yard and finished folding, carrying the basket back towards the bedrooms. She would tuck Miklós in and then finish putting the clothes away. Setting the basket down near his doorway she entered his room. Miklós was already in bed, sitting up waiting for her. As usual, he had picked out a favorite toy to take to bed. Tonight it was a wooden horse that his grandfather had whittled. "Read me a bedtime story Mama" requested Miklós. Their only children's book was a Hungarian translation of Aesop's fables. Books were expensive and precious, this one taken care of like all others in the home. A little more worn than the rest, perhaps, as favored books are apt to be. Tonight's story would be *The Tortoise and the Hare*. Margit climbed onto the bed with Miklós and he laid his head against her arm, clutching his horse. As she read he looked at the words, not yet able to read, but absorbing the story. When they were finished she leaned over and kissed him on the forehead. "Good night little one, I'll see you in the morning. Sweet dreams." Tucked in, she blew out his lamp and went to finish the evening's chores. Afterward, she prepared herself for bed. Lying awake recounting the day's events she began thinking about what might come in the days to follow, and not realizing how exhausted she was, soon fell fast asleep.

* * *

As the sun rose with a new day Margit awoke to the realization that she needed to attend to her guests in the attic as soon as possible. A lot was on her mind. Putting on her robe and slippers she made her way to the outhouse. There was a warm breeze this morning. Summer was on its way. It hadn't yet occurred to her that now even an outhouse would seem a luxury to the families in the attic. Sitting there thinking she realized the need to stock up on food, given all the mouths to feed. Continuing this train of thought she planned additional trips to the market, alternating with Klara as needed. If she bought more than the usual quantities it might appear out of the ordinary. Best to return a couple of days each week, rather than trying to bring back large amounts with fewer trips. Miklós was too young to help carry much anyway.

She stopped at the well on the way back to the house, using the hand pump to fill a bucket. Back inside, she washed up and got dressed. Miklós was still asleep.

She thought it best to let him awaken on his own. Walking back to the corner under the attic ceiling panel she tapped it lightly with a broom handle in a prearranged pattern, their code for the all clear.

Moments later the panel lifted. Mihály's face peered over the edge. "Well, good morning sunshine. Nice to see your pleasant face this morning" he said quietly. Margit smiled glad to see Mihály still had a sense of humor considering the circumstances. His subdued voice implied others were still asleep. "I have some fresh water for you. Have you anything for me?" she inquired. "Well, yes, unfortunately. Hold on." Mihály disappeared for a moment. A bucket appeared, lowered by rope. It was the waste bucket. "Sorry about this Margit" he said. "If you like, I can come down and take care of that for you." "No, that's all right. I need to do it" she replied. The bucket had a lid secured to the top, avoiding mishaps. Once down, she untied the rope then attached it to the bucket of fresh water. As Mihály began lifting it Margit said to him "I'll be right back after I take care of this. Close the ceiling while I'm gone, just in case. I'll send up the bucket when I get back, and you let me know if you need anything else." Margit took the bucket to the outhouse and disposed of its contents, then rinsed it out.

Securing the lid, she brought it back into the house. Again tapping on the ceiling, the rope dropped for retrieval. "Anything you need?" she called up. "No I don't think so - except for a good cup of coffee" Mihály quipped. "I'm going to bake some bread this morning" Margit told him. I'll send some up when it's done. And as for the coffee, I'll see what I can do." The comment barely registered with Mihály, figuring she was merely humoring him. Coffee had become a distant memory of the times. "Thank you, Margit. Again I can't thank you enough for what you are doing, risking everything and going to all of this trouble." Margit was too modest for such talk. "Shush! You need to stop speaking now. You'll wake the children." Mihály smiled, nodded, and closed the ceiling. Margit turned her attention to baking, but first she dug out the stash of coffee she and József had, just to surprise Mihály.

With the bread in the oven she checked the coop for eggs. With scarce little supplies of protein the children could use some. Wisely, that past summer, they had let the hens keep many of their eggs in order to replenish their chicken population. *Good decision*, she thought to herself. *With so many mouths to feed now we'll need all the eggs we can get.* Finding four that morning there would be enough to give everyone a little bit. On the way back to the house she decided a trip to the market was in order after breakfast. Her parents probably wouldn't be around again until Sunday at the earliest. Having a couple of farms outside of town, they often provided Margit and her family with additional food.

Miklós was awake now, passing his mother on the way to the outhouse. "I smelled the bread Mama. I'm hungry today." "Well hurry back in and wash up. I'll make some eggs to go with the bread." Returning to the kitchen she boiled water for coffee. It smelled good. The aroma of coffee brewing in the house was rare of late. They usually saved it for company and, well, now she had company.

By the time he returned his mother was removing the fresh loaf from the oven. The fragrance of coffee and freshly baked bread filled the kitchen, and with the sun shining, a couple of simple pleasures helped mask life's troubles for the moment. She boiled the eggs and set them aside to cool. Removing the shells, she placed them in a bowl to mash with a little cooking oil, salt, black pepper, and paprika making a spread. This way everybody could share in the limited amount. Margit fixed Miklós and herself a plate. "Miklós, I'll need you to help me serve breakfast to our guests." She poured herself a small cup of coffee, and then went to tap on the ceiling. Sliding open moments later, Mihály peeked over. "Drop me the basket, Mihály. Breakfast is served." "Mmm, smells delightful" he responded. Tilting his head with a quizzical look he asked "Wait, is that coffee I smell?" Margit smiled. "Well, don't get used to it. You better savor every drop. I don't know when we might have it again." "Yes ma'am, you bet I will!"

"Miklós, after breakfast we'll be heading to the market for some things." "I thought we just went Mama. I was going to play with my new bug cart. Do we have to go?" "Yes. We'll be back in plenty of time to do other things. Having guests we'll need to keep more food around. When you are finished get dressed and comb your hair. I need help carrying things home." "Igen mama" Miklós responded disappointingly. Before leaving Margit gathered everyone's dishes, informing the others where they were headed.

Along the way they encountered several acquaintances, stopping to chat. Margit, in a hurry, made excuses not to linger. Finally they made it to the market, a classic open-air variety found throughout the world both then and now. Vendors were about, some displaying their goods on wooden tables or stands, others simply using baskets on blankets, hocking everything from the blankets and baskets, to foodstuffs, clocks, and toys. It was busy already. Given the times little disposable income was available, shoppers gravitating mostly toward the essentials. Not a good time to be a clock or toy maker.

Though they cultivated a large home garden, the growing season was just beginning. Nothing to harvest now, produce being limited to what was canned the previous season. József still earned an income, enabling Margit to afford some things. Others weren't so lucky. There were more and more army widows, the Hungarian government having joined forces with Germany to fight in Yugoslavia and Russia, hoping to regain territory lost after World War I. Almost every week came news of another husband, son, or brother lost, if not from this town, then from a neighboring one. Correspondence from the front could be delayed months, families left wondering the fate of loved ones. Fascism was taking its toll on everyone and everything.

Mother and son carried two baskets each, Miklós the smaller two, his arms unable to hold larger ones out far enough to keep from bumping his legs. They wound their way between various market stands, stopping for salt, paprika, and flour. There was even some meat for sale, looking better than what had been available of late. As Margit eyed the cuts, the roar of diesel engines suddenly drowned out the sounds of the market. Everyone turned to see several covered military trucks roll into view. Stopping along the street just outside the market area soldiers began jumping from the back of each one. Shouting orders, a man appearing to be in command climbed down from the cab of the lead vehicle. The troops dispersed throughout the marketplace, taking up positions to form a perimeter, guarding against anyone that might try to leave. People stopped what they were doing to watch. Confused conversations sprang up all around, for no one could reason why the sudden military presence.

The commanding officer, flanked by two soldiers carrying rifles, made his way to the pavilion stage. Located near the far end of the market, it was normally used by musicians and street performers during festivals and wedding receptions. The officer turned to face the crowd, hands folded behind his back, the emblem of the Arrow Cross affixed prominently to his uniform. He waited a moment for the crowd to quiet before speaking. Several people tried to slip away, but soldiers turned them back.

"We are here as agents of your government to search for anyone of Zsidó (Jewish) descent. It is believed that a group of Jewish agents has been conspiring to commit crimes against the state and all Jews are wanted for questioning immediately. While we have been able to round up ..." "Mama, what is he saying?" Miklós asked tugging at his mother's skirt. "Shush, hagyj békén!" she scolded in a whisper. "*Be quiet.*" Returning her attention to the announcement "... are unable to locate several known Jews living in the area.

If anyone ..." Margit's heart sank, an uneasy feeling beginning to form in the pit of her stomach. Her legs went weak. A sudden nausea overcame her as adrenaline, mixed with fear, began coursing through her body. She struggled to keep her composure. It was really happening. All along she had feared the inevitable, but had still held out hope that somehow it would all work out. The announcement rang in her ears. "... caught aiding and abetting any Jewish conspirators, they will be arrested as enemies of the state. Soldiers will be stationed around town during our sweep. If you have any information that would aid in the apprehension of these criminals you are required to pass this it on to the nearest soldier you can find." With that, the officer looked over the crowd for a few moments as though expecting someone to come forward. People began chatting quietly amongst each other. Upon seeing no one responding to his requests he exited the stage and returned to the waiting vehicles. All but two of the soldiers followed, climbing back into the trucks. The two that remained kept an eye on the market.

Margit went back to looking at the meat so as not to arouse suspicion, a means to pause as she collected her thoughts. After a minute or so she looked at the vendor and pointed to a large cut. The woman wrapped it in paper as Margit counted out payment. Placing her purchase in a basket she decided they had what they came for. "Come Miklós, I think we have everything." As they made their way out of the market Miklós eyed one of the soldiers. He had never seen one up close before. Walking past, Margit glanced at him with a meek smile. The soldier looked down at

Miklós, who stared back up at him with curiosity. The soldier smiled and nodded, then went back to watching the market.

Walking home Margit's thoughts ran wild. *Criminals? What this government is doing is criminal!* She was nervous, the seriousness of the situation suddenly hitting home. If discovered their lives would be over. *Were they doing the right thing taking this risk? What would become of Miklós? József doesn't even know they're at the house.* The thoughts kept racing. *Enemies of the state? Are they mad? These people are just trying to get along in the world like everyone else!* That last thought strengthened her resolve. She knew they were doing the right thing.

"Mama, what were those soldiers doing? I didn't understand what that man was saying." "They are looking for some people" she said looking down at him walking beside her. She wasn't sure if Miklós associated the families staying at the house with what had been said at the market. "Why are they looking, Mama?" She knew this discussion would be difficult given her state of mind, not to mention they were walking down the streets of town in the middle of the day. "Let's wait until we get home. Mama can't talk about it right now dear." Another military truck rumbled by them, full of troops likely to be deployed about town. They walked the remainder of the way home in silence.

Once there, they set about preparing the food for storage. Margit made marinate of salt, paprika, and olive oil to season the meat. Slicing it thin, she allowed it to marinate several hours. When ready, she stoked the oven to low heat. The slices were hung on a rack and placed in the oven to slow cook, eventually becoming jerky. The process preserved the meat, allowing them to have a little every day until she could come by more. "Miklós, I need you to bring in some firewood and water. Then you can go and play, alright?" "Igen mama." Miklós scrambled out the back door tending to his chores.

Margit finally got up the nerve to relay the bad news to her guests. She tapped out the pattern on the ceiling. This time Jakab appeared at the opening. "Szervusz Margit." "*Hello Margit.*" "How are things?" Margit looked at him and then down at the floor, shaking her head. Finally, looking back up, she said "Nem jó." "*Not good.* They're here searching for Jews. Soldiers came to the market this morning and announced that you were considered enemies of the state, and therefore now fugitives. Part of a conspiracy I believe is what he said. Soldiers are going to be stationed around town, at least for a while, and anyone with information is supposed to report to the nearest one they can find." Jakab could only stare down at her expressionless. The gravity of the situation was setting in. The others came now, gathering around the opening to listen. Finally Jakab responded. "Margit, surely you don't believe that?" "Of course not, these people are evil! How did we ever get anyone like this in charge of the country?" Miklós was coming back in now with his first bundle of firewood. "How many soldiers were there?" This was Ilona. "Three trucks showed up at the market. There were probably a couple dozen or so, with the one officer making the announcement. Another truck passed us on the way home. That one was uncovered and had another dozen in it." A long silence followed with everyone at a loss for words. Suddenly boot steps were heard coming up the front porch. They quickly closed the opening and moved away from it.

"Ki az?" Margit called out walking toward the front door. "*Who is it?*" A soldier entered with rifle in hand. "Excuse me. Sorry to bother you, but we're looking for some people wanted by the government. Have you seen anyone acting suspicious?" Margit's adrenaline kicked in again. She struggled to stay composed. "No. I heard the announcement at the market today. What have these people done? Are they dangerous?" "Oh, you were there? I don't know their exact crimes. I don't question my superiors on such matters. May I have a look around?" Margit's first impulse was to decline his request, but what could she do? She hadn't had time to make sure everything was in order, but denying him access would raise suspicion. Resisting served no purpose for he would simply return with others, forcing the issue. "Go right ahead. I'll be in the kitchen." The soldier walked off toward the bedrooms. As she made her way to the kitchen she could hear another man's voice in the yard. *Miklós! There must be another one out there talking to him.*

"Szervusz kicsinyek." "*Hello, little one.*" "Mi a neved?" "*What's your name?*" Miklós had been gathering another bundle of kindling when startled by the voice from behind. Still clutching the firewood he turned to see a soldier standing there, a rifle in the crook of his arm lying across his chest. Yet another close encounter with a soldier. He couldn't tell if it was the same one he saw in the market. Surprised by the sound of the soldier's voice he had missed the question. "Mi?" "*What?*" "Mi a neved?" the soldier repeated. "Miklós" was the response. "Oh, that's a fine name. So what are you doing out here? Gathering firewood?" "Igen uram." "*Yes sir.*" "It's for my mother. She's getting ready to cook." The soldier was smiling, but Miklós declined to return the gesture. Young ones sometimes have an instinct, skeptical of dubious authority. It seemed Miklós was so inclined. "We are looking for some people - bad people. Have you seen anyone suspicious?" Miklós looked at him ponderously. "Gyanús?" "*Suspicious?*" "I don't know what that means."

In the house Margit went about her meal preparations as naturally as possible. Everything appeared in order. With the cupboard placed under the ceiling's access panel nothing seemed awry. The soldier returned to the kitchen. He looked at her questioningly. "Where is your husband, working?" Startled, she turned toward the voice, her mind preoccupied with Miklós and the soldier outside. "Oh, yes, he works at the coal mine." She returned to kneading the dough for dinner's bread. "Did I hear you talking to someone as I came up the steps?" Margit froze momentarily. *He could hear our voices from outside*. "Igen." "*Yes* you did. I was speaking with my son. I asked him to bring in more firewood" she fibbed. He noted the bundle near the stove then looked at the back door. Glancing back to Margit he headed in that direction, deciding to check her story. Stepping out onto the back porch he spotted his partner with Miklós. "Hé Balázs, menjünk!" "*Hey Balázs, let's go!*" The soldier with Miklós turned toward the voice, acknowledging with a nod. Margit followed out onto the porch, wiping her hands on her apron. Turning back to her, he said "Sorry to have bothered you ma'am. We'll be going now." He tilted his helmet in a gentlemanly gesture and walked down the steps.

The soldier with Miklós turned back toward him saying "Well, I've got to go now. Get that wood up to your mother. Remember, if you hear or see anything that seems strange, come tell us, alright?" Miklós nodded, continuing to stare silently up at him. The soldier nodded back, turning to join his partner already walking toward him, thinking s*trange that one; never once smiled.* As they made their way out to the road, the soldier that had spoken to Margit asked his partner if he had gotten anything out of the boy. "Különös?" "*Anything?*" "Nem, nulla, és te?" "*No, nothing, and you?*" "Nothing either. Let's move on to the next house." Miklós stood there watching them walk away. The soldier that had been speaking with Miklós glanced back to see the boy still staring at him, clutching a small axe by his side. *Was he holding that the whole time?* He couldn't recall. Turning to his partner he said "I will say this, though, that kid gave me the creeps!"

Margit remained on the porch until the soldiers had gone. "Miklós, hurry, won't you?" Looking up toward his mother, he acknowledged "Igen mama. I'm coming." Margit went back into the house and leaned on the counter. *Thank goodness they're gone*. She felt exhausted, still trembling from the encounter. The day was taking its toll. She took several deep breaths to relax, thinking she could really use a glass of wine. Then, thought better of it, needing to keep her wits for the time being. Suddenly there was a sound at the back door. She wheeled around to see Miklós coming in. She let out a big sigh. "Oh Miklós, it's you." After he put the wood down she called to him in a hushed tone. "Miklós, come here." He walked over and she knelt down, looking him in the eyes. "Tell me what the soldier asked you. Did you tell him anything?" "He asked if I had seen anyone sus... suspi... I don't know what that word is mama." "Suspicious; he must have asked if you had seen anyone suspicious. What did you tell him?" "I told him I don't know what that word means. He said that meant they were looking for bad people. I told him I hadn't seen any bad people." You can't always be sure what the little ones might reveal out of innocence. Most children don't really know how to be anything but honest at that age. Margit felt relieved. She was ready to stand up and resume baking when Miklós continued "I know they're looking for the people in the attic. I know they're not bad. I don't like the soldiers. They don't seem very nice. I won't tell them anything. I promise." Margit just stared at him, her eyes beginning to well up, and then frowned. After a moment she gave him a kiss on the forehead and hugged him for a while. She really needed József, the situation becoming too burdensome for her alone.

Finally she stood, wiping away her tears, and returned to cooking. "Miklós, you can go and play now. You deserve it. It's been a long day." "Alright, I'll be out by the barn." He ran out the back to resume his afternoon plans. Margit stoked the oven, wondering how to covertly feed everyone in the attic. The presence of soldiers had altered the situation, increasing the risk of discovery. Doors would have to be secured, curtains drawn, and lights dimmed. It wouldn't do to have someone peering in. Perhaps tonight her guests would have to fend for themselves from the limited emergency stores in the attic. Surely they had heard the soldiers.

* * *

That evening as Margit set the table for her and Miklós she heard a truck's brakes squeaking to a stop in front of the house. She froze hearing male voices. A metal door creaked open then shut. *Oh my God, they're back! They must have suspected something.* Steps were heard coming up the front porch. It sounded like one set, but she wasn't sure. The truck began moving again. She stared at the front door, paralyzed with fear. The lock turned, and the door opened. "Szervusz, valaki itt, én vagyok otthon!" "*Hello, anyone here, I'm home!*" It was József. What a relief, and an emotional one at that. "Papa, papa!" Miklós came yelling down the hall from his room. He ran headlong into his father's leg, almost knocking him over as he grabbed hold of him. "Well, they finally gave us a day off. Everyone was ready to collapse and the superintendent figured that wouldn't do." He hung his coat and hat and Margit came over to give him a kiss and hug. He picked up Miklós, carrying him into the kitchen. "Mmm, something sure smells good. I see you all have prepared a delicious meal. You weren't going to start without me, were you?" Miklós shook his head smiling and then put his arms around his father's neck, hugging him cheek to cheek.

József couldn't help but notice that Margit had cooked more than enough food. "Expecting company?" he asked. Margit turned from what she was doing at the counter, and glancing up at the ceiling she replied in a hushed tone "We *have* company. Jakab, Helena, and Ilona are here with the children." József's eyes got big. He whispered back "When did they get here?" "Yesterday. Late evening. Miklós and I went to the market this morning to get some things and a couple dozen soldiers showed up, making some announcement about Jews being wanted as criminals." József commented "That would explain why we were stopped at the outskirts of town by a patrol. They searched our truck. Didn't say what they were looking for. I saw several more on the way home." "That's not the worst of it" Margit continued. "After getting home two soldiers showed up going door to door questioning people. One came up the steps in the middle of a conversation as the attic was open. We managed to get everything closed up by the time he came in. While talking with me another was around back speaking with Miklós as he gathered firewood. It was a close call. I don't think they suspect anything, but when I heard the truck, and then you coming up the steps just now, I got scared, thinking they had returned." József walked over and hugged her, the stress showing on her face. She hugged him back, feeling better now that he was home. The tears began streaming again. After a few moments she looked up at him and said "I didn't know if I would be able to send up dinner for them tonight. With soldiers around I've been worried." "We'll manage. One of us can keep watch. Besides, I need to say hello to our guests" József said with a smile. His confident, cavalier, attitude always seemed to calm her. He had a way about him, making it seem like just another day in the life.

József set his son down and went to clean up. Miklós followed his father to the wash basin in the back room. "So, what did you think of the soldiers?" József asked as he washed his hands and face. After thinking for a moment Miklós replied "They don't seem very friendly. I don't think it would be much fun to be a soldier." József chuckled "Well, I agree. I don't think I would enjoy being a soldier either." He dried his face and hands, the two of them heading back to the kitchen. Approaching Margit, József said "Why don't I go outside and have a smoke and take a look around. If the coast is clear, I'll let you know and you can send dinner up while I keep an eye out. When ready, come and get me so I can say hello to everyone before they sit tight for the night. Miklós can stay in and help while I'm outside."

Stepping onto the front porch József paused, waiting for his vision to adjust in the darkness. Seeing no one, he lit a cigarette and walked around the side of the house looking toward the barn. Satisfied, he returned to the front porch and opened the door enough to stick his head in and signal Margit the all-clear. Margit knocked at the ceiling panel with the broom handle and a few moments later it slid aside, revealing Jakab. She could hear a child crying in the background. "I have some dinner prepared. Sorry it's late, but I was worried with the soldiers around. József is outside keeping an eye out while I send up food." "József is here?" asked Jakab. "I hope to say hello." "Oh, he's looking forward to it. I'm supposed to let him know when to come in to see you." Jakab caught a whiff of dinner's aroma wafting up through the opening. "Smells delicious, Margit." The child must have smelled it as well, for the crying quickly ceased. She and Miklós emptied the basket of breakfast dishes passed down from that morning, then sent dinner up. As the basket was raised Margit had Miklós peek out the front door.

"Miklós, go get your father. If any one else is there, you go on out with him. If he's alone, wave him in. Understand?" "Yes mama." Miklós opened the front door just enough to peek out and see his father sitting in a chair under the porch overhang. He was smoking another cigarette when the crack of light appeared, turning to see who it was. Miklós, upon seeing his father sitting alone, figured it was clear. Sticking his hand out he waved for his father to come inside. József stood up, took one last drag, and flicked the butt into the yard. Entering, he spotted Margit standing under the opening then locked the door. Margit stepped away to finish setting the table for the three of them. "Well hello, Jakab. I'd like to come up and pay a visit, but given the circumstances I don't think that would be such a wise idea." Jakab smiled. "No it wouldn't, I have to agree. Good to see you. Been working a lot Margit tells us. She has been amazing, dealing with all of this. We can't thank you enough." "Is that József?" Ilona could be heard saying. "Yes, come and say hello." Soon all the adults had come to greet József through the opening, with the older children having a peek as well. The conversation was kept brief, József saying his goodbyes. They wouldn't risk another conversation that evening. József would be off to work early, for how long nobody knew. The family sat down to dinner, thankful to have him home for a change. With any luck there would be no disturbances that night.

The days passed, Margit adapting to the routine of her newfound responsibilities despite the heightened stress of military presence. Eventually most left town, deployed to far flung locations, their officers satisfied no "conspirators" remained in Csékút. A dozen regulars were stationed to keep watch, rarely patrolling the streets, mostly manning posts at primary roadways in and out of town.

* * *

As the weeks passed, the group in the attic began growing restless. The quarters were becoming dank, and none of them had experienced daylight since arriving. Soon the summer's heat would be upon them, and if the political and military situation remained unchanged in the coming months there would be no leaving once winter set in. They began discussing alternatives. "A lot of people were heading for Yugoslavia" said Jakab. "We may be able to meet up with others having already fled, perhaps settled already." Helena wasn't so sure. "What if all the soldiers that left here went in that direction? Surely they would have gotten wind of people heading that way, just as we had. Maybe that was the reason for leaving in the first place, to capture those making their way south." "Truth is we don't know where the soldiers went" commented Mihály. "I agree they likely would have headed south, perhaps toward Yugoslavia. There is fighting down that way. And we surely can't go west as the government is allied with Germany. North into Slovakia is out. The last I heard it was under Hungarian control. The only sensible choice we have is south." "Or stay here. That remains a choice as well" Ilona added. They all looked at each other. She was the most apprehensive of the group when it came to leaving. They sat in silence, inwardly debating the limited options.

Though the parents were restless, the children were even more so. Living in their confines was like eternal evening. The only sense of days passing was sunlight that peeked through the vents at either end. Both couple's daily conversations became preoccupied with escape plans. After days of deliberations it seemed heading for Yugoslavia was the lesser of evils. Making it on foot was out of the question. Rail travel was risky, and doubtful they could find enough fuel to take a vehicle all the way, even if they came by one. Either of those methods would attract scrutiny from the authorities. After considering the alternatives it seemed that horse drawn cart was the most practical.

They spent several days forming a plan, beginning discussions with Margit regarding their intentions. She was adamant they stay, but they were just too weary of the situation. If they didn't leave during fair weather they would be stuck for the winter. Margit understood, but feared for their safety. "I've heard many stories coming out of Yugoslavia about the fighting there. I fear it will be much too dangerous." "Margit, what choice have we?" asked Helena. "We cannot stay here, and everywhere else is occupied." "I know, but there will be soldiers along the way. You'll be lucky to avoid them." Ilona responded "Hopefully they will be too busy fighting to worry about a couple of families in a horse cart. We'll take the back roads and camp when it's safe. We'll be gypsies. If we cover the wagon I think we'll be alright".

Margit paid a visit to Klara and Pál to discuss the matter. Of course they were against the idea as well, thinking it too risky just as Margit had. Not having experienced life in cramped darkness for weeks on end they had difficulty relating. Margit retold bringing up the same objections, but contemplating their reasons she could not help but agree. "Listening to them, it's difficult to be unsympathetic. They're cooped up without daylight, or even an opportunity to go outside for some fresh air. As I thought about it, frankly, I would go stir crazy myself." Margit gradually made the case for the families leaving. "If they don't leave before winter, they will be stuck here at least until spring. They're asking for our help again, and I don't know what else we can do. They're desperate."

Klara and Pál eventually came around. "Perhaps it would be best to help them leave". Still, none of them could really convince themselves things would turn out well in the end. Survival depended on avoiding the authorities and finding food. Klara and Pál had tended to the horse left in their care, the wagon hidden in the barn. Just as they had prepared safe haven in the attic, now too they would have to plan for escape.

Again, Margit would have to act without József, tasked with preparing food for the journey. Venturing to the market she purchased some beef, potatoes, canned tomatoes, cabbage, and meal, then made jerky and several loaves of bread.

Pál shoed the horse, then gathered oats and a bundle of hay. Preparing the wagon next, he inspected all its components; the yoke and tongue where the horse was hitched, fixing or replacing anything worn, like leather rigging, and applying grease to the wheel hubs. Then he slipped the curved planks from his own wagon, known as wagon bows, up and into slots on either side in order to support the bonnet, the cover that would provide shelter. He made adjustments where necessary since his had not been fitted for this particular wagon. Pulling out his wagon's bonnet he inspected it for any damage incurred during storage. Aside from a mouse nest it seemed fine. He cleaned the cloth and fitted it over the bows. However, leaving it in place would attract attention since Pál used his own wagon primarily for work. Disassembly would be required before heading to his sister's, where it could be reassembled. Then, under the cover of darkness, everyone would descend from the attic and slip into the barn before making their way out of town.

While Pál was doing his part, Klara prepared the wagon as a combination travel cart and sleeping quarters. She and Pál placed a small wooden chest aboard to be used for dry store, a couple of pails for water, some pots and utensils, matches, a compass, the map Jakab had brought with him, and some bedding. The sideboards, already installed, would hide the wagon's contents.

Preparations completed, they waited for sunset before going to Margit's, where she was already waiting in the barn, pacing alongside Miklós. As darkness fell she hung a lantern, turned low to prevent prying eyes from noting their activity. Hearing them arrive, Margit and Miklós opened the doors as Pál guided horse and wagon in. "Miklós, bevágja az ajtót." "*Close the door.*" They went to the wagon as Klara and Pál climbed down. Tibi remained in the seat holding the reigns as his father unhitched the horse. Klara went to hug Margit. "We didn't run into anybody, and no one seemed to be following." Miklós climbed up to see Tibi. "Did you get to drive?" "No. Not tonight. My father did. He said it was too dark for me to be driving." "Grandpapa let's me sit in his lap and drive to church sometimes" added Miklós. "He won't let me do it by myself yet, like he does you. Sometimes while we're going the horse farts or does a big poop!" They shared a good laugh, poop and farts being popular topics among boys their age.

Pál interrupted, "Boys, fetch me a pail of water, would you?" Climbing down they scurried out. "And close the door behind you!" Klara unloaded some oats and hay from the back of the wagon before she and Margit began unpacking the things Klara had brought for the night. The plan had them staying into the following evening preparing for their guests' escape.

The women had a lot to prepare. There were twelve in the house that night. It would likely be the last decent, peaceful meal the departing families would share for sometime. With all there was to do they kept the meal simple. Margit had stockpiled food for the journey that week. In the morning the wagon would be provisioned. Preparations would have to be completed before the families came down to leave. There wouldn't be time to linger over long goodbyes.

The boys came in. "Miklós, after you wash up please set the table and then go get your uncle." Pál was setting the last of the wagon bows when the boys came into the barn. "Papa, Dinners ready!" Tibi called. "Alright, I'll be right there. What's for dinner?" "I don't know, we didn't ask" replied his son. "But I'm hungry." The boys closed the door and ran back in the house. Pál wiped up, grabbed the lantern and returned to the house through the back door. "Smells good in here!" he exclaimed. "What's for dinner?" Klara was draining water from a pot. "Margit's made a couple of chickens with mashed potatoes, and the cabbage is boiling. We're getting ready to send food up. We haven't gotten to visit since they arrived." "Yes, it will be nice to see them. I really wish it were under better circumstances."

Margit tapped out the signal. A few moments later the panel slid aside. Pál had positioned himself right under the opening and was looking up smiling. Mihály peered over and was startled to see him. "Oh, jeez, now there's a sight! How the hell are you old man!" "Mihály, I'd like to say you're looking good, but you never have looked good!" Mihály chuckled. "Good to see you're as ornery as ever. Haven't changed a bit, you old dog." Klara walked over and put her arm around Pál, looking up at Mihály. "Klara darling, you're a sight for sore eyes!" He blew her a kiss. She smiled. "How did you ever end up with this guy, were you drinking?" She giggled and shrugged. "Alright, you've used enough of my time. Where's everyone else?" Pál asked. Mihály said "Hold on" and disappeared. Helena appeared and her face lit up. "Klara, Pál, so good to see you two old friends." "Enough with the 'old' thing already" Pál said. "Between you and Mihály I'm beginning to feel old!" After pleasantries were exchanged dinner was passed up. "Mmm, Margit you've outdone yourself tonight - thank you!" "Well, I don't know how long it will be before you'll get a decent meal again. Are you sure you won't reconsider leaving?" Margit was trying to hold back the tears. "No, we've made up our minds. I know it's difficult to understand, but it's something we must do." Once the attic was closed, Margit and the others sat down to eat. Holding hands they said grace and a prayer for those about to embark on their risky journey.

Miklós sensed his mother's sadness. She was barely keeping her composure. The adults understood the gravity of the situation, dining in relative silence. The boys were famished, digging in enthusiastically. With the lack of meat lately, chickens were kept mostly for egg production. Tonight's meal was a treat. "I want a leg!" Tibi exclaimed. "Nekem is!" chimed in Miklós. "*Me too!*" "Well, it's a good thing chickens come with two legs or you two would have to split one!" Klara told them. "Wait a minute, I want a leg too" Pál feigned. The boys turned and stared at him in surprised, disappointed silence. "Oh, don't listen to him boys. He's just teasing!" Klara revealed. Pál smiled and chuckled, pointing at them. "Hah, got you!" The boys looked at each other with relief and laughed. Margit finally cracked a smile. It was hard to resist Pál's sense of humor.

After dinner, Pál returned to the barn as the boys went to play, the women staying to clean up. "Margit, I'm still worried. I don't know if they've really thought this through. My biggest worry is the children. What becomes of them if the parents are arrested?" Klara stared down at the dishes, trying hard not to imagine such things. "Klara, there's no easy way to say this, but I don't think these people differentiate between children or adults." Klara nodded slowly in stunned agreement. It was hard to imagine anyone being cruel to children, no matter who's they were.

Pál finished fitting the bonnet to the wagon bows. All that remained was loading of the provisions. The women would begin that task in the morning. Finished, he went to clean up and prepare for bed. His wife was waiting up for him in the kitchen. The boys were sleeping in the living room, and Margit, exhausted, was already asleep. Klara and Pál settled into Miklós' room for the night. Though everyone was tired, sleep was fitful, their minds restless with what lie ahead the following day.

* * *

Pál arose for work at sunrise. Klara followed soon after, fixing him breakfast, then kissed him goodbye. Entering the barn to get his bike he left the doors open, looking over the wagon in the morning sun, making sure nothing had been missed in the dim light of the previous evening. Checking the lashings, fasteners, and hubs, everything appeared in order. He tended to the horse, spooning out some oats and setting out more hay then refilled the water pail. Finished, he walked his bike out and secured the doors. The air was cool that morning. The change of season was coming, looking as though it might bring some rain.

Margit awoke, shuffling into the kitchen to join Klara,

already preparing another loaf of bread. The boys began to stir in the living room, the sunlight streaming in through the windows onto their faces. "Pál elmegy munka?" "*Pál leave for work?*" "Yes, he just left. I made him a little breakfast and packed him a lunch." Klara was rolling out dough. "I feel bad I didn't get up sooner" said Margit. "I have a little coffee stashed away and I'm sure he could have used a cup this morning." "Oh, that's nice of you but he'll be fine. He'd rather have food than coffee in the morning anyway. We've gotten used to living without." "So have we I'm afraid. Well, since I have company this morning why don't I make everyone else some." Klara declined, saying "Margit you needn't bother. I'll be fine without it. Save it for you and József." "No, I insist. Besides, now that we've been talking about it I want some!" Margit brewed enough for everybody. Who knew the next time any of them might taste coffee. She set a pot of water on the stove to boil, reminding her that she ought to boil some eggs for her guest's journey. Easiest way to carry them without worrying about breakage, and should last for a day or two.

Miklós was up now, appearing in the kitchen, sitting on a stool near Klara as she rolled dough. His hair was sticking up as he blankly stared at her hands going through the motions, still semi-catatonic, having just awoken from a deep sleep. She tossed a little flour his way, making a puff as it landed in front of him, pulling him from his trance as he looked up at her. She was smiling at him, and he smiled back, suddenly conscious. He proceeded to write his name in the flour. "Miklós, I see you're writing your name now. That's very good!" He smiled and nodded, then realized he hadn't peed yet and hopped up, running to the outhouse. Margit yelled after him "Miklós, put some shoes on please." She turned to Klara. "He does that a lot. Doesn't realize he needs to go to the bathroom for a few minutes after he gets up, then goes running outside without any shoes on." "Mine did that at his age too" said Klara. "He'll grow out of it."

After breakfast Klara cleaned up the kitchen as Margit tended to the families above. The boys dressed and decided to go out and play. "Stay close Miklós, we're going to need your help today." "Alright mama, we will" he said running out the back door. The ladies sat down to finish their coffee and plan their day. The Kokhner's and Szabo's had traveled lightly given their hasty departure, bringing mostly clothes and a few keepsakes, like photographs. Anything indicating their Jewish heritage would be left behind and disposed of. Margit and Klara had desired a photograph of everyone, but sadly they couldn't. It would be unwise to possess anything linking them in the event authorities took them into custody.

Finished planning, they opened the attic. The men lowered items to be packed; suitcases, bedding, the few children's toys. Margit and Klara loaded the wagon, going back and forth between the house and barn, enlisting the boys as necessary. Food and water would be provisioned just prior to departure that night. As the afternoon went on clouds rolled in. "Looks like rain" Klara said, noting the changing conditions of the sky. Margit stopped to look, nodding agreement. On the one hand rain might make travel uncomfortable. On the other, it would provide additional cover for escape diminishing the likelihood anyone would witness their departure. The women quickened their pace to finish before the weather set in.

As they brought the few remaining items to the wagon drops began to fall. "Boys, go inside before it rains any harder." They had been playing in the yard throughout the afternoon when not helping. "Mama, we're hungry." Margit and Klara had been rushing to beat the weather, skipping lunch in order to finish. "Alright, help yourselves to some jerky and bread. But don't take any from the stack in the corner! Understand?" "Igen mama" "*Yes Mama*", Miklós yelled as the boys ran in the house. "I feel bad we didn't feed them" said Margit. "I do too, but we need to finish. They'll survive. Besides, they're eating now. I could use a little something myself." Margit agreed feeling famished as well.

* * *

That evening Pál returned as the sun was setting. The temperature had fallen steadily throughout the day, accompanied by a steady drizzle, making travel by bicycle difficult. He rounded the house, storing his bike in the barn. Leaving the doors open for light he started a lantern. Scrutinizing the wagon he could see the ladies had been busy. *Well, it looks like things are just about ready* he thought to himself. He fed and watered the horse, allowing the group to travel the night without tending to the animal. Extinguishing the lantern he closed up the barn and went to the house.

Departure was planned for just after sunset, maximizing travel time under cover of darkness. Pál knocked, coming in through the back door. Giving the ladies each a hug he said "I would've been here sooner but the wet roads slowed me down." Margit brought him a towel. "Why don't you go and put some dry clothes on. You'll catch a chill." "No, that's alright. I'm just going to get damp again anyway running back and forth to the barn. Darkness came early with the clouds and rain. I think we can start loading what's left and get them out of here." The women looked at each other, realizing the time was drawing near, then looked back to him and nodded. Baskets of food were carried out. Pál filled a couple of small water casks and loaded them, then proceeded to hitch the horse to the wagon. The women went back into the house to alert the families it was time.

Klara pulled the curtains and locked the front door, turning down the living room lantern. Margit rapped the signal on the ceiling for the last time. The panel slid aside, revealing somber faces. Margit looked up at them and said "Az van menetidő." "*It's time to go. Bundle up. It's cool and drizzly out there.*" Jakab nodded and lowered the ladder. Everyone donned coats and hats left unpacked. Mihály wrapped up Petronÿa and placed her in a basket. Helena and Ilona each took a turn backing part way down the ladder, waiting for Jakab to help each of the other children to them. Each mother walked a child to the barn one at a time under the cover of darkness. Jakab climbed down next. Mihály tied the rope to the basket containing a bundled Petronÿa, lowering her to Jakab. Finally, Mihály grabbed their lantern and blew it out, brining it down with him. Setting it aside, he climbed back up to replace the ceiling panel then stashed the ladder in a bedroom. Jakab handed Petronÿa to Mihály, father and daughter making their way outside. Klara whispered to Miklós and Tibi "Boys, come with us. It's time to say goodbye." Both she and Margit were tearing up. "And put on your coats. It's cool and damp out there."

Once gathered they closed the doors before making final preparations. The children were arranged in the wagon, Helena and Ilona climbing in to help situate them. Mihály handed up the basket containing Petronÿa, which would serve as her bassinet. "Pál the wagon looks great!" Jakab walked around performing a cursory inspection, pulling, pushing, and tugging on things to make sure all was secure. "Margit, Klara, we have all the comforts in here" exclaimed Helena. Not really, but they did have the essentials. Pál held the horse, adjusting its rig. "I've fed and watered him. He should be good for the night. I would stop for water by morning, though, if you pass a stream. Don't use the water onboard if you don't have to." "Thank you. We will" said Mihály, walking up to join the others standing by the horse.

* * *

While arrangements were being made in the barn József was dropped off in front of the house. From the porch he could see only the faint light inside, unable to make out anyone through the curtains. He tried the door but it was locked. Knocking produced no response. *Maybe she's around back.* He rapped again, this time a little louder, and still no response. *I wonder where they could be.* A momentary sense of panic swept him, thinking the worst, hurrying around back to have a look, the closed barn doors concealing its occupants. Entering through the back door he called out "Szervusz? Van ott valaki?" "*Hello? Is anybody here?*" No reply.

He walked into the kitchen. Everything seemed in order. Heading down the hall he happened upon the ladder. *Why is the ladder down here?* Hurrying back to the kitchen he grabbed the broom and tapped the code against the ceiling. No response there either. *They're gone!* He put his hat back on and hurried out the backdoor for the barn. Approaching, he heard voices inside. Within earshot he called "Szervusz!" The women suddenly froze, the voice missed by the men who kept right on talking. "Shush! Someone's out there!" Margit called in a sharp whisper, scurrying up to the men with her finger over her lips. They paused, looking at her, listening intently. "Szervusz!" József called again. Margit couldn't be sure if it was József's voice she heard through the falling rain. There was nothing they could do. The barn doors opened, a collective smile of relief crossing everyone's faces. "József!" they exclaimed almost simultaneously. "Hey, hey, look who it is!" Jakab said. "Thought you could leave without saying goodbye, did you?" József asked smiling. Margit let out a big sigh and went over to give him a hug. "You always seem to make a grand entrance" she said, giving him a light jab in the ribs. József grabbed his side in mock pain and chuckled, then looked at the others spreading his arms and jokingly said "This is the thanks I get for being a good husband!" The ladies and children kissed him on the cheek, and then he shook the men's hands. "Your timing couldn't have been better. They were just about to leave" said Pál. "I gathered that by the look of things.

I guess I've been gone a while. When did this happen?" "We've been planning for almost a week, just after you left" said Mihály. "We just couldn't stay any longer. Your hospitality has been wonderful, and we are forever in your debt, but we decided collectively it was time. We didn't think it possible to remain in the attic all summer, and once cold weather set in we would have to stay until spring." "We tried changing their minds" said Klara. "But in the end, we agreed. Put yourself in their shoes. I don't blame them. We just did what we could to help them." József paused, looking into each of the men's eyes one by one. Pál didn't appear so sure, looking down and shrugging. Jakab and Mihály stared back with calm determination. József could see they were ready to do this. Sizing up the situation for a moment József nodded then said "Well, I hate to see you go. When all this is over you better come back and visit!" "You can count on that!" Jakab said with a smile. And with that the men gave each other a big hug and a customary kiss on each cheek.

Jakab and Mihály climbed aboard. Jakab would drive first shift. "Boys, open the doors" József instructed. The ladies were at the rear of the wagon crying and hugging. Pál called back "Alright, time to go." Margit and Klara separated from the wagon waving, the wagon's occupants waving back. Pál led the horse out of the barn and stopped, then looked to the men up front. They waved and Pál patted the horse and waved back. The rain had intensified the last few minutes. Jakab snapped the reigns and they were on their way. Everyone continued waving in the darkness, the two families watching the wagon fade from sight.

The Kokhner's and the Szabo's were never heard from again.

3 Andreas and Frances

As summer turned to autumn, so turned the weather and the leaves. Time once again for school. There was but one in Miklós' village. All grades, kindergarten through eighth, attended class in the same schoolhouse. It was staffed primarily by nuns from the convent and some nurses from the town's infirmary. A few clergymen lectured higher level courses from time to time, but typically served in administrative roles. Miklós' walk to school was about a kilometer, joining other children happening by the house on their way. Many students resided in the countryside far outside of town, walking or riding for miles, leaving home early and returning late.

Miklós was excited. As much as he enjoyed summer's adventures there was a certain thrill in returning to school to learn new things and reunite with friends and teachers. His mother had just woken him. "Miklós, time to get up, first day of school." Opening his eyes, he sat up looking at her. "Iskola?" "*School*?" Jumping out of bed with the sudden realization he ran out the back door, his mother barely getting out of the way. "My Miklós, if only I could always get you out of bed that easily!" Well, it was the first day of school after all! Running outside to the outhouse he quickly took care of business.

Margit waddled back toward the kitchen. She was with child again, six months along. This would be her third, and she was hoping for a girl. She already had given birth to two boys. Their second son, Andreas (Andrew), had been born four years earlier. Andreas had been a happy little boy, full of life and not unlike Miklós in those early years. He rarely cried, and was a bit more mischievous than his brother. Miklós enjoyed having a little brother, looking forward to the things they would do together someday.

Two winters earlier they lost Andreas. Just past his second birthday a particularly virulent strain of influenza spread throughout the region. Among the first in the village to contract it, the entire family eventually succumbed. When the symptoms first appeared, it seemed a typical flu; fever, fitful sleeping and crying. Then his temperature spiked dangerously. Margit had awakened to his crying the second night and went to pick him up. "Oh my God - József, József!" Her husband shot up and ran to the baby's room. "He's on fire. We need to get him to the doctor." Josef felt his son's forehead, instantly recognizing the severity of his condition. They hurriedly dressed to rush him to the doctor, the commotion soon awakening Miklós. Standing in their bedroom doorway he was rubbing his eyes and clutching the toy he had fallen asleep with. "Mama, what's wrong?" "Miklós" said József, "Quickly. Put on your coat and hat. You can stay in your pajamas. We need to get your brother to the doctor." Just then Andreas started heaving, vomiting as Margit rushed him to the kitchen, dampening a cloth to put on his forehead. He was choking and crying now. Margit was on the verge of hysteria. Trying to remain calm she dipped a towel in water and squeezed some onto his face. Andreas gave a couple of quick shivers, hissing in his breath, startled, his eyes opening for the first time in minutes. He looked up at his mother bewildered, the agony showing on his face. He began crying again as she wiped him. József came running to them as soon as he was ready. "Miklós, come on! We must leave now!" Miklós came shuffling out with his coat unbuttoned, having trouble getting his hat on. "Alright, let's go" József called out. He closed the front of Miklós coat and picked him up. There was no time to dress him further. Margit wrapped Andreas in a blanket as they were rushing out the door.

A heavy snow was falling. They hurried through a fresh six inches of powder. Andreas' crying had quieted. Margit could smell his diaper. Likely his pain was intestinal as well. Vomiting, diarrhea, severe fever; this was serious. They arrived at the doctor's home 15 minutes later. In the dark it was not immediately apparent which house was the right one for snow had blanketed everything. Finally locating it József pounded on the door. After waiting a few anxious moments he resumed pounding. Finally a voice from behind the door asked "Who is it?" "It's Margit and József.

Andreas is bad sick, on fire with fever. Please..." The door opened before he could finish his sentence.

The doctor rushed everyone back to the examining room, his wife immediately filling a small basin with water as the doctor undressed the baby. Taking the boy's hat off his fever was obvious. Andreas screamed at the top of his lungs. Margit was sobbing, feeling helpless as she held her hands together in fists against her chest. József put his arms around her, feeling he might begin sobbing himself any moment. Miklós was awake by then, though not fully comprehending the seriousness of the situation. The possibility his brother's condition could be fatal never entered his mind.

The doctor placed the boy in the water, his crying momentarily reduced to a whimper as the shock of tepid water overwhelmed his senses. His muscles tightened and again his eyes opened. He looked around searching for his mother. Suddenly he began screaming again. Seeing the soiled diaper the doctor asked if there had been any vomiting. "Yes." Margit sobbed, "Just before we left." Hydration was now the priority. His wife poured from a pitcher into a small shot glass. She dipped her finger into the glass, transferring drops into his mouth. The exercise was repeated over and over for several minutes. At times Andreas would gag, but she continued. Slow, but steady absorption was the key. Too much at once and the water would just come back up.

After an hour Andreas was just too tired to cry any more. Overcome by exhaustion he fell into fitful sleep. In and out of the basin several times, they worked to reduce his temperature. Between dips Margit tried to comfort her son, wrapping him in a towel to be walked around, other times cradled in her arms as she sat in a rocking chair. "I'm sorry there's not more we can do" the doctor finally said. "Keep him hydrated and if his temperature should spike again moderate it with a bath." After a couple of hours they left for home, around four that morning. The snow had passed, and the moon shone bright. The footprints they made on their way over had vanished under freshly fallen powder. A cold wind blew steady, chilling them through their wool coats.

The flu was particularly hard on both the young and the elderly, as is often the case. The entire family struggled with it. Dehydration and malnourishment eventually beset Andreas, weakening him severely. Unable to keep food down, water with what little else was absorbed kept him going for a while. Soon he developed pneumonia. There was nothing the doctor could do to save him. Within days of contracting the sickness he passed.

Funerals are always difficult. When for a young child, it seems even more so. A large number of townspeople attended to pay their respects. The Falvai's were familiar to many throughout the area, friends and acquaintances coming to show their grief and lend support. When the priest finished, the small casket was laid to rest in the church cemetery. Margit broke down, overcome with grief, falling to the ground. She was so heartbroken she didn't know if she could ever bear another child. Yet, here she was, enthusiastically expecting again. Perhaps time had healed that emotional wound.

Margit was preparing breakfast for the three of them. With winter coming József would be especially busy. Coal was the region's major source of heating fuel. He managed to get home only a day or two each week this time of year. As he sipped his coffee Miklós came running in the back door, still excited about the first day of school. Passing his father, József reached out and grabbed him by the arm. "Slow down, son. You're going to wake everyone up." József gestured beyond Miklós with his eyes. Miklós turned about toward the kitchen. A couple of the German soldiers were still up, a little grumpy after a late night patrol. They were sipping coffee and glancing at Miklós with a look of irritation. He looked back at his father and nodded. He slowed his pace to the wooden chest containing the family's clothes, removing from his little corner the things he would be wearing, his mother having arranged them there the night before.

The war had dragged on for some years, food becoming scarce. Most of what was available the soldiers took, and at times even they lived on rations. Families, Miklós' included, would often have to pick through what little the soldiers threw aside just to get by. The breakfast Margit was preparing that morning consisted of bread and some reheated fat drippings poured from a tin can, collected whenever she prepared meat. The can was nearing the bottom now, having been over a week since last she cooked meat.

Even with occupation and conflict some semblance of normal life persisted, such as school. The area had not yet experienced any direct combat, save for the occasional air battle. Miklós was looking forward to returning. He hurriedly dressed, gave his parents each a kiss and went out front, waiting to join other children passing by. Margit followed Miklós onto the front porch, waiting for him to leave, taking advantage of the delay to straighten his collar and tuck in his shirt. Young boys tend to disregard their appearance. Seems that trait sometimes carries into adulthood as well. His cousin Tibi soon happened by with their friend Péter that lived a few houses down from Miklós. He waved goodbye to his mother and ran to join them, the boys instantly striking up a lively conversation.

"I wonder if we'll study music this year. I like playing the piano" Tibi chimed. "The piano - when did you ever want to play the piano?" asked Péter. "Last year sister Frances said she would teach me in the fall. She gave me some scales to take home this summer and memorize." Miklós asked "What are scales?" Tibi tried to explain "That's how musical notes are put on paper. It tells you how to play a song." Péter was skeptical. "I'll believe it when I see it." Miklós was more disinterested than skeptical.

As they continued on more children joined the procession. Some rode bikes, others hitched rides on horse drawn carts coming in from the countryside. It was a sunny morning, a pleasant start to the school year. Inclement weather would appear soon enough, sometimes making the winter trek to and from school difficult. Heavy snows made walking impractical for children from the surrounding farms, the older ones skiing cross-country when weather permitted.

Climbing the school's front steps they entered the main

hall. Children were running about calling out to one another, their laughter and footsteps echoing from the wooden floor and walls. The nuns were sorting through everyone, guiding the wayward to their classes. Multiple ages and grades were assigned to each room, the school's accommodations simple.

"Sister Frances!" Tibi called out as he caught sight of her. "Hello boys!" she smiled back waving at them. She had been conversing with a couple of young girls, one of which was crying. The boys ran towards them dodging parents and other children along the way. Sister Frances was attempting to comfort the one in tears, kneeling down and gently holding her arm. "There, there Anna. It will be all right, we'll have fun today, and every day. No need to cry." It was little Anna's first day of school ever, and she was experiencing separation anxiety. Holding her older sister's hand was her sole comfort for the moment. They were to be separated into different classrooms and Anna did not want any part of it.

The boys, having made their way over, began their greetings. "Well, look who we have here this morning, all bright-eyed and bushy-tailed, ready for school. Now that's what I like to see!" They were all beaming. Sister Frances was their favorite. Probably everyone's favorite for that matter. She gave them all a hug. This seemed to improve Anna's demeanor a bit. "Remember you said you'd teach me how to play the piano this year?" Tibi asked. "Now, did I say that?" she mocked, touching her finger to her chin, looking sideways into the air as though trying to recall making such a statement. "Oh please, please, please Sister

Frances! You said you would, remember?" Tibi pleaded, jumping up and down. "And that I did Tibi. I do remember" she said, placing her hands on his shoulders. "I was just teasing you. Did you practice your scales this summer?" Tibi nodded and held up the sheet music. She could tell he had indeed, the pages appearing quite worn. Turning to Anna, "Do you like the piano?" Anna nodded shyly, sucking her thumb, remnants of tears still streaking her face. She seemed to have calmed down. Sister Frances stood up, clapped her hands twice, and said "Alright then, everyone to their classrooms. I believe you boys are in the same one as last year, which coincidentally is mine! Now step lively. We'll see you later for music lessons!" Tibi's face lit up and the three ran off to their room. "Come Anna, I'll show you to yours personally." Anna's hesitation gave way, finding it difficult to resist Sister Frances charm. Moments later the two walked down the hall to Anna's classroom holding hands.

Sister Frances, twenty three, pretty, petite, and full of life, entered the sisterhood at sixteen. She had lived in the convent since soon after her fourteenth birthday, having been orphaned then. A fire had swept through her family's home one night while they slept. Of her three siblings and parents, she was the only survivor.

Having delivered Anna to her classroom she hurried back to her own. Father Márton's voice carried down the corridor "All right children, let's be seated and settle down. I'm sure Sister Frances will be along any moment." He had wandered upon the unattended classroom, situating the children before her arrival. "Thank you, Father" she said hurrying in. "You're welcome, Sister. I'll be on my way now. I trust they are in good hands." She frowned and tilted her head as he walked out, quickly closing the door behind him.

The classroom was a simple rectangular room with a wooden floor and a high wooden ceiling. The walls were plaster, and a few tall, narrow windows lined the outer wall. On a day like this the windows provided ample light. Seating consisted of simple plank benches lacking backrests. A wood stove stood in the corner near the front of the room. Various paintings of saints and church figures, including the current pope, were hung neatly along the inside wall. The customary crucifix of Jesus hung over the chalkboard.

"Alright everyone, first we're going to introduce the newcomers to the class, then everyone from last year. We'll do this by seating everyone in alphabetical order, starting at the front of the room. After that we'll start with this week's firewood assignments. It's never too early to start stocking up for the winter!" Students were assigned certain days each week to bring firewood for heating their classroom. She looked the children over, gauging their overall health, the scarcity of food shown in their gaunt faces.

Each morning Sister Frances sat at the piano, leading the class in a hymnal, then allowed those wanting to take turns playing. Badly in need of tuning, the children were too young to notice. As paper was in short supply, most of the day's lessons took place at the chalkboard with small groups of students taking their turn. Though this sufficed for spelling and math, it hampered teaching penmanship, another small, unfortunate casualty of war. With the occupation, lessons now included German language, a Nazi requirement to avoid school closure. Surprisingly no other demands were made upon the curriculum. There were other indirect hardships, however. Food, clothing, and heating fuel that the church would otherwise supply to the school and its neediest students were often usurped by the military.

As the days grew shorter and colder winter tightened its grip. At times heavy snow prevented children residing in the countryside from attending. Worse yet was when snow precipitated while school was in session. There was no way to accurately predict when the weather might turn severe, making the walk home hazardous, children sometimes staying overnight at the convent.

* * *

One winter morning a knock came upon the classroom door. Sister Frances stopped her lesson as everyone turned to look. The door creaked open as the reverend Márton peeked in. "Sister Frances may I speak with you for a moment?" "Excuse me class while I speak with the Father. I'll be right back." The two disappeared into the hallway. "What is it?" "Sister, we just received word that Miklós' mother is in labor. She would like someone to bring Miklós home since there appears to be no one else there." Sister Frances looked concerned. "She's alone?" "I was told the doctor and his wife are there to help deliver" he replied. "Miklós' father, József, works at the mine for days at a time. Often Sunday is the only day he is home. I would like you to take Miklós home and stay to help out after the doctor leaves. I'll run your class in the meantime."

Sister Frances pondered what might be required. "Alright, I'll take Miklós now, and when I get a chance I'll grab some overnight things from the convent. Can we get word to József?" Father Márton had already considered this. "I've got people looking into it as we speak. It's a matter of finding someone capable of delivering a message out there. And I believe Miklós' grandparents live on a farm outside of town. We're trying to notify them as well."

They reentered the classroom. "Class, I am leaving you now. Father Márton will take over during my absence. Miklós, please come up here. You will be accompanying me." Everyone looked at Miklós. The first thought that came to his mind was *what did I do?* "Uh-oh, you're in trouble!" his classmates chided. He glanced about nervously at the voices of suspicion. Sister Frances addressed the class to clarify. "Everyone, Miklós is not in trouble. He just needs to leave early. Miklós gather your things and come with me. I'll explain on the way." The class appeared unconvinced given the tone of their whispers and giggles. While Miklós gathered his belongings Sister Frances filled in Father Márton on where she had been in the lesson. Grabbing her coat, she exited the classroom with Miklós in tow. Closing the door Father Márton could be heard to say "Now, by a show of hands, who can tell me what..."

The two strode down the hall, Sister Frances holding Miklós' hand. She leaned over to him, explaining in a low voice "Miklós, your mother is having her baby. She wanted someone to bring you home. Father Márton asked me. Depending on how things go I may be staying at your house for a little while." It was not uncommon for clergy to stay at the homes of parishioners in need of assistance. "You're going to spend the night at my house?" Miklós inquired. This seemed, for the moment, a more interesting question than how his mother, or the baby, was doing. "Esetleg." "*Maybe* - we'll see. For now though, we need to worry about getting you home." She straightened up, quickening her pace. Miklós was practically running to keep up. "I hope I get a little brother" Miklós wished aloud. "Wouldn't you like a little sister as well?" she asked. "I guess" Miklós said halfheartedly. "But I think I would have more fun with a little brother!"

Exiting the schoolhouse there was a light but steady snow beginning to accumulate. Soon they had slipped and slid their way to the house. Miklós recognized his grandparent's horse and wagon tied out front. "My grandmamma and grandpapa are here!" he exclaimed and began running, scrambling in the front door, leaving it open behind him. Sister Frances followed, closing the door, only to hear screams and groans coming from the back of the house. Margit was still in labor. Miklós grandfather was pacing in the kitchen, surprised to see the two of them. "Miklós, you're here! Your mother is having the baby!" "I know grandpapa, Sister Frances told me. Can I go see mama?" "No. Not right now. The doctor and his wife are with grandmamma helping her deliver. But you can come here and give me a hug!" Miklós took off his coat and ran to his grandfather. Picking up Miklós he gave him a big hug and a peck on the cheek. He turned to Frances. "Sister" he said nodding. "Good to see you. Thank you so much for bringing him home. Margit was worried. I don't know why, I could have gotten him when it was time, but she insisted he be here. Sorry to trouble you." "Oh it was no trouble. Glad to be of help. That's my job in life, to serve God by serving his children" she said smiling, taking her coat off. She turned to him and continued "I'm relieved you and your wife made it. Father Márton thought it would be just the doctor and his wife here." She tamped her wet shoes on the mat by the front door.

"We just arrived ourselves" Miklós grandfather explained. "We came after getting word. Apparently Margit started labor and went to find a neighbor. Walking down the road she stopped for a contraction, leaning on a fence post when someone happened upon her. They got her back to the house and went to fetch the doctor. From there word was sent on to the church. Of course Margit didn't know we'd be here yet. Lately, we've been coming by every morning to check on her. Coincidentally, we were planning on staying overnight beginning today. We were already packed, and I unloaded the wagon after our arrival. We would have been here earlier, but we waited until this morning to finish packing." Sister Frances smiled and said "Well, I'm glad you're here. I'll go back and see if they need help."

She tiptoed back to the bedroom and peeked in. "Hello" she said quietly through the doorway. Margit's mother and the doctor's wife turned toward the voice at the door. Miklós grandmother was holding her daughter's hand. The doctor recognized the voice at once, having crossed paths frequently. She had assisted with deliveries on several occasions and often accompanied priests when calling in on the sick or administering last rites. "Sister Frances" he said without turning his head. "Glad you're here." Margit was too busy pushing, barely acknowledging the nun's presence. "Anything I can do?" Frances asked. "We could use some more hot water and towels" the doctor's wife replied. "There should be some water boiling on the stove."

Once she was in the kitchen Margit's father inquired about his daughter's condition. "How's she doing? Is everything alright?" "Seems to be" replied Frances. "She's in a great deal of pain of course, but everything is going fine. I'm just getting more hot water." "Oh, how I wish József were here" he said to himself pacing, arms folded. She poured the pot's remainder into a basin and refilled it to boil more.

Returning to the bedroom she heard the doctor say "I can see the crown. Alright Margit, you really need to push." Margit took a deep breath and squeezed her mother's hand with a pained, determined face. After pushing she let out a groan of agony, panting heavily as her mother dabbed her face with a cool, damp cloth. Sister Frances brought the basin to the doctor's wife, who was preparing towels to wrap the baby in. The doctor could see most of the head now. "Alright Margit, a few more pushes and we should be there." Margit began pushing again, and before long the baby was out. The doctor cleared the baby's mouth and it started screaming. "Good, his lungs are working!" he chuckled. "It's a boy!" he yelled toward the bedroom doorway so that the others could hear. He handed the baby over to his wife for cleaning.

She soaked a towel and began washing him. He had

black hair and a loud cry. The footsteps of Miklós and grandpapa were heard down the hallway. Margit was lying back, panting, while her mother continued damping her face. Miklós appeared in the doorway, his grandfather behind him, hands on Miklós' shoulders. Margit turned to Miklós, holding out her hand, and gently said "Miklós, gyere ide." "*Come here.*" Walking slowly to his mother, he stood at her bedside. She put her arm around him, pulling him close. "You have a little brother now. Did you hear?" "Yes, mama, I did." The doctor's wife brought the baby, wrapped in swaddling, to Margit. She laid the infant in Margit's arms, greeting her new son. "Hello, little József." Miklós leaned over, smiling at his brother. Everyone gathered around the bed to witness the new arrival. He was still fussing a little, but relatively calm. "Thank you for bringing Miklós home, Sister. I wished him to be here for this." "My pleasure" she replied. "I'm so glad I was able to be a part of it. He's beautiful!" Everyone nodded their agreement. Grandpapa patted Miklós on the shoulder and asked "So what do you think of your little brother?" "I didn't think it was really going to happen. And he's so tiny. Was I that little mama?" "Yes you were. We were all that small at birth."

Gazing upon little József brought back a flood of memories for Sister Frances. Drifting off in thought, the experience took her back to the birth of her youngest brother. Not unlike the birth of little József, doctor and wife in the home aiding the delivery. The oldest of four, it remained vivid in her mind - relatives gathered, nervously waiting through her mother's labor, followed by the collective relief of the baby's cry.

Helping raise her brother, she recalled the dressing, feeding, and bathing, memories of him as a toddler, running through the house playing hide and seek or clumsily making his way through freshly fallen snow, with his innocent smile and giggles of joy. Unfortunately, her brother would not live to see his third birthday.

No one knew how the fire began that January night. Back then homes were lighted by oil lamp and warmed by flame. Perhaps her father had fallen asleep smoking in bed. Frances awakened to the sound of glass breaking, their house a single story structure. A neighbor with insomnia noticed the flames dancing through her window as she sat knitting in her rocking chair. Dropping her handiwork she quickly roused her husband from his slumber. He dashed over in his nightshirt and boots, all the while calling out for help from neighbors, only to find the front door engulfed in flames. Running around the side he picked up a split log from the wood pile and began breaking in the only window without fire behind it. Calling out he heard Frances reply. Clearing as much glass from the frame as he could, she climbed out to him. They continued calling but no one else responded. Eventually they had to back away as the flames became too intense. Frances continued calling, screaming for her family, even as the home collapsed in a pile of flame and embers. Crying hysterically, and helpless to save her family, she was restrained by neighbors to keep from running back into the inferno.

She had been orphaned with no place to turn. Taken in by the church, she remained in shock for a week. Over time she recovered, coming to live at the convent. Eventually life among the sisters grew on her. At fifteen she decided to become a nun, beginning her liturgical studies. Some thought it a shame, thinking she would have been a good wife, instead deciding to marry God and do the bidding of the church.

"I noticed you named him József" the doctor said drying his hands, his voice yanking Frances back from her daydream. "Yes, we thought this may be our last one" responded Margit. "So if it were a boy it would be József, and if a girl, she would have been Klara." "Speaking of József" Margit's mother said "is anyone on the way to let him know?" Sister Frances answered "Father Márton is sending word with someone to the mine. I hope he can travel home tonight. By the way, I'm here for you as long as needed." "Oh, thank you Sister. That would be wonderful, but my parents are staying. I don't want to impose. The children would miss you greatly at school. Miklós speaks so fondly of you." "There's no imposition really, and besides, someday when I'm teaching József I'll be able to tell his story to the class!" Miklós looked up at her and smiled. She looked down at him, tilting her head to the side, smiling back in that sweet way she always did.

Looking out the window Miklós grandfather realized he had forgotten something. "Oh, I better go get the horse in the barn. The snow is really coming down now. Miklós, why don't you come help me while we let your mother rest. We'll grab some more firewood while we're out there."

The two bundled up and headed out. "It wasn't snowing when we got here. Poor horse, he must be feeling miserable out here. Come on boy - let's get you in the barn to dry off and get you fed." The world around them had quieted with the newly fallen snow. The horse was led in and unhitched. Miklós closed the doors as his grandfather lit a lantern. The snow immediately began melting from the horse's back. They set some water and oats and covered it with a blanket.

Heading back, the baby's faint cries were heard coming from inside. "Well Miklós, it sounds as if your baby brother is awake. You'll be getting up a lot, too. Babies often eat in the middle of the night you know." Grandpapa looked around as though making sure the coast was clear. "And those German soldiers are just going to have to deal with it!"

Entering the through the back door they found the doctor and his wife gathering their belongings. "Thank you for coming sister. You've been wonderful. Staying with them would be a tremendous help." "Yes, I'm sure they can use it." The couple bundled up for the walk home, the doctor's wife adding "I suppose the officers will be in for a surprise when they get back." Sister Frances brushed it off with a wave of her hand. "Oh, don't worry. I know how to handle them. They shouldn't be any trouble." She walked them to the door. "Thank you so much. Everyone seems to be doing fine." "If there is a problem, be sure to come get us right away, no matter what time, night or day." "We will doctor. I'm sure everything will be fine."

***

About this time brothers Benedek and György were

nearing the coal mine, tasked by Father Márton with notifying József. The monks had been traveling in one of the church's covered wagons for several hours. Snow was falling heavy, almost blinding. Fortunately there was little wind, so drifting had not hampered the journey. They were warmly bundled, but with the sun setting fast, the cold began penetrating their skin. With neither of them ever having ventured to the mine they lost time making a couple of wrong turns. The directions given them relied on landmarks now covered with snow. Desperate, they stopped at a farm house seeking help, the farmer volunteering to guide them to the mine's entrance using his own horse. With a few kilometers remaining and darkness setting in, the brothers would probably have been lost into the night.

Arriving at their destination the farmer stopped, climbed down, and walked over to the brothers. "Down the hill, about half a kilometer, you'll come to a set of buildings. Someone there should be able to help you." "Thank you for your generosity. I don't know if we would have made it in this weather without your help. We might have frozen out here" Benedek said. "No bother. But you two better stay here for the night. With the weather as it is there's no way you'll make it back to Csékút in the dark. Good luck." The farmer waved and turned his horse around, fading into the falling snow. "Thank you again" yelled György.

The monks continued through the entrance. Negotiating the incline the horse began losing its footing. Benedek decided it best to get out and guide, only to discover the footing was no better for him. It was difficult to tell which was fairing better, him or the horse. Fortunately the grade flattened out as they approached the complex. Following the sound of faint voices through the falling snow they eventually recognized silhouettes walking between buildings. "Hello" Benedek yelled in their direction. "We're brothers Benedek and György from Csékút. We're looking for Falvai József. Would you know where we might find him?" The figures changed direction upon hearing his voice, walking toward the pair. Coming into view, one of the men in the group pointed to the building they had just come from. "He's in there. Just go in the big door on the right. Is there something wrong?" "No, actually it's good news. His wife is having the baby. We were sent by father Márton to inform him." "Oh, so József is a papa once again!" The men started cheering and applauding. "We'll have to share a drink tonight in a congratulatory toast!" "That sounds really good to a couple of cold, tired monks." The smell of food cooking drifted in the air from somewhere, the thought of a hot meal lifting the brother's spirits. The workers happened to be on their way to the mess hall when hearing the monk's call. "Is there somewhere we can put up our horse for the night?" A couple of men volunteered to guide György to the barn. The rest of the men took Benedek to the machine shop, sharing the news with József.

Alone, he was finishing paperwork before joining the others at the mess. Hearing the commotion outside, he looked up confused. The door opened, everyone stomping the snow off their feet, exchanging enthusiastic banter. "Hey, József you old dog, someone here to see you." The man yelling at József turned to Benedek extending an introductory arm, then looked back at József. "Good news! Your wife's having a baby!" József's eyes opened wide with surprise. "What?" "Hello, I'm brother Benedek" the stranger said, pulling his hood off and extending his hand. "Father Márton sent brother György and me to bring word." They shook hands. "We don't know if she's delivered yet. We were dispatched upon receiving news of her labor." "Is she alright?" "I can't say. We were sent so quickly. The weather hampered our progress." "You're not going anywhere tonight József" one of the workers said. "The snow is really coming down. You're stuck here, at least until morning." "Well" yelled yet another, "I suppose this calls for a celebratory toast since everyone's stuck here anyway!" The man went over to a shelf full of machine parts, reached behind a box and pulled out a near empty bottle of vodka. He held the bottle by the neck and jiggled it to gauge its contents, then shook his head. Setting the bottle back on the shelf he reached a little further back behind from where he had retrieved it. Out came a full bottle. Looking at it, the man gave a single nod, turned to the others and yelled "A toast to József!"

The men all cheered, scrounging up enough tin cups to share in a toast as the others returned from putting up the horse. Laughter and conversation echoed off the walls as they walked in, drinks being poured all around. A generous shot was doled into each cup and passed along. Once all were handed out, one of the men raised his, announcing "A toast to József and his new baby!" Everyone raised cups in unison, said their toasts then took a long pull. The usual "ahh's" and "woo's" followed, homemade hooch being a bit less refined than the commercial stuff. In difficult times you make do.

A second round was poured, emptying the bottle, everyone giving József a one-armed hug or a pat on the back. It was nice receiving some good news for a change. Life here was often monotonous and gloomy, the stress of extended hours taking a toll. Providing for another child would sink in on József later. Tonight would be one of those rare moments of late when there was genuine call for celebration. "Alright," someone said, "I think we emptied the bottle. Let's get something to eat before they close it down." Everyone was hungry, but feeling good, not only from the effects of the vodka, but their happiness for József as well. The monks would welcome a warm meal. They had not eaten since leaving the monastery and were beginning to feel the effects of the alcohol.

The group shuffled through the snow, their commotion carrying into the mess hall. As the door opened those inside turned their attention toward the group, noting a couple of unfamiliar faces among them. "Hey everybody" one of the men entering shouted. "József's wife is having another baby!" The cheers went up. "Hurray!" The revelers grabbed tin meal trays, sending József and the monks to the head of the line. "What's on the menu tonight?" József joked to the cooks. "József, if we knew your wife was having a baby we would have made you something special!" "That's alright. I'm so hungry I could eat anything right now. Make sure you take care of my friends here, brothers - Benedek and György – right?" "Oh, welcome brothers. I suppose you're the messengers bringing the news?" "Yes, thank you!" said György, holding up his tray to be served. "We barely made it. All the landmarks given us were covered by snow and the sun was setting fast. Fortunately, a farmer was kind enough to guide us here. Otherwise, we'd probably still be wandering around!"

The meal was simple; boiled pork, potatoes, and cabbage, lacking seasoning yet satisfying nonetheless. Looking around it appeared news of the delivery had helped lift the worker's spirits, if only briefly. The brothers seemed younger than anyone working the mine, most of the laborers older, the younger men having been conscripted into military service. Many had lost sons to the war. Enjoying the worker's companionship they noted the positive reaction to their presence, feeling their chosen path in life worthwhile. Just the sort of mission they had envisioned upon committing their lives to the church.

After dinner the shift turned in for the night. Dormitories were arranged in rows similar to that of a military base. The interior of each structure consisted of a large central area surrounded by bunk beds. The monks slept among the miners, utilizing one of the empty bunks. József usually slept on a cot in his office. Had anyone been scheduled to go home that night the weather would have prohibited safe travel anyway.

* * *

Thankfully, the morning sun arrived bright. József was anxious to depart. Rising, he threw a couple of logs in the stove, and started some coffee. Peering out the window he noted the previous night's snow blanketing the landscape below a clear blue sky. Getting dressed he bundled up warmly for the ride home.

Others were stirring now, exiting the dormitories, making their way to breakfast. The brothers were still sleeping soundly when József entered with his pot of freshly brewed coffee, shaking the two awake. Opening their eyes, squinting, they were a bit disoriented having been roused so suddenly. "Good morning. Hope you slept well." The two had indeed rested well considering the accommodations. The previous day's journey had worn them out, a belly full of food and vodka helping enhance their slumber. Another hour or two of sleep would have been nice, but József was anxious. "I've brought some coffee. I made it a little stronger than usual. We've got a long ride ahead of us." He poured each of them a cup, having brewed his extra ration normally brought home to Margit. "I'll tend to the horse while you two get breakfast. They'll be serving for another half hour or so. I'll head over to grab a bite when I'm finished." The brothers rubbed their eyes, sitting there a few minutes to empty their cups of ambition before heading out.

After breakfast the three went to hitch the horse. The air was cold and crisp with little wind. The sun shone brightly upon the white landscape. At least the journey home would be shorter. József knew the way home, snow or no snow. He had packed them a lunch of dark bread and cheeses for the ride back to Csékút. Despite traveling in snow the early start would leave them plenty of daylight.

4 The Curtain Draws

The Soviet Union was repelling the German army all along the eastern front, the campaign into Russia having decimated the German military. Fighting on two fronts, East and West, there was no alternative but to retreat and make a stand. After June 6th, 1944 - D-Day - Germany had been put on the defensive in the West. In late June, the Soviet Union launched a successful offensive into Belarus, from there pushing into Poland. Then in October a massive Soviet invasion commenced into Hungary, lasting into February, when Budapest, the capitol of Hungary, finally fell. The Soviet army remained, occupying the country, driving out or capturing the last of the German troops during the spring of 1945.

As the offensive approached Miklós' village, the residents pondered their fate. On and off, day and night, the sound of artillery rounds pounded in the distance. Week by week the volleys grew louder. Military hardware rolled through town regularly. Bombing raids and aerial dogfights became more prevalent.

One night Miklós and family awakened to a column of heavy mechanized vehicles rumbling past their home. The sudden pounding of boots running up the front steps and through the door gave Margit and József a start. They looked at each other in the dark, neither making a sound. Boot steps were heard going every which way through the house. Someone was yelling orders in German, other voices responding in kind. Lanterns were lit, their glow's shadow play visible on the wall outside the bedroom's doorway. Miklós and family listened from bed, nervously waiting. Minutes passed before József decided to have a look. "József!" Margit barked in a hushed but sharp tone "Get back here! You need to stay away from there."

József tip-toed to the edge of the threshold and peered around the door frame to catch a glimpse. Soldiers were gathering gear; packs, utensils, maps, anything they could carry. The officers residing in their house continued barking orders as two men in the kitchen stuffed whatever food they could find into backpacks. Chickens began squawking outside. Apparently the coop was being raided as well. Miklós could not stand it any longer, and József suddenly felt his son peering out from between his legs. "Miklós don't be like your father. Get back in bed!" No use. Margit's requests fell on deaf ears. Finally, with a big sigh, she joined them to see what all the fuss was about. Sticking her head under József's arm she leaned against the door frame. "What are they doing?" Margit whispered. "It looks like they're in a hurry to leave" replied József. "I think the Russians must be close." Moments later the whistle of artillery pierced the air, followed by its impact, the closest one yet. Pictures on the walls shook, plaster falling about them as the floor vibrated. Instinctively they ducked and huddled. "Papa, I think you're right" Miklós said. The Germans froze, ducking as well, the look of concern showing on their faces. The officer in charge started waving his arm toward the front door, yelling "Schnell, schnell." "*Hurry, hurry.*" The men took what they had gathered, rushing out the door into their waiting vehicles. They departed at once toward the south, opposite the direction the Soviet army would be advancing, apparently in some sort of retreat. Another large boom shook the ground, not as close as the last, but close enough to give one pause. The family hurried outside and down into their cellar for cover. Chickens were running around the yard. Whoever had gone into the coop left the door open. József thought *won't that be fun trying to round them up. If we live through the night!*

Once safely inside the small cellar József secured the top as Margit set the baby down to make some light, preparations having been made in advance for such a situation. Rations, candles, matches, and blankets had been stashed there shortly before the occupation. The thunder of shells began fading in the distance. Perhaps the fighting would pass them by. Best to stay put. The situation could worsen rapidly.

"It seemed the Germans were on the run" said József. "Let's hope they've all left town so there won't be any fighting here." Margit spoke more like a mother. "I hope they didn't take all the food. They rummaged through the cupboards stuffing their bags with whatever they could find." "Well" József responded "I think that maybe they're gone, hopefully for good! We'll be alright. We have at least a day or two's worth of food down here." A couple of successive booms echoed, sounding closer than the last. Miklós looked around nervously. József, noting his son's apprehension, attempted to take his mind off the artillery thunder outside. "Speaking of food, let's have some of these." József opened a jar of dried figs that had come from their tree, offering some to Miklós and Margit. The three of them chewed on the dry fruit and Miklós smiled, distracted for the moment.

Soon he laid his head on his mother's lap. She gently stroked his hair as he fell asleep. The sound of shelling had finally ceased. "Do you suppose you'll be going into work tomorrow?" Margit asked. "No. Everyone will be taking shelter like us. After a night like this nobody will be going to work in the morning." "Just as well. I'd rather you not go. I prefer you here with me and the children." "I think that would be best" he replied. "Besides, if the Russians are on their way who knows what might happen if we ran into them. Fighting could break out anywhere. We should lay low for a while." József slid next to her and she laid her head on his shoulder. Before long they too were asleep.

* * *

They were awakened next morning by a mechanized column rumbling past the house. The baby stirred and began crying. Margit rolled over tending to him. József sat up rubbing his eyes, listening to the sounds of machinery rolling by outside. He decided to take a peek. Standing up he unlatched the cellar door. "József, where are you going?" "Just having a look-see." "Do you think it's safe? I don't think you should go out yet." József wasn't swayed. "We can't stay down here forever. I'm just going to see if anyone's out there. I want to know if it's the Germans or the Russians." "Alright, but don't be seen. I don't want to attract attention." "Don't worry, I won't." József lifted the door a crack and peeked through. Because the door swung overhead his field of vision was limited to one side. Scanning the limited view there were no signs of activity. The sun was bright but dust and smoke from the passing vehicles clouded the air. A few stray chickens still loitered about the yard. József decided to climb out to better assess the situation. "József get back here. Don't go out. I thought you were just having a look." "I am, only I'm doing it from outside. Don't worry." "Oh, you're going to get us in trouble" she worried aloud.

József swung the door open, turning in the direction previously hidden from view. He froze, staring straight down the barrel of a rifle. Standing over him was a pair of Soviet soldiers. "Nye dvee guy tyes. Pod nyaats strel ka!" "*Don't move. Hands up!*" yelled one in Russian. Patrols on foot were sweeping the village as their column passed through. As luck would have it these two happened by just as József was lifting the cellar door. One of the soldiers approached, holding his rifle in one hand and pointing to the ground with the other as his colleague stood cover. "Who are you? Come out of there - on the ground" the man ordered. József knew little Russian, but comprehended the gesture and tone of the commands. Placing his hands on his head he climbed out. Margit felt the onset of panic, hearing the bark of orders and seeing József staring toward the voices. She knew it to be soldiers yelling at József, recognizing the Russian accents. Sensing what he was being instructed to do, József lied facedown. The soldier yelling knelt down on one knee, frisking him while the other gave cover. Satisfied József was not a threat he stood and went to the cellar stairs. He paused, aiming his rifle down into the stairwell, allowing his eyes to adjust to the darkness below. Staring into the small space a few moments he could finally make out Margit and Miklós gazing back up at him, little József in his mother's arms.

Using hand movements the soldier gestured for them to come out. Margit instructed Miklós to climb up first. "The soldier wants us out. You go first and I'll be right behind you." Miklós glanced up at the soldier, then back to his mother with a look of apprehension. "It's all right. He won't hurt you. I'll be right behind you. Your father will be there too." Margit tried to mask her anxiety. Miklós tentatively made his way up the steps, emerging from the darkness of their subterranean quarters, squinting in the morning light. Margit followed with baby in arms. Miklós went to sit beside his father, still lying on the ground. Once Margit had exited, the soldier aimed his rifle into the cellar and descended the stairs, searching for any potential threats. Satisfied, he emerged to let his partner know the area was clear. "Poi dem." "*Let's go*. It's just a family." The soldier providing cover lowered his rifle, joining his partner to continue their sweep.

Once the soldiers were out of sight József stood and tried to hug Margit. Instead he was met with a slap on the arm. "I told you not to go out!" she scolded. "It wouldn't have mattered" he responded. "They would

have opened the cellar and searched it anyway. I'm sure they searched the house before coming out here. They're looking for German soldiers, booby traps - any useful information that may have been left behind."
"Well the whole thing just about scared me to death. I wish you wouldn't do such things. You have children to think about you know!" József thought it best not to argue. They had more pressing matters, like getting back in the house to take stock of their situation. Between the German's rummaging through the house the night before, and now the Russian patrols, who knew what state their home was in. "Let's get inside and check things out" József said. "I'm not sure I really want to know" Margit quipped.

The ground trembled under their feet as the column continued rolling through town. The rattle of tank tracks and the sound of roaring engines made conversation difficult. Diesel exhaust and road dust hung heavy in the air. Coming up the back porch they could see the door had been left wide open. As József suspected, someone had indeed been through the house. Approaching first, József turned to the others and said "Wait here on the porch in case someone is still inside. I don't want us all going in at once and startling anyone with a gun." "Be careful József. You've already had an encounter with guns this morning." József nodded once and turned to go in. Stepping quietly across the threshold he paused to listen. Only the rumble of passing hardware was audible. József didn't know much Russian but knew a couple of greetings, having haggled in the past over mining equipment. He called out "Privet?" "*Hello there?*" Then in Hungarian "Szervusz?" No response.

Venturing a little further he scanned the kitchen. Most of the cabinets hung open, utensils scattered about as a result of the retreating Germans rummaging for supplies the night before. It looked like any food that could be readily carried in a pack was gone. The front door was open as well, allowing exhaust fumes and dust to drift indoors. He walked through the front room and closed the door. The house quieted a little. He listened once again for any sounds from within. Not hearing anything he called out once more, again with no response. József quietly made his way to the bedrooms to make sure. No one there either. Satisfied the house was unoccupied he went to bring everyone in. "It's alright, no one's here. The place is empty, but what a mess. Soldiers wrecked the place last night, and the shelling cracked a lot of plaster. The front door was left open and there's dust all over everything."

As they followed József in Margit was shaking her head, wondering where to start. Miklós ran to the couch by the front window and climbed up, kneeling on a cushion. Leaning on the sofa back he peered through the sheers at the parade of vehicles and soldiers making their way past. Turning back to his parents, "Papa, can we go outside to watch?" "I don't see why not". "József, haven't we encountered enough soldiers for one day?" Margit pleaded. "Oh, it'll be alright. How threatening do we look as a family? Besides, most of the village has been swept by now. The way this column is moving they seem to be in a hurry. Come on Miklós let's go out." Hopping off the couch he ran to his father. Taking Miklós' hand József opened the front door and they stepped out onto the porch. Margit decided she might as well follow.

Loud didn't begin to describe it. Vehicles of all sorts were rumbling by; tanks, halftracks with artillery in tow, trucks full of soldiers. Miklós stood in awe. He had never witnessed such a thing. Little József clung to his mother, the anxiety showing on his face, the sights and sounds overwhelming him as they stepped outside, not caring for the ruckus one bit. Margit tried calming him, bobbing him up and down, swaying, and speaking comforting words softly into his ear. Some of the soldiers waved as they went by, Miklós returning the gesture. In either direction down the road other villagers could be seen watching the parade of vehicles. "Looks like the Germans retreated in a hurry" József yelled above the noise. "We haven't heard any fighting since last night and the Russians seem to be moving quickly." "Thank goodness" Margit responded. "I hope we never see those Germans again. Good riddance!"

Regrettably, the Russians would not be the liberators hoped for. Having extricated another invading force from their homeland they remained to carve out a buffer zone across Eastern Europe. This war would end, only to be followed by a much longer one; the Cold War.

***

Although combat operations had officially ceased in Hungary by the summer of 1945, a large contingent of Soviet military remained on Hungarian soil. Elections were held in November. An independent party won over half the vote, compared with less than a fifth for the Hungarian Communist Party. Hungarians, for the most part, did not fancy themselves socialists, though neither monarchy nor fascism had served them well. Despite their overwhelming victories at the polls, the Soviet commander of Hungary refused the independents majority control, instead forcing the formation of a coalition government with the communists. Though the victorious independent candidate ascended to the presidency, a majority of key government posts were doled out to individuals chosen by the occupiers. Socialism, Soviet style, was being established forcefully. The transition from fascism to communism had begun.

The Yalta talks produced treaties essentially dividing Eastern and Western Europe, and splitting Germany. With war still being waged in the Pacific a quick resolution to the reconstruction of Europe was called for. Roosevelt had assumed the loose alliance with the Soviets to defeat fascism would carry forward as goodwill in reshaping the continent. This would not, however, be the case and the people of Eastern Europe came to resent the outcome. By allowing control of the East by the Soviet Union, the West had doomed countries such as Hungary to decades of heavy handed socialism.

In 1948, with the support of Soviet troops, the Communist Party wrested control from what remained of the coalition government. The following year Hungary was proclaimed a People's Republic, transitioning to a one-party state, setting the stage for the country to become part of the Soviet dominated Eastern Bloc. As the world entered the Cold War the Eastern Bloc countries would come to be known collectively as the *Iron Curtain*.

Most industry became nationalized, including the coal mine employing József. Although he maintained his position within the operation, management's priorities changed. Quotas were set for both domestic consumption and export, requiring surplus production to meet the newly created demand for currency from outside Hungary's borders. The 1947 Treaty of Paris required Hungary to relinquish all territory acquired since 1937, and to pay $300 million in reparations to the USSR, Czechoslovakia, and Yugoslavia. All Hungary had to offer in the way of exports were commodities, such as coal, metal ores, and agricultural goods. In their haste to increase production communist agencies created economic imbalances typical of state-run economies.

Agricultural lands were collectivized into state farms. This meant Margit's parents would be farming under government supervision, required to meet quotas, and forced to employ people on land that had been in the family for generations. This was a devastating turn of events. No longer could they freely choose what or when to plant, but were now beholden to appointed bureaucrats. Because of their agricultural background they were kept on to manage what were formerly their farms, but responsible for meeting the government's quotas despite lacking authority.

The people of the region soon came to harbor deep resentment at the confiscation of property, farms, and businesses. Opposition was quickly suppressed, and those involved often found themselves harassed by the secret police. The terror employed was patterned after that of the USSR's Stalinist regime. The campaign peaked in 1948 with the trial and life imprisonment of Cardinal József Mindszenty, leader of Hungary's Roman Catholics, outspoken on the issues of church freedom and political persecutions. As a result he was arrested, tortured, and in 1949 sentenced to life in prison following a show trial that received worldwide condemnation and a United Nations resolution protesting the actions against him. By the late 1940's political opponents had been systematically eliminated, either through deportation, imprisonment, or execution. Indoctrination would become a key factor in controlling the populous.

And who better to indoctrinate than the impressionable minds of youth.

5 Transition

As time passed many aspects of life were integrated with the new regime. Although the communists had lost the original elections, the Soviet influence eventually assimilated much of Hungarian society through brute force and social inertia. Isolated pockets of resistance occurred occasionally, but were swiftly and efficiently dealt with. After two world wars and a second occupation by a major power, the country's resources were strained, and its people too weary to resist.

Miklós' school remained staffed by a few members of the clergy, but the educational agenda was now set by a socialist administration. Oversight was ever present, lesson plans inflexible. Communist doctrine eliminated religious teachings from the curriculum. Those lessons would be left for church and Sunday school, which fortunately, the Marxist government had yet to eliminate.

Propaganda, subtly introduced into the courses of older children, became gradually more overt through the younger grades. Over time, as the cold war progressed and intensified, so did misinformation. Younger children were taught that Westerners, especially the United States, were war mongering, constantly preparing for the eventual invasion of the East. Western culture was portrayed as militaristic, the citizens living underground and in tents to keep mobile. Photos and newsreels of racial injustice, industrial accidents, military training, and nuclear testing were the only real exposure of western society youngsters received. In a carefully planned manner, the older the class, the less half- truths were dispensed. Aware that most of the older students possessed knowledge of the world outside their borders, the ministers of misinformation were mindful to prevent creating an atmosphere of exaggeration and disbelief.

Most people knew otherwise. Many families with relatives residing in the West had communicated with them regularly prior to the war. Miklós had relatives living in Detroit, Michigan. Correspondence with the West was still allowed, but letters could be opened and censored, or even discarded. One had to be careful of the written word for fear of bringing scrutiny upon one's family.

One evening over dinner Miklós broached the lesson topic at school that day. "Papa, why do the Americans want to fight us?" József paused. "Where did you get such a notion, Miklós?" "Today in school they were showing us pictures of the American army, and all their bombs, and the way they treat people. Most everyone there lives underground and..." "Miklós, that's not true" his mother scoffed. "Do you remember the pictures of your aunt and uncle and all your cousins from America?" "Yes." "Well, do they seem like that? You saw the pictures of their house and all the children in the yard playing, and bicycles, and furniture and things. Do you really think they look like soldiers?" "No mama, I guess not, but then what about the stories? Why would the teachers tell us such things?" The couple glanced at each other, pondering an explanation. "Miklós, I know it's hard to understand" József finally said, "but sometimes people don't always speak the truth. I know you expect teachers to tell you the truth, but our government doesn't like the Americans. They are a threat to them. Your teachers are made to tell these lies. Just go along with what they say, but you don't have to believe it. Tell us about what you are taught and we'll discuss it with you." "And don't argue with anyone about it" added Margit. "Like your father said, just pretend to believe. It wouldn't do to get in trouble, or have your grades suffer." She felt the need to make one more point, however, pausing for a moment, holding back her tears of contempt and sadness, "But remember this as they speak; they are the ones that took away grand mamma's and grand papa's farms 'to serve the greater good'."

Miklós was perplexed but understood. He was experiencing an epiphany of sorts, and didn't care for it. You grow up with a certain set of core beliefs, and it's not usually until early adulthood that one begins to distinguish the brilliance from the bull. Miklós was experiencing such thoughts, albeit in the mind of a third grader. Fortunately, his parents were not unlike most, both cynical and skeptical of the current system. There were, of course, opportunists that "embraced" the new regime, seizing the opportunity to gain privilege from the powerful. Opportunists are present in all societies, regardless of the moral or ethical implications. After all, it wouldn't be possible for governments, no matter how despised, to function without some support from the populace.

That night, when time for a bedtime story, Miklós lacked interest. Margit entered his bedroom, grabbing Aesop's fables and sitting next to him in bed as she did most nights. Lately Miklós had been doing most of the reading, his mother helping with the more difficult words. "So, which shall we read tonight?" "I don't know" he sighed. "Miklós, what's wrong. Are you feeling alright?" Margit reached over to feel his forehead. "I'm fine mama. I'm just not in the mood." "Tell me, are you worried about something?" "No. I'm just thinking about things." His mother sensed what was bothering him. "It's what we talked about at dinner, isn't it? I know it's hard now, but as you get older you'll appreciate such matters more. You won't always understand why things are the way they are, just like I don't, but you'll be able to comprehend more. Would you like to talk about it?" "No, I think I just want to go to sleep." "Alright dear, I'll see you in the morning. Good night." Margit kissed him and turned out his lantern.

Miklós lay awake for a while staring at the ceiling, occupied by his thoughts on the day. *Why would they lie? Don't they know we'll find out the truth? I wonder what everyone else thinks?* Miklós decided he'd talk to

Iron Cross, Iron Curtain, Iron Will

Tibi about it on the way to school in the morning. Sleep came late, but it finally came.

* * *

On the walk to school the next day Miklós was silent, alone in his thoughts. He wished to talk with Tibi about what was on his mind, but wasn't sure how to broach the subject. Tibi was busily chatting with several other children. After a couple of minutes Tibi noticed Miklós' unusual silence. Walking up beside him, he asked "What's wrong? You're quiet today." "Oh, I'm just thinking about stuff." "What stuff? Did you get in trouble?" "No." He looked around to see if anyone was listening. "I talked to my parents last night about the things they've been telling us in school, you know, about America and all. My parents say they're lying to us, but that I should just listen and pretend to believe." Tibi laughed. "So why does that bother you? I talked to my parents about it a while ago and they said lots of people lie and not to worry about it. As long as we know the truth, that's what's important." "But doesn't it bother you? Teachers aren't supposed to lie!" "Which teacher's lying?" one of the other children asked. Glancing over his shoulder Miklós realized he had spoken a little too loud. "Oh, no one" he responded. Speaking softer he returned to Tibi. "Doesn't it bother you?" "It kind of did at first, but I just talk to my parents about it now and then." Miklós gave him a long look. Tibi just shrugged and returned to the conversation with others.

Before long, Miklós joined up in conversation as well. At that age it is easy to get distracted. They arrived at school and began making their way toward class. The bulletin board had an announcement that morning, catching Miklós' attention. He stopped in the middle of the hall to read it, almost getting knocked over by some older boys walking and talking without noticing him. He stumbled aside and approached the posting. "Miklós, come on, we're going to be late" Tibi called back, noticing his cousin no longer behind him. "Hold on, I want to read this." Miklós removed his hat while reading the chalkboard announcement. *Tryouts will begin tomorrow for the wrestling team. Those interested between the ages of ten and twelve should contact coach Laszlofi.* Though not yet old enough, the thought intrigued him. Coach Laszlofi had been teaching gymnastics and wrestling in gym class during the winter months. Miklós, unbeknownst to his parents, was a natural at gymnastics. However, he had always had an affinity for wrestling, his father teaching him the rules and some finer points from a very young age.

Miklós decided to talk with coach during gym that day. He ran to catch up with Tibi, who was almost to class. "What were you looking at" he inquired. "They're having tryouts for the wrestling team tomorrow." "Are you trying out?" "No, I'm not old enough" Miklós replied disappointed, "but I'm going to ask the coach if I can come and watch the team." They arrived at class just in time, hung their coats and hats, and took their seats. Miklós began wondering what the ministers of propaganda might be lecturing on that day.

* * *

After lunch the younger students attended gym class, segregated by gender. Even at this age the students were required to dress out. The clothes weren't uniforms, but had to meet certain requirements. The drill for wrestling was pretty much the same as gymnastics; after dressing out everyone participated in setting the mats out appropriately, and then lined up for stretches and warm ups. As Miklós dragged a mat by the instructor he asked "Coach Laszlofi, would it be alright if I came to wrestling practice?" "Miklós, you're a fine athlete but you're not old enough yet." "I know, but I just want to watch and learn." Coach had noticed Miklós' athletic abilities, but hadn't thought about inviting him to practices. After a moment's thought it didn't seem such a bad idea, really. Indirectly coaching those with potential while young, and getting them interested and enthusiastic at an early age, could potentially make the school's teams more competitive in the long run. The coach began walking along with Miklós. "I think that would be a fine idea. Tell you what, if it's alright with your parents you're welcome to stay after school and come to practices." "Really!? Thanks coach. I'll ask when I get home today. I sure hope my mom says yes." Coach chuckled, admiring the boy's enthusiasm. "Alright!" he yelled out. "Get those mats in place and line up for warm ups." After his talk with the coach, Miklós was looking forward to class with renewed enthusiasm. Today's lesson would mean more now that he considered himself a student of the sport.

On the way back to the changing room after class coach stopped Miklós. "You were looking good there today. Don't forget to talk to your parents tonight." "Oh, I won't coach. I'll remember." "Alright, see you tomorrow." By the time Miklós got into the changing room Tibi was almost dressed. He looked up at Miklós and asked "What did the coach want to talk to you about?" "He said it would be alright for me to stay after school and come to the wrestling practices if I get my parent's permission." "Oh? So you're really going to do it?" "I hope so. I don't see why my parents should mind."

Arriving home that afternoon Miklós went running in the door to find his mother. He couldn't wait to ask her about wrestling. "Mama, mama! Coach says I can stay after school to watch the wrestling team practice. Can I go, please!" "Whoa, wait-wait-wait! Where did this come from? What are you talking about?" The subject seemed to Margit to have been conjured out of thin air. "Since when did you want to stay after school for anything? Wrestling? Are you trying out for the team?" "No, I can't try out for the team yet. I'm too young. But the coach thinks I'd be a good wrestler. I saw an announcement for tryouts beginning tomorrow and I asked him in gym class today. He said it would be alright. Can I go mama?" Margit was in the middle of fixing dinner. "Miklós, I'm cooking and can't talk about it right now. Go wash up and set the table, please. Your father should be home soon. We can discuss it with him then." Margit watched him run off and shook her head, contemplating this new wrinkle in life that her son had just brought home. *Yet another thing to worry about* she thought to herself looking upward.

When Miklós finished he went back into the kitchen to see what was for dinner. József happened to come walking in the front door. "Papa!" Miklós went running to hug his father. Little József started making yelling sounds as well and waddled over to see his father. "Oh my! What a greeting from both my fine sons!" József managed to pick them up and carry them to the kitchen. On the way Miklós had to start telling his father about wrestling practice. "Papa, guess what? Coach says I can stay after school to watch the wrestling team. Mama said we could talk about it when you got home." "I said we could discuss it over dinner with your father, dear" she interjected. József gave Margit a kiss on the cheek and went back to listening to Miklós. When he finished József asked "Aren't you too young for the team?" "Not to be on the team, but just to watch and learn. The coach thinks I'm good and told me it would be alright to stay after school and watch the practices." "Hmm" his father pondered with a frown, "so you want to be a wrestler, huh? Well maybe tonight after dinner you can show me some moves." "Alright, I will papa. Today we learned the single and double-leg takedowns. Coach says I'm pretty good. I even took down Tibi! "Oh-ho, so you did? Well, just have to try those moves on me then!" Rough-housing with the boys was one of the things József really enjoyed about fatherhood. He put the boys down and went to see what Margit was cooking.

She still had her worries, and thought József was being a little cavalier about the matter. After all, she wasn't quite ready for her son to get involved in competitive contact sports. "József, you're encouraging him before we've even discussed it. He just mentioned this two minutes before you walked in the door. I haven't even had time to think about it yet." "Oh, what harm could there be. It's not like he'll be on the team. He's just going to be watching. I think it will be good for him." József reached for a nibble of what Margit was preparing and got his hand slapped. "You go sit. I'm busy in here. You're distracting me." He could tell she was bothered by Miklós request. József smiled and slipped his arms around her waist while she was still chopping and began kissing her on the neck. Margit tilted her head, giving in and giggled a little. "Now stop that, or dinner will never get done!" She wiggled to the side out of his grasp and he chuckled. Then turning toward the boys, József put his arms up like a bear attacking and started growling. The boys promptly squealed, running for the living room where József took up chase around the furniture, snarling and stomping as the brothers laughed hysterically. Margit couldn't help but chuckle along. After a few minutes of this she finally had to break up their little brouhaha. "Somebody set the table please – dinner's almost ready." The three of them stopped and looked at Margit, then looked at each other. József yelled "Last one to the kitchen is a rotten egg!" As they began running József grabbed them both by their shirt tails, holding them back triggering further laughter, then pulled them backwards on either side of him before running ahead into the kitchen.

At dinner they discussed Miklós and the wrestling team. "I'm not so sure I want Miklós walking home by himself after school" Margit worried. "Well, school isn't that far away" József responded. "It's not like he doesn't go farther when he's playing." Margit wasn't convinced. "But soon it will get dark early. I don't want him walking home in the dark." "Alright then, how about he has to come home before it starts getting dark? That means he'll have to leave before practice is over, but at least he can stay a little while and learn some things. What do you think about that?" Margit had to admit to herself it wouldn't be so bad if Miklós came home while it was still light out. "I suppose that would be alright. But Miklós, you have to make sure you leave on time. Watch the clock. And remind the coach that you have to leave early. Maybe he'll make sure you leave on time." "Thank you, thank you. I can't wait! Can I stay tomorrow? Please, please?" "Yes, I suppose you can, but I want you home in time for your chores and supper." Well, that was settled. Miklós was on his way to beginning his wrestling career, his mood causing him to eat ravenously.

***

As the years passed Miklós became more involved in sports. At age 10, he became a member of both the wrestling and gymnastics teams. While quite capable at gymnastics, he excelled in wrestling. The wrestling team would have competitive meets with other schools from surrounding towns every week. The matches were conducted in the traditional Greco-Roman style. Miklós had no trouble bettering his opponents through the first half-dozen meets or so. But there came an opponent that would become a thorn in his side for years to come.

His name was Imre, and had been on a tear much like Miklós, the only undefeated members of their respective teams. The day finally came for their first match, both teams eagerly awaiting the contest. The coach spoke with Miklós before the match. "This guy Imre is undefeated too. He must be pretty good. I've never seen him wrestle. Don't worry, though, I imagine his coach is telling him the same thing. Just wrestle the way you always do and show him what you've got!" Miklós was ready, and not about to lose.

The whistle blew and the opponents came out to meet in the center of the mat. They sized each other up then shook hands. The referee backed away, and at his instruction the boys took their opening stance. The start whistle blew and the match began. Immediately they began circling back and forth in quick steps, each looking for an opening. With timed rounds, as many points as possible needed to be scored in each of the three two-minute periods. The teammates were yelling now. "Gyerünk Miklós!" "Rajta Imre!" "*Come on!*" "Menjünk!" "*Let's go!*" Miklós reached in first, trying a double-leg takedown. His left hand missed Imre's right leg but his right arm landed a tight grip on the left leg behind the knee. "Lift, Miklós!" coach called in. Miklós knew instinctively what to do. He pulled his challenger's leg up to his chest and began to twist left, pushing against his opponent's body with his other arm. Miklós drove Imre to the mat on his side, scoring a point, surprised at how easily he had performed such a maneuver on an undefeated rival, yet disappointed he had not landed him on his back for an additional point. Imre was quick to recover, however. Just after hitting the mat he immediately countered by turning onto his stomach, straightening the leg in Miklós' grasp. Miklós lost the leverage he had and Imre sprawled out to prevent having his shoulders being pinned and ending the match. Miklós climbed over him, attempting to twist Imre onto his back to expose his shoulders to the mat, but was unable. The stalemate continued for the remainder of the first sixty seconds. The whistle blew and they now had to assume the par terre, or ground-wrestling position. The referee motioned them to take their positions, Miklós having the advantage posture with the lead. The whistle blew and Miklós immediately went for the waist to overturn his opponent. Imre sprawled again, managing to keep himself down on the mat. When Miklós momentarily relaxed his grip to have another try Imre seized the opportunity. Before Miklós realized what happened he was on his back, his rival now on top, his face pressed into Imre's back. Arms still tight around Imre's waist Miklós tried to shift him off, but his opponent managed to plant his left leg and arm on the mat, turning with sufficient leverage to loosen Miklós' grip, then spun to his right, pinning Miklós' right shoulder with the heel of his hand. Immediately he gripped the shoulder with his fingers and pushed downward quickly. At the same time he dropped his forearm onto Miklós' left shoulder and pressed hard. *Bam, Bam, Bam*! The referee slammed the mat.

It was all over before Miklós knew what happened. He had been pinned. The whistle blew and the match was finished before the end of the first period. Miklós lay there stunned. *What just happened* he thought to himself? *How did he do that*? Miklós sat up. His teammates had grown quiet as Imre's cheered. The referee motioned for Miklós to stand. The three gathered in the center and the referee raised Imre's arm. It was over. They walked back to their respective benches. Coach came to speak with Miklós. "What happened? That guy put a spin move on you like I've never seen at that age. Did you lose your grip?" "I don't know what happened. I was getting ready to try and pull him over again and before I knew it he was on top of me. I never had anyone do that to me before." The coach was disappointed for Miklós and his team, but he had to chuckle. "Well, that's what it feels like to lose". Coach smiled and walked away to get ready for the next match.

When Miklós walked in the front door at home that evening he was subdued. "Miklós, is that you?" his mother called from the back of the house. Getting no response she peeked around the corner toward the front door. "Hello sweetheart! How was the match?" "I lost" Miklós mumbled. "What, I didn't hear you." She sensed the outcome by his funk. "I lost my match" he hollered back. Margit finished folding the article of clothing in her hands and went out to talk with him. "So the team lost?" "No just me. Luckily the team won, but not because of me." Margit frowned and gave him a hug. "Oh dear, you can't expect to win every time." "I know. But now he's the only one undefeated. I don't know how he did it, but he was quick. He pinned me in the first period!" József junior heard the conversation from back in the bedroom and came running out to greet his big brother. Margit hugged him again. "Oh Miklós, you'll have another chance. I'm sure next time you'll be ready, especially now that you know what you're up against." Little brother ran headlong into Miklós, hugging him around the leg and catching Miklós by surprise, nearly knocking him down. Looking up at Miklós he asked "Did you win?" "No, I lost." "Oh, well you can wrestle me. You always beat me!" And with that his brother tried pulling him over. Miklós couldn't help himself and picked his brother up, turned him upside down and pretended to do a takedown. Little József was squealing hysterically. His mother smiled and started walking back toward the unfinished laundry, calling out on the way "Be careful you two. I don't want anyone getting hurt. When I'm done folding clothes you boys need to go out for some water and firewood and then wash up while I prepare dinner." There was no telling if her requests had gone in one ear and out the other as the two rolled about on the living room rug.

* * *

Weeks later Miklós was prepared for his next encounter with Imre, determined to win. Imre was well aware of the resolve Miklós would have going into their next match, and still undefeated, was responsible for Miklós' lone defeat.

Both dispatched their opponents handily in the preliminary rounds, advancing to the final match. They greeted and shook hands, Imre smiling and Miklós merely staring down his opponent. The whistle blew and the first period was under way. The two circled each other, probing and grabbing, neither committing. The period was nearly half over when Imre made the first move. He reached in for Miklós' legs but Miklós was too quick, straightening his legs and grabbing Imre around the waist over his back. Miklós tried to take Imre to the ground but couldn't. Miklós strategy was to ride Imre until he lost footing then hopefully land on top of him, remaining straightened to avoid Imre's grasp. Miklós struggled to keep them in the circle but Imre managed to drag them both out. They now had to assume the par terre, advantage Miklós.

Miklós was concentrating, knowing what happened last time they met. The whistle blew and Miklós managed to pull out Imre's arm and slam him to the mat. With his other arm tightly wrapped around Imre's waist, Miklós hoisted him a couple of feet into the air, and in one swift move rolled him over, slamming him to the mat. Point to Miklós. He attempted to maneuver his opponent back on his shoulders to pin him but Imre managed to flip, crawling and dragging the two of them out of the circle again. Whistle blowing, they had to resume at center mat once again. Time expired for the first round. Miklós was up by two. He had only to hold on and prevent Imre from scoring.

Next round the two circled, grabbing and probing, each managing to push the other out of the circle a couple of times, no points scored. The third and final round Miklós, still up by two, decided he should try and score at least one more point to ensure victory. His strategy was to try the same move he performed in their first encounter, thinking Imre would not be expecting the same maneuver again. Miklós reached in for the double-leg takedown. This time he was quick enough to get both of Imre's legs, having worn him down for two and a half rounds. Miklós had found Imre's weakness. He had never gone the full length of a match before and was tiring. *Bang*, onto the mat Miklós slammed Imre, momentarily stunning him with the impact. Point to Miklós. Miklós followed through and was beginning to pin him, *boom-boom* went the referee's slap on the mat. Imre managed to roll his shoulder, denying Miklós the pin before the referee reached three. They were spinning around on the mat now, Miklós trying to pin him and Imre struggling to prevent it. *Whistle*. It was over. Time had expired. Miklós had defeated Imre three to nothing. Not as satisfying as a pin, but it was the next best thing - a shutout on points. They stood, the referee taking each one by the wrist. He looked to the scorers and lifted Miklós arm, the victor. Miklós shook Imre's hand and went back to his cheering teammates, everyone hooting and hollering, patting him on the back. They needed that match for the team win.

As the years went by Miklós and Imre would face each other many times, exchanging victories and defeats. No animosity ever existed between the two, each looking forward to their next encounter, hoping to best the only opponent up to the challenge, and their rivalry becoming well known in the region's wrestling circles.

6 Passage

The summer after Miklós turned twelve his father arranged him a summer job in the mine's machine shop. Margit was reluctant. "I don't want him going down in those mines. You know how dangerous it is." "He wouldn't be working in the mines" József responded. "He's too young. And besides, I wouldn't want him down there either. He'd be working with me in the machine shop. We need someone to help with framing. We're expanding the shop and need some extra workers to help erect an addition. I think it would be good for him. He knows how to swing a hammer and he'd be learning skills every boy should know." Margit, the ever protective mother, wasn't convinced. "I agree it might be good for him, but he could still get hurt. And I know some of the men that work there. I don't think they would be the best of influences on him." József could tell he almost had her convinced, the arguments becoming weaker. "Well, growing up it's inevitable that he's going to be exposed to things. He needs to work over the summer. Would you rather him work somewhere I'm not around?" Margit sighed. "No, I suppose not. He does need to work and I guess it would be better if he was working with you nearby, rather than with strangers." So it was settled. When school was out Miklós would begin work.

He would ride to and from work with József in the truck. Miklós looked forward to it. He had never been to see his father's place of work. This would be a new experience. And never before having a paying job it felt kind of grown up.

The day after semester's end Miklós was up early, dressing for work and having breakfast with his family, excited about the day ahead. "So, ready for your big day?" József asked. "I think so. Do I need to bring any tools?" "No, don't worry about that. We have everything you'll need. Saws and drills, metal fabrication equipment, furnaces, air compressors, you name it. You have to be careful with power tools, though. You'll eventually be using those while framing. Some of the men will have to supervise you a few times before using them on your own." *Oh great!* Margit thought to herself. This was just the sort of thing she really didn't want to hear. All this time she's thinking about the mines and big machinery, and now she had to worry about Miklós using power tools. *He'll come home missing a finger or a hand or something, I just know it!* She couldn't help herself any longer. She piped in "Miklós, I want you to be very, very careful. There will be many things all around that can hurt you. I want you watching out all the time." "I will mama. I'll be careful, I promise." "And for my sake too!" József quipped, giving Miklós a wide-eyed sideways look, implying mother would be making father sleep in the barn for a long time to come if anything bad happened to her son. "I want to go too!" chimed in little József with a mouthful of oatmeal. "No, your not quite big enough yet little one" his father told him, tussling his hair. "Ah! When will I be big enough to go too?" "In a few more years, József, a few more years." "Not fair!"

A truck was heard coming down the road. "Well, I guess it's time we were going. Ready, Miklós?" "Ready!" "Alright then, grab your things." They left the table, grabbed their lunches and hats and kissed little József and Margit. József junior and mother walked out behind them to wave goodbye from the porch. "You be careful, Miklós!" his mother yelled over the idling diesel flatbed waiting in front of the house. "You first Miklós" József told him, opening the door on the passenger side. "Good morning Miklós! Ready for your first day?" Jani (pronounced Yaw-nee) greeted with a smile. Miklós was grinning ear to ear as he climbed into the cab, scooting across the bench seat to make room for his father. It was a bench seat in the literal sense. Being such an old truck, it had a modified wagon bench; wooden planks making up the seat and back with padding adhered to them, mounted on leaf springs. "I am!" responded Miklós. József climbed in next to Miklós, pulling the door shut. The truck trembled, smelling of diesel, oil, sweat, and dirt - the sort of thing young boys take to instinctively, setting in motion a rush of testosterone when experienced the first time. Perhaps the next best thing to getting a woody! Miklós stared out the windshield smiling, ready for his first day as a man. "Wave goodbye to your mother and brother" his father reminded him. Miklós popped out of his trance. *Mother? Oh yes, mother.* Miklós turned, waving toward the window as Jani released the clutch, putting the truck in gear. It roared and lurched forward a couple of times before winding up.

Miklós had never ridden in a truck before. He noticed how high it was, looking out over the long, black hood. "So Miklós are you ready for a long, hard day at work?" inquired Jani. "Yes, my dad says he's even going to show me how to use power tools." "Is that so? Well, I hope you brought along a big, hearty lunch. You're going to need all the energy you can get. Your father is quite the slave driver you know!" Jani leaned forward, looking over and giving József a big grin. Miklós looked up at his father, who just smiled and shrugged. Miklós looked back over at Jani who gestured the same. Miklós kept smiling and went back to watching the countryside pass by, caught up in the moment.

The drive to the mine took about an hour if no livestock got in the way and the creek crossings weren't swollen from rain. It was a bumpy, rural ride along dirt roads through farm country. Occasionally they were delayed while waiting to pass a horse-drawn wagon or a tractor. As they drew closer the ruts became deeper from the heavy machinery coming and going. Miklós had never been so jostled in his life, but still enjoyed the ride.

Passing through the mine's entrance Jani shifted to a lower gear, anticipating the coming incline. Miklós began to make out the various structures scattered throughout the operation. Large, elevated conveyors and smokestacks stood out, dwarfing the surrounding buildings. Dust and smoke hung in the air, a haze obscuring much of the forest that lay beyond in the surrounding hills. Most everything was coated in a dingy layer of dark grey coal dust. Not quite how Miklós had pictured it in his mind, but fascinating nonetheless.

Jani parked the truck near the entrance of the machinery shop. They climbed out and Miklós looked around. The sound of machinery reverberated from every direction. A large, roaring earth moving machine exited the shop's garage door belching thick diesel exhaust. An elevated conveyor belt hummed a hundred meters or so away, carrying excavated material toward the crushers. Everything around him appeared in motion. He stood there mesmerized by the animated scene. "Miklós" called his father, "follow us." He ran to catch up with József and Jani, already entering the shop.

Inside was a buzz of activity. Men were shaping metal, repairing equipment, and tuning motors - the sorts of sounds that can cause hearing loss over time. The three made their way to the coffee pot. Jani grabbed an extra tin cup and gestured toward Miklós with a smile. "How about you, fancy a cup?" József chuckled "I don't think he's ever had coffee", then turning to Miklós "have you?" Miklós face lit up as though he had been asked to join some fraternity. "Sure, I'll have a cup." József chuckled again, shaking his head walking away. Jani poured half a cup, knowing how strong it was then handed it to Miklós. Placing the pot back on the boiler Jani warned him "Careful, it's hot!" He handed the cup to Miklós, who blew on it, having had hot tea from his mother in the winter. The aroma was strong. He took a sip not knowing what to expect. He grimaced slightly at the bitterness and then swallowed. Looking back into the cup at the dark liquid he wasn't sure what to think. "Good, huh?" inquired Jani smiling. Miklós looked down at his cup and then back at Jani and nodded. Jani chuckled and said "Alright, let's go see what your father has in store for you today."

They joined József who was listening to a man explaining something about a truck he was working under. They had to yell above the roar of the engine and other surrounding machinery in order to be heard. József nodded and pointed at something and the man nodded and rolled back under the truck. Jani leaned over to Miklós. "Stay close to your father. I've got to go and do some things. I'll see you later." Miklós, still examining the contents of his cup curiously after each sip, nodded and went beside his father.

They walked passed lathes, metal rolling machines, and various other heavy tools of industry. The smell of grease, metal, and cigarette smoke filled the air. Nearly every man they passed bid a good morning or gave a nod to József, who returned the gesture. Their hands occupied, most smiled and made head gestures toward Miklós, figuring him for József's son, noting the way he was following closely. Miklós would smile back when not preoccupied paying attention to obstacles in his path.

They arrived at the construction area, which was relatively quiet for the moment. József approached the supervisor and shook his hand. They turned to a couple of saw horses with planks lying across them, forming a makeshift table. József put the drawings down and made introductions. "Miklós this is Bela. He's the mine's construction foreman. He'll be your boss while you're here." Bela extended his hand. "It's a pleasure to meet you Miklós." "Bela is real good at what he does. Just follow his instructions and watch and learn." With that taken care of József walked away, tending to matters requiring his attention. Bela gestured for Miklós to follow. "Come on, I'll introduce you to everyone else."

* * *

The weeks ticked by and the structure took shape. Miklós swung a hammer most days, occasionally cutting wood when the task fit his skills. He began fitting in with the men on the job site. It was tiring, but that didn't bother him, although work had reduced time for socializing that summer. Not missing much, though, since most of his friends were working as well, either at other jobs or on the family farms.

Lately he and his father were riding back and forth to work on József's motorcycle when gasoline was available. The motorcycle made for a quicker commute than riding in the truck. That is, when the motorcycle didn't get a flat along the way. In the days of tube tires and dirt roads flats were common. The two always rode ahead of Jani just in case they needed to put the bike on the flatbed. Sometimes they didn't get around to making repairs until Sunday after church.

Miklós had always enjoyed riding with his father. When he was a few years younger József would set him up right behind the fuel tank and let him hold the handle bars. Papa would gun the accelerator enough to occasionally get the front wheel to pop off the ground, the two flying back and forth down the road in front of the house. Margit was not at all enthusiastic by this. She wanted nothing to do with the mechanized monster, but she knew better than to try to come between the boys and their toys. Other than her, the thing was József's passion. She would hear Miklós having a wail of a time as they went screaming past the house. After enjoying a few high-speed passes József would take the two of them on a leisurely ride through town, waving as they passed familiar faces or a fascinated child.

***

At the end of the shift on his last day the men gathered around to give Miklós a send off. Inviting him into the machinery bay they began pouring rounds of vodka. "Miklós come here" Jani called out, handing him a tin cup containing a generous slug of the clear liquid, then wrapped one arm around Miklós' neck. "Miklós, we certainly enjoyed having you here this summer. Everyone, raise your cups to Miklós!" They cheered as they toasted, then took a draw. Miklós, having never sampled vodka, wasn't sure what to expect. He stared into his cup much as he had with the coffee back on that first day, and then took a swig. The liquid surprised him, burning his mouth and throat, causing a fit of coughing in reaction. The men had a hearty laugh at his rite of passage. József, watching from across the room, shook his head and smiled, laughing on the inside. Jani continued "In honor of your time here, we got you this!" Extending his arm over his head, he held up a brand new hammer for everyone to see. "We expect to see you swinging it skillfully upon your return next summer!" "Here, here!" was the refrain from the other men, raising their cups again and taking another draw. Miklós knew what to expect this time, his reaction a bit more subdued. The drink made him feel warm, beginning to have its effect.

After shaking hands and saying his goodbyes, Miklós climbed on the back of József's motorbike and the two departed for home, with Jani following as usual. József decided this would be his last ride to work on the motorcycle that season, rejoining Jani in the truck. Making their way home a pleasant breeze blew at their backs. Miklós clutched his new hammer, smiling as he examined it in the glow of the sunset. He had enjoyed the work and camaraderie of that summer. Despite the calluses, splinters, and achy muscles, the experience had left him feeling this was how life was meant to be.

* * *

A week remained before the start of school, a time marked by the beginning of the Autumn Festival in Csékút, a celebration of the season and a successful harvest. It was like most fairs held around the world, where the fruits of an agrarian society are put on display. Contests in categories of all kinds were held; livestock, produce, and cooking and baking. Vendors plied their wares as performers showcased their skills for applause and a handout.

Miklós, with his new found carpentry skills, was recruited to help erect structures for the events.

Animal pens, walkways, vendor booths, bleachers, and more were required prior to opening. Encounters with familiar faces provided opportunity to reconnect with the social network neglected that summer while working at the mine.

A major festival attraction was the Hungarian version of rodeo. Two groups of expert horsemen took part in demonstrations; the Puszta (plains) cowboys, and the Magyar horse archers. Puszta cowboys worked various farms throughout the region. The term is historical, originating with the riders of the Hungarian plains, known for their legendary equestrian skills that included herding, roping, and wagon driving. The legend was kept alive both by the practical needs of working the farm's livestock, and forums such as this one that provided a venue for demonstrations and competitions. Always drawing large crowds, and never disappointing, most everyone attending the fair caught at least one Puszta event.

After the cowboys completed riding, the ring would be transformed into a target gallery, replete with obstacles. The archers, keeping alive the traditions of the ancient Magyar cavalry, demonstrated their skills from horseback. Shooting targets while on the move as they negotiated rope fences adorned with flags, then maneuvering their horses over and around barriers, wowing the crowds with their skill and grace. Wearing the traditional garb of the cavalry they appeared both regal and foreboding.

The finale to the weekend's events was a series of elimination motorcycle races. Street racing on motorcycle was new to Csékút, and had just been added to the fair that year. The increased popularity of motorcycles among the country's youth had given the sport a recent surge in interest. A surplus of post World War II bikes had been sold off or scrapped by the military, and now provided a relatively inexpensive mode of transportation for the younger generation. As with anything people ride there inevitably ends up a competition incorporating it.

Tibi's uncle, Máté, was a carpenter by trade, involved most years erecting and dismantling temporary structures at the fair. He had gotten Tibi and Miklós paid apprentice jobs, which also provided the benefit of nearly unlimited access to the fair. The boys had been working that week erecting bleachers and fencing around the equestrian ring. They were excited at the prospect of attending the motorcycle competition. "I can't wait to see the bikes race" Miklós said while driving nails. "My father has been teaching me how to ride, and now that I have an idea of what's involved I think it's going to be even more fun to watch." Tibi's anticipation was equally enthusiastic. "I know. I can't wait either. I read in the newspaper about the races coming to the fair, and how they're really popular now in Budapest and other big European cities. I think it's going to be great. I wonder on what streets they'll lay the course out?" Since paved streets were relatively new and few in town it wasn't difficult to deduce which would likely be used. The topic occupied them for the better part of the afternoon.

* * *

Opening day the boys finished what little was left to do in the morning, free to enjoy the events. They encountered quite a few schoolmates as one might expect at a regional fair. Many of their friends were involved in some capacity, whether in the agricultural competitions, helping out their families vending that week, or other odd jobs such as Miklós and Tibi had.

The sounds and smells of the fair filled the hot summer day. The boys, having just been paid for the week, indulged themselves with a sampling of the fair's treats. There were many edible choices; grilled meats, breads, soups and stews, and pastries for desert. Arts and crafts, novelties, and gifts of all kinds were on sale. Various entertainers wandered the grounds: Acrobats, jugglers, clowns, and vaudevillian acts. Eventually the two found their way to the equestrian ring as the Puszta were preparing their first demonstration. Having helped erect the viewing area they climbed the bleachers to where they knew the best view to be. They had stuffed themselves, ready to relax and watch the show. A short while later the cowboys came rushing into the ring, riding in pairs on horses, followed by two men guiding a two-horse wagon. This was the precision riding team demonstrating formations.

As the show wound down, the boys decided they would watch the upcoming archery events another day. The first of the motorcycle elimination rounds was set to start. They ran toward the grandstand at the other end of the fair, erected next to the road leading into the fairgrounds. The area nearest the track was already standing room only. Obviously many others were interested. "I can't see from here" Miklós said. Tibi thought he spied an opening in the distance. "Let's run down along the fence, I think I see a spot." The boys took off before someone else found their opening, managing to squeeze between others already lined up. Leaning over the split rail fence they looked towards the start line. Racers from the first heat were lining up their bikes. In those days the only thing that even remotely resembled safety equipment (that anyone wore anyway) was leather boots and gloves, and denim pants.

The course wound its way several kilometers through town, the start-finish line located in front of the grandstand. Viewing areas were set up at various points along the course. Most turns had hay bales stacked along the outside, intended to slow and stop any riders losing control, and protect spectators. Each heat consisted of five laps. Start positions were determined by drawing straws. Entrants would have to vie for position along the initial quarter mile straightaway before heading into the first turn.

The racers started their engines, the revving sounds filling the air. Once they were positioned along the line, the green flag dropped and the bikes roared down the straightaway. Into the first turn a couple of riders broke away from the pack, pulling ahead. The trailing riders followed into the first turn, several abreast. One of them over applied the brakes, losing traction and spinning out, sliding into the turn and taking out several other racers in the process. Screeching across the pavement, they ended up in a heap of men, machines, and hay. With no cautionary flags anyone caught behind the pile up would have to maneuver around the melee and play catch up. People rushed out to help the riders and remove the bikes. One of the riders managed to right his bike and began kicking the starter pedal. Starting it he took off, but not before a spark from his exhaust set some of the hay on fire. A couple of sand buckets were rushed out by volunteers, having been place nearby for just such a situation.

The crowd was excited, the first time most of them had experienced the roar of this many engines at once. Minutes later the leaders came racing by again, the crowd jumping and cheering as the bikes flew by in a blur. Miklós and Tibi were screaming at the top of their lungs, barely able to hear themselves above the sound of engines and the crowd. As each lap progressed fewer racers remained in the chase, some eliminated in crashes, others by mechanical failures.

Finally, the checkered flag waved as the remaining racers came down the straightaway on the final lap. Of the ten in the first heat, only five finished, the top three advancing to the next round the following day. Today consisted of the first round eliminations, with racing lasting into the evening. It wasn't until the boys were leaving after the last race that they realized soot covered their skin and clothes. "Whoa! That was great!" Miklós could hardly hear his own voice over the ringing in his ears. "I definitely want a motorcycle now." He felt that it might just be the next best thing to flying. "Well, I'll believe it when I see it." Tibi figured Miklós was simply caught up in the moment, the excitement still fresh in his mind. As they walked back toward the staging area Miklós did some mental estimation. "When I get home I need to count my forints" (the Hungarian unit of money). "Then I can work on my parents."

***

Tibi's uncle was waiting at the wagon to bring them home. "Well, how was the fair" he inquired. "Great" they agreed. "After we finished work we had lunch and watched street performers, then went to the cowboy demonstration. Those guys can really ride! I recognized one of them driving the wagon as a schoolmate's father. He's been doing it since he was a kid. The rest of the afternoon we spent watching the motorcycle races." "Yes, I caught a couple of races this afternoon myself." Máté confessed to enjoying it. "It was fun to watch, but pretty crazy if you ask me." "Miklós wants to buy one and race someday!" Tibi blurted out. "Hallgass! Tibi!" "*Shush!*" Miklós admonished. Máté chuckled. "It's alright, Miklós. Your secret's safe with me. Besides, if you ever really want to get one you know you'll have to convince your parents." "I know" Miklós admitted. "I just don't want to bring it up until I have enough money. It'll be difficult enough to convince my mother as it is. I don't want her to use that as a reason against the idea." The streets were quieting as fair goers dispersed toward home. The clop-clop of the horse's hooves and the crackling of the wagon wheels over pebbles were soon the only sounds. The boys sat, legs hanging off the back of the wagon, admiring the sunset. Tibi retrieved some jerky left over from the fair and shared it with Miklós. The two chewed on it the rest of the way home, relaxing in the moment.

That night after dinner Miklós opened his money stash to count. Unsure what a motorcycle cost he decided to ask his father. Finding the rest of the family in the living area he sat on the floor to join them, picking up part of the newspaper his father wasn't reading. Papa puffed his pipe, relaxing in his chair with a nightcap, feet propped up on the ottoman. His mother and brother sat on the couch reading from a story book. After finishing the paragraph she had been reading aloud with József, Margit paused to look at Miklós. "How was the fair today?" she inquired. "Did you and Tibi get to do anything fun?" "Oh yes, we finished work early and got the rest of the day off. We ate lunch, walked around looking at stuff, watched performers and the cowboys, and then caught the motorcycle races. It was a lot of fun. We're going back tomorrow to see if they need us to help with anything. We want to catch the archery show and then watch some more elimination races if they don't need us." His father looked up from his paper. "How were the races? Were there many entries?" Miklós' set the paper down, his face alight. "Yes, today was just the first round, about ten riders in each heat. Tomorrow there will be more, and then the championship on Sunday." József went back to his paper. "I'll have to catch a race this weekend. It sounds interesting." Margit let out a sigh of relief looking at József. "For a minute there I thought you were thinking about racing the way you asked him how many entries there were." József lowered his paper, looking at her over his reading glasses. "Dear, I'm much too old for something like that", adding after a sufficient pause, "without your permission", then smiled and returned to his paper. This elicited a sarcastic "Ha-ha!" from Margit.

Miklós figured this was as good as any a time to bring it up. "Papa, how much did you pay for your motorcycle?" "Oh. Not too much. It's old and I had to put a lot of work into it." Again József lowered the paper, looking over his glasses in Miklós' direction this time. "Why do you ask?" "Yes, why do you ask?" He had drawn Margit's attention as well. Miklós realized his plans to broach the topic in a subtle manner hadn't worked out quite as hoped. He glanced from one to the other. "Well?" his mother asked impatiently. He finally managed a response. "Oh, I was just wondering. I was thinking about getting one someday." "Hmmm" was the response from his father, wisely going back to his paper, aware of what was coming. Mother's response was more direct. "So you watch some crazies drive around town like madmen and decide you want to be like them?" The boys got wide eyed and looked at Margit. Papa decided it best to remain hidden behind his paper for the moment. Little József turned, staring back at Miklós, waiting in anticipation for his brother's response. Miklós was tongue tied, not knowing quite how to dig his way out. Finally, "It wouldn't be for racing really, it would be just to ride around for fun like papa does." "It wouldn't be *really*?" Poor Miklós struggled to explain, but it wasn't working. "No, it wouldn't be for racing like you're thinking. I meant like racing up and down the road like papa." Margit continued looking at him with a stern face of suspicion. József decided it time to interject. "So, how much money have you saved?" Miklós told him. "Well, you're going to need at least another summer's wages before you can even begin to shop around." Out of Miklós' view József gave Margit a glance from behind the paper, letting her know where he was going with this. "And even then there won't be that much to choose from at that price." He put the paper down to empty his pipe. "Well there you have it" was Margit's response.

The discussion was followed by a long period of silence. Miklós feigned he was still reading the paper. As much as he wanted to, he thought it best not to pursue the subject. He would just have to wear them down over time. *Like papa said, maybe by next summer I can afford one* he thought. In the meantime he would keep an eye out for any that happened to come up for sale in order to get an idea of the cost.

7 Descent

High school was a far different matter than grammar school. Access to higher education was limited, and only the top in their class were allowed to move on. Only about one in ten attended high school at all. Once there, maintaining at least a B-average was necessary to stay in good standing and remain eligible for attendance. Those not advancing were left searching for work, hoping for acceptance into a trade apprenticeship.

"Mama" Miklós called out, sprinting through the front door one day toward the end of the academic year. Having rifled through the contents of the mailbox as usual, he discovered the letter from the school board. Setting his things down, he opened it before going inside. Quickly scanning the correspondence a broad smile appeared across his face. His grade point average and entrance exam scores had gained him acceptance. Dashing up the front steps, he left his brother behind, now curious as to what had made Miklós take off running. "I got accepted to high school. Look, here's the letter!" Miklós held it out to his mother. "Oh Miklós, that's wonderful" Margit responded, drying her hands to read the letter for her self. "This is what we have been hoping for."

Their district's high school was located in a different town, about thirty miles away. Dormitories housed the students, separated by gender. Between semesters, travel to and from school and their village was done via train. Other than holidays or semester breaks there was little contact with home and family except through letters.

After reading the acceptance letter Margit gave him a hug and a kiss on the forehead. "Miklós, I'm so proud of you. I can't wait until your father gets home. He's going to be so thrilled. I suppose we should begin making plans soon since you'll be going away in the fall." Indeed, there were things he would need to take. Mostly clothing, though no more than a rucksack's worth would be allowed. Bedding was provided by the school dormitory. As joyous as the news was, once it began to sink in with Margit a small bit of sadness came over her, realizing her son was essentially leaving home at such a young age.

* * *

The summer after turning thirteen Miklós returned to work at the mine. His age now permitted working underground. Having experience from the previous summer Miklós was tapped for subterranean work. Demand for carpentry in the mines was continuous, mostly for structural work like framing and bracing. Occasionally the projects were of a larger scale, such as an elevator shaft or a trestle.

One evening over dinner József decided to broach the subject of Miklós venturing into the mine. He was not so concerned about Miklós' reaction, but more about Margit's. "So Miklós, what would you think about doing some work underground this year?" Without a chance for his son to respond Margit paused, mid reach, with a full serving spoon of vegetables in her hand. "Földalatti?" "*Underground?*" She looked at József with concerned surprise on her face. "Miklós? I'm not sure I want him going down in that filthy, dangerous hole in the ground." She glanced at Miklós then resumed filling her plate. József had, of course, anticipated this. "Well, thirteen is the age when you can start working the tunnels. Not everyone has the opportunity to go on to high school as Miklós does. They have to find work. Yes, he would be among the youngest there. And he wouldn't work down there every day, nor would he be in the most dangerous areas. Those require more senior workers. Believe me, deep underground you don't want to rely on anybody green." Margit still objected. "Why haven't you brought this up before now, only a couple of days before he goes back?" József nodded, understanding her apprehension. "Well, it had only just come up. They've started tunneling through a new vein and they need experienced carpenters. Miklós would stay closer to the surface in more of a support role, taking over some of the tasks the more experienced men normally do."

Miklós listened to their conversation, not yet having the

opportunity to respond. Finally he interjected "What if I don't like it? Can I change my mind and do something else?" József had expected the question. "I suppose that's possible. I have the pull to do that, though I think if you agree to try you would be expected to stick it out. It wouldn't look good to the others. You would likely lose their respect, appearing to be receiving preferential treatment." Miklós took a bite, pondering his father's response. He looked at his mother, who was looking at her plate, busy cutting food. He looked back down at his own plate for a moment then answered "Rendben." "*Alright.*" His parents looked up at him. "Why not, it sounds interesting. Papa's been working down there all these years and has told me many stories about it." Margit still had her misgivings, but sensed the conversation's momentum shifting against her. She decided to try a different tact. "Do you remember when you were young and your father came home telling of what happened to István after a cave in? Are you sure you want to face that possibility?" Miklós stared at her for a moment. Margit stared back, letting the question sink in. Little József piped in. "Mama is it dangerous? Can Miklós get hurt in the mine?" She looked at him, then at her husband, then to Miklós, and back to her husband. "Would you like to explain it to him, or shall I?" József set down his fork, put his elbows on the table and folded his hands. "Well son, it can be dangerous. Occasionally people have died while working down there. It's been many years since that's happened. I go down there regularly myself, and I'm still here." Little József made a long face as though about to cry. "But I don't want Miklós to die!" His father tried reassuring him. "Nobody is going to die. It's actually very safe. People die from many things, and sometimes it can't be helped. People sometimes die from getting sick, or in an accident. But if we all try to take care of each other then it shouldn't happen. Okay?" Little József nodded as though he understood but still appeared sad, on the verge of tears, and stopped eating. "Don't worry. I won't let anything happen to Miklós." Looking up at his father little József asked "Te ígér?" "*You promise?*" Placing his right hand over his heart, and his left hand in the air by his side, palm out, his father replied "Igen, én ígér" "*Yes, I promise*".

They continued eating in an awkward silence. Finally, Miklós broke the ice. "Papa, would I be going down in the mine right away?" József paused. "Well, that all depends on the need that day. You'll be briefed on safety procedures and issued gear before you are allowed down." Miklós pondered this. "What sort of gear? Like pick and shovel?" "No, no nothing like that. You wouldn't be digging. You'd get a miners helmet with a light, a tool belt, a flashlight, a whistle; those sorts of things." Little József was curious. "What's the whistle for?" "That's just in case you need help. You can blow the whistle to get someone's attention." Margit added "Or if you're in trouble."

József went on to explain more of what Miklós might expect that summer. "I was thinking you could do some work in the shop too. Maybe some mechanical work, you know, run some of the machines. Metal forming, tool making, that sort of thing." Miklós liked that idea much better. He still wasn't sure about working underground, but he trusted his father.

Besides, he had never been one to shy away from a challenge.

* * *

Miklós first morning back, he and József rode with Jani in the old truck. The spring thaw came late that year, making the roads too sloppy for the motorcycle. Even the truck slid here and there, the wheels occasionally losing traction when negotiating an incline, rain slowing the commute. Warm days had been sparse that spring, overall the weather cooler than normal. Trees were in bloom, but mornings were still cool and overcast.

Along the way they happened upon people stranded in the mud, helping pull wagons and less capable vehicles out of their predicament. It might be a long wait for another truck or a tractor to come along. It was mid morning by the time they turned up at work, the mine already humming along. Ore was rolling out of a tunnel to the crusher, making an awful noise, all quite familiar to Miklós now.

They hopped out of the truck and trudged up to the shop. After banging the mud off their boots and putting up their things they stopped for coffee. "Are you up for a cup of our wonderful brew?" Jani kidded Miklós. "Of course, Jani, how could I get through the day without it?" "We all might be better off skipping it I sometimes wonder" Jani chuckled back. József smiled at the banter, then turned to Miklós "Come on, I want to show you what we've done with the expansion you worked on last year. See you later Jani." Raising his cup Jani responded "All right, be here when the whistle blows!"

As they walked the shop Miklós took note of the changes made since last he was there. Unfamiliar equipment hummed away, operated by a few recognizable faces, some waving back. Passing the metal fabrication area József stopped, pointing out equipment Miklós would likely be working with. "These rolling machines here are typically used to form vent pipes and chimneys. The lathes over there are for making parts when equipment needs repair, or for fabricating specialized tools."

Arriving in the addition Miklós had worked on he realized its purpose. The heavy equipment service bay, used for repairing gear such as trucks and bulldozers, had been relocated to this new section, now cluttered with rail cars, vehicles, and mining equipment in various states of disrepair. Maintenance indoors, away from the elements, was far more pragmatic than working on these behemoths outside.

After being shown around and getting reacquainted with colleagues, Miklós followed his father to another building that housed the miner's personal equipment. Near the front door they came upon a few desks arranged in a makeshift office, unoccupied for the moment. Another doorway led into a large meeting area with seating for up to fifty at a time. "This is where you'll be briefed on mine operations and safety. We have new hires joining us this week so you'll attend the same session as them. Let's look around and see if we can find someone that can add you to the schedule."

***

Miklós arrived on time for training the next morning after stopping for coffee. There were roughly a dozen new recruits joining him, some about his age, but most were older. The instructor came in and introduced himself. "Jó reggelt!" "*Good morning*! I'm Imrus. I'll be conducting the mine safety class this morning. We'll cover the basic procedures, and what to do in case of emergencies. For some of you this will be the first of many classes, depending on your assignments."

The lecture lasted a couple of hours. When finished they were escorted to the equipment room for gear and locker assignments. Afterward, it was back to the classroom for fitting and familiarization, then off to the main shaft entrance

A tunnel not far from the main shaft gate rumbled with loaded coal cars. The recruits would go down the lift in groups of six, alphabetically, as a way of taking roll. Imrus would accompany the first group, with the lift operator returning to bring down the others on subsequent trips. The instructor had to yell to be heard above the surrounding machinery.

They walked down an incline toward a large opening carved into the rock. Descending, the clatter of machinery from above began to fade. Groundwater seeped from the rock over them, making the ramp wet near the entrance. Continuing under the face into a cavity carved in the hillside, they stepped onto a metal platform leading to the lift, gathering near a wire mesh gate to await descent. Imrus addressed the group. "Everyone turn your helmet lantern on. Always make sure it's working before heading underground." They followed his instructions and confirmed each other's lanterns were working properly. A moment later a large electric motor, mounted in a cage to their right, began humming. Serpentine belts and cables wound through wheels and pulleys hanging above their heads. The lift arrived topside, operated by a man donning a hardhat, someone unfamiliar to Miklós. He unlatched the gate and slid it open. The first group boarded. Their stop was about 10 stories down at the shallowest of tunnels. Not that deep as compared with much of the mine, but deep enough for a first visit. No need to spook the new hires their first time. A short descent helped ease them into the unfamiliar surroundings.

A while later the elevator reemerged from the dark opening. Miklós would ride with the second group. The lift stopped and the operator slid the gate open, gesturing for them to step aboard with a nod. "Légy óvatos, ügyelj magadra!" "*Be careful, watch your step!*" Making sure everyone was safely positioned he then secured the gate. The lift dropped slightly as the brake was released, prior to the motor kicking in, everyone experiencing stomach butterflies for an instant. Instinctively they all grabbed a rail. The shaft was dark, save for the few dim lights at the top of their cage. One of the young men looked rattled, backing his way into a corner, leaning back and clutching the rails with both hands. He began moaning under his breath, a look of panic forming on his face. The lift operator recognized the reaction at once. Not unusual for first timers to experience some form of claustrophobia.

The lift slowed as they approached their stop. Opening the gate the operator gestured for everyone to exit into the shadowy chamber, keeping an eye on the panic stricken youngster that appeared determined to remain aboard, shaking his head, speechless. The operator looked at Imrus and shrugged. Imrus stepped back aboard to see if he could talk the guy out. "Son, are you alright? It's time to get off now." The young man just stared into the tunnel, still shaking his head, white knuckle gripped to the cage rail, refusing to budge. Imrus gestured to the lift operator, pointing up toward the surface then addressed the other recruits. "I have to take this young man back to the surface. Wait here and I'll be back on the next trip."

Those in the tunnel watched the lift ascend, disappearing into the darkness above. It was disturbingly quiet underground compared to the surface. The barely discernible sound of machinery could be heard from some unseen tunnel. The two men aboard the lift watched the scared youth in silence as they climbed. Upon reaching the surface the operator unlatched the gate. The others waiting were a little surprised to see Imrus return with the young man. Before the operator could get the gate fully open the panic stricken youth dashed onto the platform, pushing everyone out of his way as he ran into the open. He stopped, threw his helmet off, crouched over and began hyperventilating. Soon he was leaning against the rock face vomiting. Imrus grabbed a phone from the wall and contacted the operator, requesting the infirmary. An escort was needed to help the youth back up to the office. Some of the other recruits appeared troubled by the scene. Witnessing something like that gave one pause before descending into the abyss for the first time. When finished with his call, Imrus turned to the others, sensing the apprehension on their faces. He explained "Not everyone is comfortable in closed spaces. Sometimes it's the lift, sometimes the tunnels. It's a condition known as claustrophobia. It's nothing to worry about. Most everyone will experience a little apprehension their first time, some worse than others." He turned his attention out the tunnel entrance. The others turned to follow his gaze. A medic had just arrived to escort the youth up to the infirmary. Continuing, "It would appear our friend had a severe reaction. Nothing caused by the mine, I assure you. It's all in his head. It happens to someone new every now and then. He'll be alright in a few minutes. Probably not cut out for a career in mining, though." His attempt at humor was lost on them. They looked at each other with nervous gaze. Imrus pointed in the direction of the lift. "Alright, everyone aboard, the others are waiting below."

Those already in the tunnel anxiously shuffled about, curious about the situation at the surface. They were relieved to see the lift returning. Imrus stepped off, quickly getting things moving. "Let's go, follow me! We're running behind." He turned to walk backwards while addressing them. "We're expected down the tunnel." Moving quickly they came to a chamber carved from a coal vein that once occupied the space. There they boarded a set of small rail cars that would take them further into the hillside.

The tunnels, nearly circular in shape, were roughly ten feet in diameter, reinforced with steel I-beams fashioned from railway tracks, bent to follow the curvature of the tunnel. Rough-hewn wooden beams were inserted behind the steel along the tunnel face, insulating the tunnels from dirt and rock that might otherwise fall inward. Along one side electrical cables and communications lines were strung in a bundle, incandescent bulbs hanging from them. The mine generated its own electricity using a small, coal-fired power plant, the miners preferring to rely on their own power generation, shunning the spotty reliability of the government managed grid. Installed on the opposite side was a narrow duct work for circulating air from the surface. The hum of fans emanated from inside at various points. As they walked György explained various aspects of the tunnel's construction and the mine's infrastructure.

The large chamber carved from the rock was an intersection of connecting tunnels. Two of these tunnels had rails running through them, narrower than standard railroad gauge. A majority of cars leading into one tunnel were coal trucks. Miklós recognized them at once, having seen them move in and out of the mine almost continuously. A couple of men were waiting next to a small car, referred to as a miner's carriage. It had a thin steel box for a body, with simple sliding doors for shelter from the elements when needed. They sat on plain wooden bench seats bolted to the frame. Propulsion was provided by a gasoline locomotive hitched to the carriage.

Coal trucks moved differently. Hitched together, they

were pulled in and out of the mine via a system of steel cables, powered by what is known as a winding engine. The same mechanism moved the lift up and down through the mine's vertical shaft. An operator would set the direction of the winding engine based on whether the coal trucks were moving in or out of the mine. In this way, coal was transported out of the mine without the need for separate locomotives. These trucks made a round trip on the same track by reversing the direction of the winding engine.

Once everyone was aboard the carriage the operator engaged the locomotive and they began moving. They lurched forward, accelerating nearly instantaneously as the drive mechanism engaged quickly. Braking was controlled by a separate lever.

Lighting in tunnels traversed by rail was sparse. Some tunnels, carved from solid rock, required no bracing. Occasionally ground water seeping from the darkness overhead splashed the carriage. It didn't take long to learn to slide the doors shut and look down while riding.

Completing the tour, they arrived back at the lift, returning topside for the walk back to the classroom. Here they would learn their crew assignments based on either their skill set, or on an as needed basis, as would be the case with Miklós. Crew chiefs posted the duty roster in the locker room each morning.

* * *

The following week Miklós was assigned to the machine shop. Various metal working machines were utilized continuously for fabrication and repair. Rollers, cutters, lathes, drills, saws, and welding torches combined in a dissonance of sights, sounds, and smells. During one's shift the buzz of activity never stopped except at meal breaks.

His first task was to operate a metal rolling machine. Sheets of metal would be rolled into tubing for various purposes in and around the mine. The length and diameter varied based on the application. As work orders arrived from different departments, they were filled based on priority.

Miklós was trained on the machine for a day, supervised by one of the senior machinists. It was large, with several stainless steel rollers turned by electric motors. The rollers would be selected and positioned by turning a threaded shaft via a spoke wheel handle, perpendicular to the machine. In this way the desired diameter was achieved by running the steel around the appropriate roller. A large cutting machine was used to dimension the sheet metal prior to forming.

One day, as Miklós was feeding metal into the machine, a fellow worker named Ádám happened by. Recognizing Miklós, he stopped to say hello, having worked together briefly the previous summer. Concentrating on his work Miklós missed Ádám standing there. Turning to place a finished piece on his stack Miklós glimpsed him smiling. Shutting down his machine, he removed a glove and extended his hand. "Hey! Good to see you Ádám. Things going well I hope?" "Jó, jó!" "*Good, good*! Glad to see you too. I see you're playing with new toys this summer." "Yes, they're letting me use something other than a hammer! Not that I don't enjoy framing, but it's nice to try something different." They had to yell over the hum of surrounding machinery to be heard. "After the project last summer I moved onto a welding crew. I really like it. I was just on my way to grab an acetylene tank." The welding shed was located directly behind Miklós' work station. "They have me welding coal truck axles today." Ádám pointed in the direction of his work station. "Sounds interesting, maybe you can teach me one of these days?" "Sure. No problem. Well, I better get going. Good to see you!" "You too" Miklós waved. Putting his glove back on, he cranked up the machine and continued working his way through the stack of metal.

Minutes later, *boom*! A horrific explosion took place with Ádám still in the shed, its thick steel door blown off its hinges and striking Miklós in the back with such force his body was thrust forward into the rolling machine. His head banged into the steel face, his arms pinned under his chest. Stunned by the impact of the door and the blinding force of the explosion Miklós was momentarily disoriented. Suddenly, in panicked realization, he felt his fingers being drawn in, his hands landing on a still spinning roller. Friction gripped the glove's fingertips where the rollers were fed sheet metal. If he didn't extricate himself quickly from the gloves his fingers would be crushed - and possibly more. He tugged and twisted to no avail, managing for the moment to keep from being pulled in. As his feet left the ground the flailing of his legs made a chance contact between his right knee and the kill switch. The machine ground to a halt and Miklós slumped in relief, dangling by the stretched fingers of his leather gloves, still captive to the machine.

He tried catching his breath, only to begin choking on the smoke and dust in the air, his ears ringing from the blast. The shock and adrenaline were beginning to wear off, replaced by the pain they had been suppressing. A dull ache emanated from his back where he had been struck by the door. The gloves were constricting his fingers, stretched by the weight of his semi-limp body. He struggled to climb the machine using his legs and feet, searching for a way to gain leverage. Finally, he was able to free his hands.

As his senses returned he realized other machines were still running, presenting a danger. Visibility was limited by the cloud created from the explosion. It was dark, most of the lighting directly overhead blown out by the force of the blast. Miklós' breathing became more regular as his panic subsided. He dropped to the floor, slipping on debris at the base of his machine. Struggling to his feet, he heard voices through the haze. Calls rang out from those rushing to the scene, mixed with cries of help from victims. Stumbling about he located a machine by its hum, leaned against it, fumbled for the switch and shut it down. Miklós barely made out the pained groans of the machine's semiconscious operator above the ringing in his ears, nearly tripping over the man. Still dizzy, he slumped to help the injured man then began calling out "Segít!" "*Help!*"

He heard the voices of workers feeling their way through the dark, demolished shop. It was hard to tell how close they were, the ringing in his ears overwhelming. Again he cried out "Segít!" Moments later he spotted silhouettes moving closer, responding to his cries for help. Someone knelt next to him "Are you all right?" Miklós, barely able to keep his eyes open, looked up at him, then at the man lying on the floor. "Help him" he managed to mumble. The man crawled over to the motionless body. After a moment he looked at Miklós. "I think he's dead." Miklós' head slumped as he slipped into unconsciousness.

* * *

He awoke to the sound of voices and the clang of metal. Blinking open his eyes, he winced at a solitary light bulb hanging overhead from a stark white ceiling. Squinting, and disoriented, he tried sitting up, only his back wouldn't cooperate. He lifted his arms to find bandaged hands. Events began coming back to him; the roar of the explosion, being struck from behind, the struggle against the machine. Miklós turned his head to look, only to experience a sharp pain shooting up his neck. Glimpsing someone next to him, he managed to twist enough for a look. Lying on what appeared to be a cot, he saw a man with his head bandaged. Rolling the other way he found a similar scene. He realized *I must be in a hospital.* Having never been in the mine's infirmary it was not immediately recognizable. "This one is awake, doctor" said a female voice from the direction of his feet. She moved next to Miklós, leaning over him. Wearing a standard white nurse's uniform she spoke in a soft voice. "Do you know where you are?" Miklós looked at her and blinked. His ears were still ringing, not quite able to make out everything she said. He feebly shook his head, attempting to point at an ear with a bandaged hand, indicating his trouble hearing. She understood his gesture and asked again, this time a little louder. Again Miklós shook his head. "You're in the infirmary. There was a terrible accident. You've been here since yesterday. How do you feel?" Miklós shrugged and managed "Alright I guess." His voice sounded muffled inside his head. Lifting his hands to have another look at his bandages he was distracted by a man's voice at the foot of his bed. It was the doctor reading Miklós' chart. "Ah, Miklós, glad to see you're awake. We've been worried about you. You have a nasty bump on your forehead. It must have knocked you out." He looked over the chart for a moment. "Nurse, bring him some water and something for the pain. Then if you would, go out to the waiting area and get his father. He's been waiting all night to hear about Miklós. "Yes doctor" she replied and hurried off. Looking back at Miklós, "I'll be right back."

The doctor came over to examine him, probing various parts of his upper body with a stethoscope, listening for signs of respiratory issues. Satisfied there were none, he pulled back the cloth bandage wrapped around Miklós head to check on the bump. Miklós had not realized his head was bandaged. "Yes, that's a nasty little egg you have there. But, I think you'll be alright. You may feel a little groggy for another day, at least until the swelling goes down. As for your hands I see you can move them. They're a little raw. Looked almost like burns. We applied some salve then bandaged them. You'll have to wear those for a few days. Your hands should be fine." Miklós responded "My back hurts, though. Something slammed into me when the explosion happened. I can't sit up, it's too painful." "How about your legs, can you move them?"

Miklós lifted his legs slightly, wiggling his feet. "Jó."
"*Good*, it looks like your spine is intact." The doctor hung the chart back on the cot by Miklós feet and left to check on another patient.

Minutes later his father appeared by his side. "Miklós, thank God you're alright. I've been worried sick. How are you feeling?" "Not good, but not so bad either. The doctor says I need to wear the bandages for a few days. My back really hurts, though." His father nodded. "We found the steel door to the shed by your work station. The blast must have thrown it against you." "How's everyone else?" Miklós inquired. József formed a grim look on his face. "We lost three so far. Another is critical. Don't quite know if he'll make it yet. Mama is probably worried sick. They sent word of the accident out to the villages. You weren't awake yet. I'll try to let her know today somehow. Maybe we can take you home tomorrow." Miklós nodded. He wondered how his mother was doing. She had to be worried for the both of them.

"So what happened?" Miklós asked tentatively, not really sure he desired an answer. "We're still trying to figure that out" József replied, looking around the makeshift ward. It wasn't the first time this many people were infirmed at once as a result of an accident. "All we know is there was an explosion in the welding shed. All those flammable gases went off like a bunch of bombs. We're still trying to figure out what caused it." Miklós suddenly remembered his conversation just prior to the explosion. "I talked with Ádám just before he went in there. He was getting an acetylene tank." József looked down at Miklós. "We found him, likely killed instantly. We identified him this morning, the only one unaccounted for. Otherwise we never would have..." József stopped mid sentence, shaking his head. It didn't make sense to upset Miklós by describing Ádám's remains. "He was a good kid. Everybody liked him. He had a lot of potential. I'm guessing it was dumb luck he happened in there then. Likely a leaky valve on one of the tanks was the cause. I don't know what would have set it off though." Nothing anyone could do about it at that point. Mining was a dangerous business. For that reason it paid more than many other vocations due to the inherent risks. Men wanted to make a better life for themselves and their families, feeling the risk worth the reward. Unfortunately, the risk sometimes outweighed the reward.

Miklós was sent home the next day. His back was still badly bruised and sore but he managed to walk. Jani and József helped him into the truck for the ride home, each bump and bounce along the way amplified by the pain. The ride was relatively quiet, each man alone in his thoughts.

Upon arriving home Margit came running out to the truck with the younger József. Still not knowing what to expect she nervously held her head in her hands. The men helped Miklós down and she started shaking her hands, crying, unsure whether she should touch him or not. "I'm alright mama, just sore. My back hurts a lot, and I have these." He held up his bandaged hands. Margit was shaking her head, crying, mumbling "Oh my God! What happened? Look at you!" She couldn't resist any longer, finally grabbing him for a hug. "Ouch-

ouch, easy, watch the back!" She eased up a little then leaned back and grabbed him by the elbows. "What happened to your hands?" "My gloves were caught in a machine because of the explosion and tore my skin a little. The doctor says I should be able to take the bandages off tonight." Margit was relieved to hear his injuries were not more serious. "I see a bump on your forehead, and a bruise!" she said pulling the hair back from his forehead. "Was that from the accident too?" "Oh, I forgot about that" he fibbed. He didn't dare tell his mother he lost consciousness from the bang to the head. That would upset her even more.

They helped Miklós in the house and onto the couch. His mother doted over him a while before deciding to finish preparing dinner. Jani needed to leave and said his goodbyes. "Won't you join us Jani?" Margit insisted. "No, the missus is expecting me. She's worried I'm sure, anxious to hear all the news. I'll see you later. Take care Miklós!" "Viszlát Jani." "*Bye*."

Inside, Miklós asked "What's for dinner mama? I'm starving!" Margit's tears were beginning to subside, feeling her son was probably no worse for the wear. "Your favorite, but don't worry, I made plenty in case you want seconds - or even thirds!" Miklós lifted his arms brandishing his bandaged hands, chuckling "I don't think I'll be able to hold a fork with these. I'll have to take them off to eat." Papa said "Let's go look at your hands." The two went into Miklós' room, József lighting a lamp. "Let me know if it hurts." His father began firmly but gently squeezing the bandages in various places, probing for particularly tender areas. Miklós did not flinch, so József removed the bandage from one hand. Marks from the glove were visible, the fingertips raw. Bruising showed through the middle three fingernails. József commented "Looks like you may lose a nail or two. Not too bad, though. You were lucky." Turning Miklós' hand over, he examined the palm. Some bruising on the finger tips there as well. "Can you flex?" Miklós did so without issue. They repeated the exercise with the other hand. "You better show your mother. She'll be relieved."

She took his hands and examined them for herself. "Oh Miklós, are you sure you want to go back to work in that awful place?" "I think so. Papa has been there all these years and he's made it this far." She hugged him, knowing there really was no alternative. "Ouch-ouch-ouch!"

The saying of grace before dinner took on special significance that evening, together as a family for a joyous, yet reflective, reunion. Miklós was a little awkward with the utensils at first but adjusted, giving his brother the giggles. Everyone couldn't help but laugh with him. Margit's tears were masked by her relief. The thought that she could have lost both Miklós and József in a single accident had kept her up the last few nights.

Miklós returned to work the following week. The machine shop was still in shambles. He was assigned to the crew involved in rebuilding and refitting the area. He had a new found respect for the inherent risks of the things around him. The experience had matured him. Changing the occasional flat tire no longer seemed the imposition it once had.

8 Away

The day arrived for the new batch of freshmen to embark on their journey for high school, the next phase of their academic life. It was a bright summer Saturday, the last before fall semester. Those accepted from around the region were to meet at the rail station, boarding a train bound for the county seat of Veszprém (pronounced Ves-prem).

When Miklós' family arrived at the railway station the crowd was already growing. Students and relatives waited in anticipation, anxiety expressed on some faces more than others. The boys were to be segregated from the girls, riding in separate rail coaches. Then, upon arrival at the Veszprém station, buses would carry the students on the final leg.

As departure time approached the crowd swelled. Numerous extended family members had tagged along to bid farewell, adding to the ever increasing crowd. This was, after all, a big event for the families of the students accepted. Most the parents had not themselves attended high school. Given the limited enrollment, such classes were made up of the best and brightest the region had to offer. Friends and family congratulated one another, hugged, gave their best, and shed the occasional tear.

The train soon arrived, right on schedule. Additional passenger cars had been hitched to accommodate the students. As the cars screeched to a stop the conductor and several porters stepped off, followed by the assistant dean to the freshman class, and then the girl's head mistress. They would oversee the students for the remainder of the journey.

Margit had managed to maintain composure up to that point, but emotions finally got the best of her. Her mother Maria, Miklós grandmother, had come along to join in the farewell. She too began to well up as they wrapped their arms around him. "Mama, ne sírj ma." "*Mama, don't cry.*" "I'm not going away forever. I'll be back before you know it." Miklós hugged her tight, making an effort to hold back the tears, lest the other boys see him. The women had already pulled out their handkerchiefs. "I know you'll be back, but you are so young! You're only thirteen!" Miklós finally managed to squirm from their grip. "Mama, I need to go. They're going to be boarding soon!" he pleaded. She grabbed his head with both hands, planting a couple of big kisses on each cheek. Turning to his father, he caught him grinning. He gave Miklós a wink and a big bear hug. "Make us proud, son." Miklós nodded. "Minden

tőlem telhetőt megteszek papa." "*I will do my all papa.*"
Then he hugged his brother just as they began the
boarding call. "Someday you'll follow in my footsteps.
Be good." Brother József smiled and nodded. Turning
back to everyone else Miklós said "I've got to go now."
He blew them a kiss. "Szeretlek mindenki. Viszlát!" "*I
Love you all. Bye!*" His mother and grandmother each
blew him a kiss back, waving.

The students gathered near the assistant dean to
board as their names were called in alphabetical order,
the girls first to be seated in the front car. Eventually
"Falvai Miklós" was heard. Heaving his rucksack over
his shoulder he got in line. Porters tagged and
checked bags to be claimed upon arrival at the
dormitory. Making their way to the front of the line
each student identified themselves to another porter to
be checked off the roll. About to board Miklós turned
and waved to his family. As he disappeared into the
car his relatives strained to catch a glimpse of him
through the windows. All around people were sobbing,
waving, and yelling out words of advice and
encouragement to a departing child.

Miklós sat with Péter, his neighbor friend and wrestling
teammate. Immediately they struck up a conversation
about the days ahead and days past. After roll call was
complete, and the last student had boarded, the
administrators attempted to answer the myriad of
questions they were being bombarded with from
parents. Once the train had taken on all its
passengers and freight, the conductor bellowed the
universal call of "Beszállás!" "*All aboard!*" The head
mistress and assistant dean left the crowd waving and

Iron Cross, Iron Curtain, Iron Will

hurried aboard. The conductor, seeing the loading area empty, signaled the all clear. The engineer released the steam locomotive's brakes in a loud hiss, blew the whistle, and set the train in motion. The wheels spun and the cars lurched slightly as each carriage hitch grabbed the next in succession.

Filled nearly to capacity, the passenger coaches were beginning to feel warm in the summer's heat. Soon they were rolling, creating a welcome breeze through the open windows. Movement also helped sweep away the smoke and coal soot belching from the locomotive. Outside the crowd was yelling and waving their farewells. Everyone on the train waved back, trying to spot relatives in the crowd.

Each administrator headed for their respective car to brief the students on what to expect upon arrival. They were to disembark the train the same way as boarding, through roll call. All were to gather outside their coach and wait to board buses for the final leg. There would be one more stop before arriving in Veszprém.

Miklós had ridden on a train only once before, a family trip to Lake Balaton. For many this was a first experience. The assistant dean left the boys car for a while, returning shortly thereafter with a white laundry bag. "Everyone will receive one of these caps. You are to wear it whenever you are away from the main school building." He placed one on his head. "That way we can identify you as a student. I will call each of you individually to be fitted. Please put it on before exiting the train so that we can all remain together for the bus ride to school."

The first to don his cap was greeted with a chorus of hoots, hollers, and whistles. Turning to face the others, he clicked his heels and saluted, sporting the hat as though a soldier. This elicited laughter and applause from the rest. Further laughter ensued as he marched mockingly back to his seat, the boys standing to salute him. "Actually, you don't know how accurate he is" hollered the assistant dean above the rumble and click-clack of the train. "You will be marching and singing daily as you make your way between campus and the mess hall." "What sort of songs?" a voice enquired from the back. "Mostly school songs - we have quite the repertoire to help keep you marching along."

* * *

Reaching their destination, the assistant dean stood and walked to the car's steps. "As I call your name, please put on your cap and line up outside." The freshmen, stepping onto the platform, immediately noted the scale of Veszprém's station as compared with Csékút's.

The buses were already lined up, the drivers waiting to retrieve the new arrivals for the last leg to school, a few kilometers away. Large buildings of the classic Baroque style lined the streets, exemplifying the architecture common to the region. For most of the students this was the most cosmopolitan place they had ever been.

Arriving on campus they stepped off to claim their bags and get in line. Dormitory rooms had been pre-assigned, the student's names appearing on the doors. There were four students per twelve by twelve foot

Iron Cross, Iron Curtain, Iron Will

room, each furnished with two bunk beds and four small wooden trunks. Cries of "I get the top" could be heard echoing up and down the halls, causing those not already in their rooms to scramble in hopes of claiming a top bunk for themselves. Ten minutes were allowed for locating rooms, stowing belongings, and taking a bathroom break.

Clambering into his dorm room Miklós slammed into another boy shoulder to shoulder as both tried squeezing through the doorway from opposite directions. Practically knocking each other over, they stumbled in, competing for the remaining top bunk. Miklós tossed his things aside and launched himself into the air, his gymnastics skills helping lay claim to the top. The young man he collided with regained his balance and looked up to see Miklós' sitting atop the bed, pumping his fists in the air as a mock gesture of victory. Their eyes met, both staring at each other in a moment of recognition. Miklós' jaw dropped upon seeing his former wrestling archrival, Imre. Though attending different grade schools, they had ended up at the same regional high school. Miklós lowered his arms, shrugged and smiled, saying "Imre, how have you been?" Imre, having to admit defeat this time, went to claim the lower bunk. "I'm alright, how about you?" "I'm doing well, thanks. So, we're roommates. Trying out for the wrestling team?" "Of course, I'm not about to allow you all the glory. You may have gotten the top bunk, but I'll have the top record!" Miklós chuckled. "Ha! We'll see about that."

Miklós, sizing up Imre, knew he wouldn't have to worry about competing for a spot in his own weight class.

Imre had grown since last they met. He had always been at the upper end of his flight weight-wise, but now appeared to be exceeding that. It was advantageous to be at the upper end of a weight class, providing additional leverage against an opponent. The strategy did, however, create the occasional need to go on a crash weight loss program in order to meet weigh-in requirements.

The floor supervisor's voice bellowed down the hall. "One minute, everyone. Get a move on." Miklós and Imre fell out, making their way for the front of the building, their personal rivalry reigniting in earnest. They raced down the hallway and staircase, each trying to be the first outside. Imre squeezed through the door ahead of Miklós, claiming victory.

In the days that followed, the more they talked, the more they had in common. Similar in personality, and having a mutual respect for each other's athletic abilities, they quickly became friends, and eventually wrestling teammates. Although no longer in the same weight class, they sparred together regularly.

Next they were shown to the school store where each was provided a pair of school uniforms. These were to be worn around campus everyday, along with the caps, in order for the faculty to identify students. A matching wool winter coat was included. "Take care of these. If you need additional uniforms, or replacement, you will have to pay for them on your own. Take them back to your dormitory and put them on. You will soon be called for lunch at the mess hall. If late, you will have a long wait until dinner."

After changing into uniform, the call came down the halls to gather at the front of the building for the walk over to the cafeteria. The dean was there to greet them. "Hölgyeim és uraim, jó napot!" "*Good afternoon ladies and gentlemen.*" A distinguished looking middle-aged man in a suit was addressing them. The girls had gathered there as well, escorted from their dormitory building by the head mistress. They wore uniforms nearly identical to the boys, only with a skirt and hose instead of pants. "Welcome. I am dean Zoltán." The dean appeared to be of medium build with salt and pepper hair, wearing wire rim glasses. Looking quite business like, he reminded Miklós a lot of a politician, like a mayor or something. "I wanted to introduce myself on your first day here. I won't keep you long." He went on about how wonderful the academy was, and what was expected of them.

Finishing his introductory speech the dean handed things over to the dormitory's resident supervisor, Mr. Kouach. "We will march four abreast to the dining hall everyday at mealtime. Each of you is to get in line with your roommates as a group of four." The supervisor did not look as business-like as the dean, but meant business nonetheless. He had an athletic build and was wearing a uniform similar to the students. As it turned out, he was also the wrestling coach. "If you do not know who your roommates are yet" he continued, "you are about to be introduced. As I call out the groups of four, the first group is to line up in front of me, arms length apart. For the rest, please fall in line behind the group called prior to yours."

As they lined up they were given instructions on

formation and marching by the supervisor, assisted by other school personnel. "Extend your left arm out, palm down, on the left shoulder of the person in front of you. This is to be your following distance. Next, extend your right arm and place the hand on the shoulder of the person to your right. This will be your formation spacing." He paced in the front of the formation while yelling out instructions. Assistants walked up and down the line on each side, inspecting and assisting as needed. "Please keep your hands where they are until we instruct you otherwise." He stopped for a moment, slowly turning his head back and forth to inspect the group.

"Jó." "*Good*. Now that you are all in place we will demonstrate. First we start marching in place to become familiar with the tempo." The uniformed personnel all began in lockstep. "All right, now everyone join in." Within moments most everyone was in synch, keeping up for the most part. Those lacking rhythm took a little longer. "Nagyon jó." "*Very good*, now we will demonstrate marching forward." The supervisor marched back and forth in front of the lines while his assistants marched up and down the formation. "This is the tempo we will use. Each day for the next few weeks we'll teach you a new marching song to help keep cadence, announcing to everyone around that our proud students are making their way."

The girls were led away first and seemed to be doing fine, with a straggler here and there having to make up an occasional half step to keep pace. The boys watched as the girls went by, and some began pointing and talking. "Csend!" "*Silence*! There will be no conversation while in formation, unless given permission. You are to keep your hands in position until we think you are ready to march otherwise. It may be today, tomorrow, or next week. That is for us to decide." Once the girls had a sufficient head start the boys commenced. "Rendben van, kövess engem!" "*All right, follow me!*"

They began moving in lock step, with the occasional stumble caused by the stiffness of new dress shoes. The assistants marched along side the formation keeping an eye on the student's posture and technique. Turning and marching backwards their supervisor yelled, "Repeat after me", getting them in tune with the chant already begun by the young ladies marching ahead. It was a simple rhyme, designed to keep everyone in rhythm and occupy their minds.

The mess hall was located just off campus on the outside of town, about a two block walk. The campus itself, if you could really call it a campus, consisted of a single large classroom building and two dormitory buildings - one for the girls, and one for the boys – punctuated by a central grassy area utilized for sports and recreation.

Meals were among the few occasions that the genders commingled outside the classroom. Even then, they were required to sit at separate tables. The girls went through line first, followed by the boys. Once marching ceased at the mess hall entrance the boys would often run, push, and shove to be among the first in line, vying for a place closer to the girls.

After lunch they were given a tour of the classroom

building, a singularly large structure, housing not only classrooms and laboratories, but also the gymnasium, the library, and a chapel. Constructed of brick and mortar, the interior floors were wood plank. A sprawling two story structure, about 30 years old, it had been added on to over the years. Only recently had any new construction taken place. Since the war, reconstruction and reparations had diverted school funding. This campus had recently been retrofitted with a hot water heating system, however. There would be no more handling of wood for heat as in grade school since the boiler was heated by a coal burning furnace. However, the stench and soot it produced coated a good part of the grounds during the winter months.

After the tour they returned to the dormitories to unpack before marching to dinner. Lights out was at ten o'clock. Revelry was at five every morning. Rising, they were to don their gym clothes for the morning workout, followed by a quick shower, dress in their uniforms, and fall in for a quick march to breakfast. Afterwards it was back to the dorms to gather their belongings and race off to classes for the remainder of the day.

That night, at lights out, most still couldn't fall right to sleep, the excitement of the day's events overcoming their weariness. They chatted for a while about girls, teachers, classrooms, and the food. One by one they nodded off, sleeping soundly, too tired to be even remotely homesick. As time went on their camaraderie would come to fill the void of family left behind.

Everyone took the same basic curriculum the first two years. Upperclassmen were eligible for elective classes, allowing students to tailor their education toward future endeavors at university. A B-average or better was required to maintain high school eligibility, and also to gain acceptance to university.

Class work was intense, with "homework" assigned almost every night for all subjects. Books were available only in the library, so most studying and fulfillment of assignments took place there, rather than in the dorms. With communism firmly entrenched by the Soviet-backed government, both Russian language and Marxism were required. The students were typically exhausted at the end of the day minimizing socialization during the week, save for a pick-up game of soccer from time to time.

Students were expected to write a letter home every week. Mail calls were a welcome diversion, especially care packages from home. Packages with toiletries, pastries, and other sundries were often the student's highlight of the week. Monetary contributions were especially welcome for the once-a-week trips to the nearby store. It was there they could purchase not only needed items and incidentals, but books and games as well.

Athletics were a welcome diversion for those interested. The government was placing an emphasis on sports, a policy recently adopted by eastern block countries. Participation provided flexibility when it came to class attendance and homework assignments, allowances made to support athletes. Not many sports programs were sponsored on this campus, but those available were practiced at the highest possible levels, practice and competition taken seriously. Anyone excelling had the chance of being recruited for a national team, including the coaches. The school had produced some star athletes at the national level, a few having even been recruited to the Hungarian Olympic team.

With Miklós' love of competition, he naturally gravitated toward the two sports he was practiced in; wrestling and gymnastics. He made both teams, but it wasn't easy. In his small hometown he outshined most. Now he had to compete with athletes from around the region.

Practices took place early morning before class. When competitions drew near there were two a day, morning and afternoon. This curtailed study time, making for some late nights. With lights out at ten o'clock, there was barely time to cover the material. The general store often sold out of flashlights and batteries soon after receiving a shipment. Reviewing notes under the covers was commonplace before exams, especially among athletes.

* * *

As time went on student life settled into a routine. There were, however, processes of elimination taking place, more commonly associated with universities. Despite qualifying for high school, a small percentage of students lacked the required discipline to adapt to the rigors of campus life at such a young age. Some failed to make the grade. A few were expelled for recurring disciplinary problems. Others dropped out due to personal or family issues. A non-deserving number managed to stay enrolled because their families were connected politically, or were fortunate enough to have the financial resources to maintain attendance through other means. Rumors surfaced from time to time of improprieties, but were always difficult to prove. Even if such activity could be verified it might serve to make things difficult for the accuser.

Academically, Miklós gravitated toward math and science, excelling in chemistry and physics. Not so much in the liberal arts, except for his discovery in art class of a hidden talent for sketching. This was when having a network of classmates to rely on for mutual assistance paid off. Tutoring one another in subjects when appropriate was not only expected, but encouraged. Cheating, however, could result in expulsion. Everyone worked hard to maintain their academic standing.

There was a one week break per semester, after mid-term exams, when students visited family. Other than transportation to and from the train station in Veszprém, students arranged their own passage home. Everyone was to return to school on the same day or risk losing prearranged travel from the train station.

Miklós looked forward to that first break. He was anxious to see his family and share his experiences. He was doing well, on track to make straight A's. Following his last midterm exam, he packed some clothes, his best sketches, and his gymnastics ribbons to share at home. He even had a photograph of his team in uniform, along with an individual full-length photograph of himself in his regular school uniform. His mother would like that. And she would get to see him donning his uniform, as it was required to be worn when traveling to and from school.

In Csékút, Miklós and Tibi found their mothers waiting with the boy's grandparents. It was a joyful reunion. Their fathers were at work, and Miklós' brother was in school. There was a lot to talk about. "Miklós! Oh, I'm so glad your home. How was the trip?" ""Jó." "*Good.* Everything was right on schedule. I've got so much to show you." "És Középiskola?" "*And high school?* Are you enjoying it?" She already knew the answer from his letters, but wished to hear it in person. "Igen mama. It's a lot of work but I really like it." They walked to the baggage collection area. "I brought some of my gymnastics ribbons to show you. I took first place on the horizontal bar at one meet!" Margit smiled at him. "I remember you mentioning that in a letter. I'm so glad everything is going well. I can't wait to see everything when we get home." The boys collected their things, everyone heading back to Margit's house where she had already prepared a reunion lunch.

Exiting the station the boys searched for the wagon. Their grandfather asked "Have you heard? We got a truck. We're riding that home today." "Nem, komolyan gondolod?" "*No, do you really mean it?*" Other than József's motorcycle or grandpa's tractor, it was the first real vehicle anyone in the family had ever owned. It was an old surplus diesel flatbed, around ten years old. Getting on in years his grandparents thought it a good idea for working the farm. But as they were getting older, it was really handy for coming into town as well.

Iron Cross, Iron Curtain, Iron Will

The boys were excited, knowing sooner or later grandpapa would let them drive it.

They threw their things in the back and looked the truck over, climbing inside to examine the cab. Not unlike the old truck Miklós rode to the mine with Jani and József, but newer. And the seat was actually cushioned with springs. Riding down the road the boys smiled at each other. They were glad to be home for a much deserved break. Both were looking forward to home-cooked meals and sleeping in their own beds for the next week.

Over a late lunch the boys shared their scholastic achievements with family. Athletic awards, test scores, and written compositions. Tibi was anxious to share some of his piano scores but there was no piano available there. It would have to wait until he got home. Klara declared "We'll host dinner at our house one night this week so everyone can hear."

As they were finishing lunch Miklós' brother József came scurrying in the door, home from school. "Hé József!" Miklós yelled upon seeing him. "*Hey József!*" He got up from the table to give his brother a hug. "Miklós!" József exclaimed running over to his brother, who leaned over to hug him. "Look at you. You're way too big to pick up anymore. You've grown so much since I left." "I know. Coach is already asking me when I'll be ready for wrestling. He remembers how good you were and can't wait for me to join the team." "Oh yeah! Well, let's see how ready you are!" Miklós growled, leaning over and grabbing József behind the legs, performing a mock wrestling takedown onto the rug. József laughed hysterically as he made a vain attempt at defense against Miklós' move.

* * *

The last Saturday before returning to school the families gathered at Tibi's house for dinner. It was reminiscent of the Sunday afternoon meals from days past. After dinner Tibi recited his pieces from school, having practiced during the week. As the wine continued to pour through the evening they gathered around the piano to sing along to familiar songs. Before long it was time to break up the gathering. The boys had to catch the morning train, requiring everyone rise early.

That morning a grey sky loosed the fall's first snow on the way to the station. Not heavy, but enough to wet the streets. With the inclement weather the grandparents did not join in seeing the boys off. Many more students were present for the trip back, all grades returning together. They would not be home again until winter break. Everyone's bags were laden with care packages from home, carrying as much as they could, hoping it would hold them over until the end of the semester.

As the weeks passed the students immersed themselves in study. The final push was on to complete semester projects and study for finals. In the background noise of campus life, mostly unnoticed, the seeds of change were sprouting. Nothing one could point to in particular. Whether it was the students coming of age, or more a societal change, a common thread of hope and independence began taking hold. Miklós, like other students his age, was naïve to this

Iron Cross, Iron Curtain, Iron Will

new wave of optimism, just going with the flow. The mood was catching more with upperclassmen and faculty, a movement that would ultimately come to a head several years later.

* * *

The school year ended and Miklós returned home. Again he would work at the mine. Margit was as apprehensive as ever due to the explosion that previous summer. There really was not much she could do but hope and pray that her men would return home safely each day. Fortunately Miklós' stint at the mine that year transpired without incident.

At fair time Miklós anxiously looked forward to the motorcycle races. As the competitions had gained in popularity more riders and better bikes arrived on the scene. Having saved enough money, he was anxious to begin shopping, knowing that during race week there were always used cycles for sale. Inviting his father to accompany him and Tibi, József enthusiastically accepted.

Miklós was relieved that his mother had finally capitulated. With that taken care of, his father could finally assist in locating a bike. He had his eye on an ESO Scrambler, a Czechoslovakian made motorcycle. Western bikes were unavailable in Eastern Europe, and the ESO (meaning "ace" in Czech) was the premier racing bike in that part of the world. In fact, they were considered world class, essentially clones of a successful British design, some twenty years old at the time, in which the founder of the Czech company, Jaroslav Simandl, had made some improvements. The original design was based on that of the J.A. Prestwich Company, or JAP as it was known. The motorcycle had a single cylinder engine capable of producing forty five brake horsepower, appropriately dubbed the S-45.

That morning would be "guys'" time at the fair. Miklós grandfather drove the truck to pick up József and the boys, dropping off grandmamma at the house, then on to Tibi's. The boys climbed in the back, pressing up to the cab to talk through the open rear window. On the way József coached Miklós about what to say and do regarding the negotiation process. "Miklós now let me do the talking. You haven't had much experience with salesman and haggling. These guys will tell you whatever they think you want to hear. It's easy to get caught up in the excitement and image of what they are trying to sell."

In the days leading up to the races the company roped off an area as a sales lot. There were plenty of shiny new machines lined up alongside the used ones. Walking the lot, one in particular caught Miklós eye, an early model S-45. Though the pale blue fuel tank looked like it had taken a skid on the pavement, Miklós was immediately taken by it. "Papa, look at this one." "Hmm, I see." József came walking over to get a closer look. Tibi was certainly enthusiastic. "That's a great looking bike Miklós. What do you think of it?" "I'm not sure yet. I want to try it out first. I don't see a price." József was looking it over. "It looks like it has taken a spill before. The left handle bar and foot peg are bent, and this side of the fuel tank has scrapes in the metal under where it has been repainted." Other than the obvious damage it seemed to be in good shape overall.

Built for racing, its most distinct feature was the aft indentations on either side of the fuel tank, just forward of the seat, allowing the rider's knees to be tucked inward for streamlining and negotiating curves at steep angles. The top of the tank was arched, allowing the rider to lay over it with outstretched arms to the short handle bars. The seat was a small leather pad, designed without comfort in mind, positioning the rider toward the rear of the bike, creating a low, streamlined profile.

József, a rider himself, was getting caught up in the moment as well. "Szervusz! Szabad segítenem?" "*Hello! May I help you?*" One of the sales staff had noted their interest. "Igen" "*Yes*, we're interested in this one here. Tell us about it." "Well, this one has quite a history" the salesman began. "I can tell that you are an experienced rider, and have no doubt noticed this fine machine's racing condition." Double speak for wear and tear. *Ah, nothing ever changes* József thought. *Horse salesman, wagon salesman, and now motorcycle salesmen.* The boys listened intently to the salesman's pitch despite József's coaching.

After a minute or two of the man's rambling József cut him off. "So, how much?" The salesman hemmed and hawed, but József would have none of it. He glared at the salesman with an impatient look. Eventually he came around to naming a price. József shot him a dubious glance, giving the bike another look over, and then back to the salesman with an incredulous expression. Tibi leaned over to Miklós and whispered "Is that a lot?" Miklós nodded and whispered his reply. "That would be almost everything I have." Tibi looked sideways at Miklós then back at the two men. "Tell you what. Let's have a test drive. You're asking a lot of money and I want to see what she's got." "Well, it is the best thing out there short of our newest model. Some even like the older ones better!" *Right* József thought to himself sarcastically. "Go ahead, give it a kick and rev it up. It has a full tank of gas." József opened the fuel valve, turned the electrical switch and kicked the motorcycle to life. He revved it a couple of times. It was loud. No mufflers on these babies. The salesman walked around to the boys. "Sounds great, yes?" he said with a big grin. The boys looked at him and nodded. The salesman had what sounded to be a thick Czech accent, but spoke Magyarok (Hungarian) very well, most likely a factory employee making the rounds on the racing circuit.

József revved it a couple of more times, put it in gear, let out the clutch, and slowly made his way to the test drive area roped off near the start/finish line in front of the grandstand, then zoomed off. The boys ran out from between the lines of bikes on display in order to get a better view. József zipped around the test track a few times. The bike had a lot of acceleration and cornered much better than his. József's was, after all, a much older twin-cylinder touring machine, never intended for racing. The salesman could tell József was experienced. "I can see your father has ridden before. Does he have a motorcycle?" "Oh yes. He rides quite a bit. He lets me drive it now and then." "So you ride as well?" "Yes I do. We're actually shopping for me." The salesman's eyebrows went up, knowing Miklós would be an easy sell. The young ones are always enthusiastic. Haggling with father would be the trick. "So are you ready to have a go?" Miklós looked at the man briefly, smiling, nodded and then focused his attention back on his father's test ride.

József pulled up next to the boys, leaving the bike idling while he got off, holding it upright as Miklós climbed on. József yelled into his ear above the noise of the unmuffled idling engine. "It's a little awkward with the bent handle bar and foot peg, but you should be able to compensate." Miklós nodded, looking the bike over from the rider's perspective, getting a feel for the controls and the bike's orientation. József backed away as Miklós took off, gassing it and popping the clutch, the front wheel lifting several inches off the ground. Watching Miklós zip off, József could not help but wonder if the thing had taken a spill on someone's test ride. Had it been back through the factory the bent metal would have been straightened and the scraped fuel tank replaced. As it looked, the fuel tank could have easily been touched up by any one of the support crew.

After accelerating quickly down the straight Miklós braked hard going into the first turn. He drove tentatively, the feel and handling different from his father's bike. The test course was, to a lesser extent, configured to create conditions encountered in a road race. On each successive lap he leaned a little further into the turns, increasing speed as he grew more comfortable. A small but steady group of curious onlookers came and went around the track to watch the test drives. The bikes' blaring exhaust always drew attention. After five laps Miklós returned to the starting point, wearing a smile that expressed his feelings. József had been right about the bent bar and peg. Everything else about the bike seemed to operate beyond his expectations. Miklós killed the motor and set the kickstand, circling the bike, looking it over. "So, what did you think? Pretty nice ride, no?" inquired the salesman. "Yes, that was great!" Miklós could hardly contain his enthusiasm, forgetting the advice of his father regarding the art of the deal. "Alright then, let's roll it back and talk about what it will take to get you to ride home on this thing today." The salesman pushed the motorcycle back in line with other bikes. The boys began following him but József grabbed them both by the shoulders and pulled them back, allowing the salesman time to walk ahead out of earshot.

"Remember, let me do the talking" József chided. "We need to talk him down some. We'll use the angle that the bike needs work. I think we can fix it on our own, but he doesn't need to know that. As a starting point of negotiation we'll tell him the parts will need to be replaced." Miklós grandfather tagged along, enjoying the moment, having just been through this sort of negotiation when purchasing his truck. He had grabbed a beer during the test rides. Tasting so good that hot summer day he allowed himself a second. Beer was not readily available the rest of the year, and he looked forward to imbibing at the fair. And this year it was kept on ice for the first time ever! Modern refrigeration had finally made it to Csékút.

The salesman turned to Miklós "Well, what do you think? Are you ready to take it home?" Before Miklós could answer, József stepped in. "That's a lot of money for a young man to spend. He's been working hard and saving for three summers. I don't know if he has enough. And, he'll have to spend some more to replace the handle bars and foot peg. And then there is the scrape on the tank. Who knows what other damage we have yet to notice?" The salesman responded defensively "Sir, I assure you, there is no other damage. The price of the bike already takes into consideration the minor damage." "Minor?" József shot back. "You can't expect someone to drive with a bent handle bar, or a foot peg for that matter." "Well, you two seemed to handle it pretty well out there. Tell you what. I know its tough for a young man to afford something like this. I'll knock off the price of a used set of handle bars and throw in a foot peg." József looked at him, rubbing his chin as though contemplating a counter offer. Suddenly grandpapa piped in, feeling the confidence of a couple of beers. "I think you should throw in a set of inner tubes too. We don't know what's inside those tires." *Burp*. Everyone turned and looked at him. József turned back to the salesman. "Ok, we'll take it with the handle bar discount, the foot peg, *and* the tubes." After contemplating the counter offer the salesman finally agreed. Having a slow day he was desperate to make a sale. "Alright, you have a deal. I must say you drive a hard bargain."

Counting out the money there was little left. "Well, at least you'll have some for gas and oil. Not to mention, you're going to need some spending money back at school." Miklós contemplated the pile of bills he was about to hand over, having worked a lot of long, hard days to earn it. He stared at the bike then smiled to himself *but it's worth it!* They exchanged money and paperwork. Shaking hands "Well, enjoy. You got yourself a great machine there" the salesman said smiling. Miklós was wearing an ear to ear grin. Even Tibi was excited. "Well, let's get this thing home so we can enjoy the rest of the fair" grandpapa chimed in. They headed back to the truck for the ride home.

At home Miklós could not wait to show his mother. "Oh, that looks nice. I like the color" feigning enthusiasm the best she could. Miklós was anxious to take it for another spin. "Papa, I want take it up and down the road to show mama." "Alright, take a couple of runs. Then we need to head on back to the fair. We haven't gotten to do anything at the fair other than motorcycle shopping" he said, letting Miklós get it out of his system. His brother and Tibi took turns riding on the back as best they could on the little racing seat. "How about you mama, want a ride?" "Oh, no thank you dear. That's a little too adventurous for me." That meant riding was over for the day. Papa was ready to go. "Alright, let's put it up in the barn so we can get going. Mama wants to get to the fair too."

Miklós spent the remainder of his summer break occupied with his new obsession. Every morning, upon finishing his chores, he would ride. The last Saturday evening before departing for school Miklós and his father went for a ride together, young József sitting on the back of his father's bike. Halfway through the ride they traded off, driving each other's back home.

As difficult as it was, Miklós would now have to refocus on packing for the trip back to school. He would be a sophomore. *And Tibi a senior* he suddenly realized. They would catch the train to school in the morning.

For now, however, it was time to enjoy his last home cooked meal for a while.

* * *

Although the second year's curriculum was notably more challenging than the first, the students quickly fell back into their routines. The social atmosphere on campus, however, had changed. A subtle, yet noticeable, difference in attitude regarding academics and the future crept into conversations, this momentum of optimism having carried forward from the previous academic year. Students were expressing views of their government and the state more openly. Some defended the one-party system, while others derided it. Not everyone, however, articulated an opinion, choosing to remain neutral regarding politics.

As the academic year progressed, and political discourse heated up, friction between the more outspoken on both sides of the issues sometimes became heated. Incidents of classmates and roommates fighting were expected among adolescent males, but the number of clashes so early that year raised concern among the faculty. Given some of the student's political connections it was often difficult to defend the others involved against disciplinary action, even suspensions and expulsions. Regardless of a faculty member's political beliefs they had not only to enforce the rules, but follow the orders of their superiors, even when those orders violated official policy. As an arm of the government, they often had no choice. Disregarding the rules, or just disagreeing for that matter, could be career ending - or worse.

Clearly, lines were being drawn. Roommates that clashed were reassigned. Most students got along regardless of beliefs, but cliques formed among the more opinionated. Through it all, Miklós remembered the advice given him by his parents some years earlier regarding school and propaganda. As much as he resented socialism, he knew it useless to resist under the circumstances. To arrive at a better life you had to play the game. That is a truism in any system.

* * *

Wrestling season found Miklós needing to make the weigh-in for his position on the team. Having consumed generous portions of his mother's cooking during winter break meant he would now be resorting to extreme measures. He had almost a full kilogram to lose. It was not uncommon days before tryouts or competitions for team members to consume laxatives, parking themselves on the toilet for hours at a time, a practice among athletes having to meet weight classifications. It could be an excruciating, yet necessary, way to meet competitive eligibility. Serious athletes did whatever it took to meet their weight class. Being at the upper end of your classification provided an advantage over lighter opponents, while equalizing one against opponents of similar weight and build.

Miklós was not to sit alone. Several of his teammates joined him in the community lavatory to perform the same ritual. Imre had the opposite issue, having to gain weight, resigned to moving into the next weight class. That evening he happened upon his teammates' rite. "Whew! You guys really should coordinate this so you're not all in here at once. I can barely breathe!"

The comment drew groans and some forced off-key notes from a couple of the organ recital participants. A few managed to chuckle at his remark between grunts - everyone except Miklós that is. He responded with a few choice words instead, inducing further laughter, causing a cacophony of accompanying laughs and toots. Given the circumstance, the laughter became infectious, bringing the performance to its peak. A little humor did help to lighten an otherwise unpleasant situation. "Good lord!" gagged Imre. "I'm getting out of here."

* * *

March of that year saw the passing of Joseph Stalin, the reviled Soviet dictator, only the second premier of the Union of Soviet Socialist Republics (USSR). Following the death of Vladimir Lenin in 1924 he rose to become the Soviet leader, and ultimately the man responsible for creation of the *Iron Curtain*. Though Hungary was officially in mourning, most citizens discreetly celebrated his passing, giving rise to hope that the iron fist of communist repression might soon pass. It was Stalin that had forced collectivized farming on peasant farmers in the Soviet Union, and later on the Eastern Bloc countries, ultimately leading to Miklós' grandparents losing their farms to the Hungarian government.

One of the welcome distractions for the students that semester (and for the population at large) was the Hungarian National Football (Soccer) Team. Emerging as the dominant national team of the early 1950's, they became darlings of the East Bloc media, the "Magical Magyars" capturing Olympic Gold at the

Helsinki games in 1952, captained by Ferenc Puskas. Culminating in the November 1953 defeat of the English, who were previously undefeated outside England, the Hungarian team provided a sense of national pride not felt in a long while.

* * *

As the academic year came to a close Miklós returned home for summer. Papa worked that weekend and couldn't make the reunion. After joining the family for lunch and settling in Miklós was ready to put his bike in order. "Hey József" he called to his brother, "Want to help me get the bike out?" "Sure" he replied enthusiastically. József really enjoyed it when his big brother involved him. "What took you so long?" Margit's father jokingly called after the siblings heading out the back door. "I'm surprised your mother got you to sit down for lunch!" Miklós, peeking back in, said "Grandpapa, you know how much I like to eat. I do have my priorities you know!" Returning to the kitchen he put his arm around mama's shoulders, kissing her on the cheek, adding "And mama always makes something special when I come home!" "Oh, you are such a flatterer my son" she responded, rolling her eyes and patting him on the chest. "You certainly got your father's charm!"

Walking to the barn József informed Miklós "Papa has already been riding his bike to work. The weather has been so nice he decided not to wait for you." "I'm not surprised" Miklós replied. "I would too if I were him." The boys entered the barn leaving the doors open for light. "I helped papa get his ready. He left you some gas and oil over there in the corner." The two untied the rope and folded back the cover, setting them aside.

Miklós rolled his bike into the sunlight, inspecting the spark plug and partially filling the gas tank. Having drained the fuel system for the winter it took several kicks to get the lines primed before sputtering to life. Miklós allowed it to idle a while, and then shut it down to inflate the tires, the air having slowly leaked out over winter. When finished he oiled the chain and gears, inspected the sprockets, and rolled it to test the brakes. Satisfied everything was working he kicked it to life, put it in gear and zipped up to the road. His brother followed, running behind to watch. "Don't forget to come back and give me a ride!" József yelled at Miklós' trail of dust.

He accelerated quickly and then leveled off to make sure everything was working properly. After a half mile or so he turned around, goosed it, lifting the wheel off the ground and went flying past the house. His brother watched him zoom by. Miklós got a feeling of power and freedom on his machine. He passed a truck carrying a load of coal, waved, and accelerated ahead. A ways down the road he had to break hard going around a curve to avoid cows at a crossing, then turned around to pick up József. Approaching the house he spotted his brother sitting on the front porch steps, waiting with grandpapa. Miklós slid to a stop and gestured to József. "Hop on. I'll take you for a ride." József jumped up, running out the gate and climbing on the back. The seat was not meant for two, but József was still small enough to be accommodated. A couple of laps later they returned home, József thrilled as always. Pulling up to the gate he hopped off.

"Grandpapa, why don't you ride with Miklós?" "Oh, I don't think so. I'm a little to old for that sort of thing now. I'd just as soon watch you two enjoy yourselves."

***

As summer wore on, Miklós gained confidence in his riding abilities. In addition to the commute with his father, he would practice racing on the weekends. There were other teenagers in town that had acquired bikes as well. Some were friends from grade school, others he had met since riding, a loose brotherhood of bikers. Together they hung out, heading into the countryside for hours, thrill seeking, racing, and smoking cigarettes. A couple of the girlfriends snuck off with them from time to time, riding on the back of a boyfriend's bike.

Towards the end of the summer Miklós' confidence had built to the point that he considered racing. Having turned fifteen he became eligible that year. One evening over dinner he decided to broach the subject, aware his mother would be a hard sell. "I've been thinking about racing when the fair comes. With all the riding papa and I have been doing, and the practicing I've been getting on the weekends with the guys, I think I can compete." Margit had fretted over this since the previous summer. With all his riding she figured it inevitable, the focus of his free time. Papa sat quietly, waiting to measure Margit's reaction. The younger József couldn't help himself and piped in first. "Versenyzés? Remek! Szabad résztvesz?" "*Racing? Wow! Can I come?*" Margit's reaction was naturally more subdued. "Well I for one am not thrilled about it, but I know you've wanted to race for sometime now. I think it's crazy and dangerous. You could get yourself killed." She stared at him a moment. "But you go right ahead and break your skull open if that's what you want." Not an unexpected reaction from his mother or from most mothers for that matter. Emotional guilt is something mothers dispense naturally.

Miklós did not respond right away, preferring instead to sit quietly and wait for his father's response. Finally József spoke. "Well, you're old enough now to make some of your own decisions. Its one thing to flirt with danger when it comes to work because it is necessary - and lord knows you've been through some dangerous times at the mine. It is however, an entirely different matter when choosing to do something dangerous for the thrill." He paused momentarily, hoping his words were sinking in. Resuming, "That being said I understand your desire to compete. It is thrilling. Hell, at your age I probably would have wanted to do it too, had there been racing back then." Miklós was at once both relieved and elated, but also humbled by the words of advice given by his parents. He nodded to indicate his understanding. József continued, "You are a good rider, and always safety conscious. You certainly have maintained your bike well. What worry's me is the others you would be racing against. They may be a little more prone to risk taking." Miklós appreciated his father's point. "I know. I've watched the races the last couple of years. I know some of the guys shouldn't really be out there racing, but I think I can handle them." József shot Margit a grin and a roll of the eyes, responding to Miklós' naive statement. Overconfidence and a sense of immortality come naturally to the adolescent male.

The next day Miklós couldn't wait to tell his buddies the news. Some of them had already cleared it with their parents. Others had not yet dare ask, while a few had been turned down flatly. They stopped to break from riding in one of their favored shady spots, those that smoked lighting up. One of the boys had snuck a bottle of wine and began passing it around. "Well, I got permission to race from my parents last night during dinner. They weren't too thrilled with the idea but gave in." "My mother said no way" stated another. "My father won't stand up to her. 'Whatever your mother wants' is what he told me. Maybe next year I can talk her into it." A couple of the boys were a year older and had raced the previous year. One described his experience. "I can't wait. Had a couple of close calls but made it through the second heat. Definitely have my eye on the finals this year." The oldest of the group recalled his mishap the previous year using hand gestures to illustrate. "I plowed into a stack of hay bales on turn three. The guy on my inside slid out and knocked me off the track. Luckily I hadn't started accelerating out of the turn yet and all that got hurt was my pride and my bike. The guy apologized once he came to. He was in a daze for about five minutes. He must have taken a really bad bang to the head." Racers did not wear helmets back then, or much else in the way of safety equipment for that matter, save for a good pair of leather boots, a pair of jeans, and maybe some riding gloves.

That week, Miklós and the guys he rode with went to the fair as a group. Those racing signed up for the race that coming weekend. They would be assigned heats randomly, the top three from each advancing to the next round. With more entrants that year there would be more heats, spanning two days instead of one.

They wandered the fair until early afternoon, when it was time to get home and prepare for the following day. Miklós wanted to put on a fresh set of tires and tune the engine. His friends would perform similar exercises. Before heading home they took a ride around the race route, becoming familiar with the track conditions and layout. Preparations were almost complete. Hay bales were stacked strategically at sharp turns and viewing areas. Barricades were set aside, ready to be put in place at race time. Banners were hung over streets announcing the race. People greeted them, waving and shouting words of encouragement as their bikes roared by, a telltale sign that race day was near. "Sok szerencsét!" "*Good luck*!" The boys smiled, waving back, feeling a bit like sports stars or celebrities. After a couple of laps they headed for home.

* * *

Race day Miklós awoke early having slept restlessly. The boys were to meet that morning and ride in together. His family would arrive later, prior to the first heat. There was no way of knowing which heat Miklós was in until starting positions were drawn closer to race time. Margit still had reservations with the whole thing. She was regretting having given in, but knew she really needed to let Miklós go ahead with this. Hopefully he would emerge from the experience unscathed.

Once there, the boys checked in with the race

organizers. Miklós had drawn the first heat, racing nine others for a spot in the top three in order to advance to the next round. Instructions were given on the procedures and rules, and their bikes given a cursory inspection. Each was handed a linen cloth painted with the number they had drawn.

With race time drawing closer the nerves and butterflies began. As experienced a rider as he was, Miklós had never participated in an organized event. This was the real deal. Many of the competitors were experienced racers, certain to be aggressive. He would have to rely on his instincts and physical abilities. Being athletic would certainly help.

With the racers gathered in the pit area his family came by to see him. "Miklós!" his brother yelled, running over to him. "We're here! Are you racing soon?" "Yes, I'm in the first heat." He looked at his watch "About half an hour from now." His father asked "Well, do you think you're ready?" "As ready as I'll ever be I suppose." Miklós was both excited and nervous. The adults could tell. "Sok szerencsét!" was given from everyone, with his mother and grandmother applying hugs and kisses. Miklós tried to play it down, being a bit embarrassed by the gestures, a teenage boy trying to appear macho in pit row.

With race time approaching Miklós and the others in the first heat were given the five minute warning. They walked their bikes to the start/finish line and started their engines. Spotting his family and friends in the grandstand waving, Miklós returned the gesture. Having drawn the number seven spot meant he was seventh from the left, putting him toward the outside of the first turn if he were to maintain his initial position. This would be his assigned number throughout the event. The number, painted in black on the linen square, was to be pinned to the back of the shirt and worn throughout every race. He would have to battle for a spot on the inside down the main straightaway in order to move up in the pack. The race was five laps, two kilometers (about one and a quarter miles) per lap.

The racing official walked the starting line, making sure everyone was ready. Returning to the edge, he verified all riders were behind it then moved forward to the starter's position. He raised the green flag, indicating the race was about to begin. It was loud, everyone revving their engines, ready to engage the clutch. So loud, in fact, that the riders could not hear the crowd cheering them on.

The flag dropped and they were off. Miklós got a good start, jumping ahead of the rider to his left, positioning himself a little further to the inside heading for the first turn. The rider in the number eight position had a good start too, and was coming up on Miklós' right, no doubt pursuing the same strategy. All of them accelerated quickly down the straight, having to brake hard to negotiate turn one, a ninety degree bend. Miklós was in sixth place as they entered the turn, further to the outside than he had hoped. About thirty feet ahead the bike in second place lost traction and started skidding toward the outside, crossing the road and taking down the rider in third. The two just ahead of Miklós steered wide trying to avoid the mishap. One of them went headlong into the hay, wheels screeching and smoking as he locked up the brakes, hitting with a thump, launched over the handlebars and somersaulting into the stacked bales. The other rider had to lay it down on his left side just in front of Miklós. The racer that had triggered the whole thing was rolling across the pavement, his bike having spun around with the front wheel now facing the oncoming racers. The bike and rider behind Miklós went tumbling over the bike on the ground, narrowly missing its rider. Miklós braked hard cutting left, having to lay his bike down as well. He slammed the pavement on his left side, the bike sliding out from under him into the hay, wheels first. The riders at the rear of the pack had to scatter in all directions to avoid becoming a part of the melee. Only one of them managed to maintain control and avoid the others.

Miklós escaped with only a scraped elbow and torn jeans. He hopped up and scrambled to his still running bike and righted it. Jumping on he maneuvered around a couple of bikes and riders still scattered on the ground. He could not tell if there was any significant damage to his own motorcycle, focusing instead on catching up with the others still racing. He accelerated into the next straightaway dashing to make up lost ground. He was in fourth place now, the rest of the field spread out all over the first turn. One of others left behind finally managed to get back on his bike as well, furiously trying to kick the engine back to life. After several tries it turned over and he too was able to rejoin the race, albeit from even further behind than Miklós.

A few moments later word of the crash made its way through the crowd, many having already recognized the screech of tires and metal in the distance meant an accident. Margit grabbed József's hand and squeezed, worried over the fate of Miklós. She was looking and listening frantically, wondering where he was. József looked about anxiously as well, unsure whether to get up and inquire as to the fate of Miklós and the other riders.

Miklós raced like a madman to catch up. Negotiating the track, he leaned steeply into the turns, quickly accelerating out of each one. He hardly noticed the spectators cheering him on, narrowly missing one that dashed across the street as he came out of turn four. Making his way back to the straightaway in front of the grandstand he spotted the third place rider ahead, about halfway to the first turn. Miklós, determined to catch him, accelerated so hard out of the turn his front wheel lifted slightly off the ground. This drew a loud cheer from the crowd as he shot by them in a blur. Miklós' brother József stood up pointing and yelling "Look! There's Miklós! Wow! Look at him go!" turning his head to follow the action. Margit sighed in relief, making the sign of the cross, then placed her hand on her heart and leaned against her husband. Putting his arm on her shoulder he squeezed it tight. She was not sure she had the emotional endurance to make it through the race, the stress of it already taking its toll on her.

As Miklós came into turn one he was relieved all the bikes that had taken a spill were safely aside. One of the riders involved in the crash was being taken away on a stretcher. Exiting the turn he came upon lot of heavy, black smoke. Miklós slowed down, visibility almost zero as he entered the dark cloud. Blowing through it he could make out one of his fellow competitors on the side of the road, frantically trying to extinguish the flames coming from his bike, aided by some spectators. He could not tell if it was someone that had wiped out earlier, or one of the others that had been ahead of him. Remaining focused on trying to catch the lead pack he gave it no further consideration.

Desperately trying to gain ground he pushed himself and his bike to the limit. Back at the main straightaway the race judge was waving the flag that indicated one lap remained. Miklós had lost sight of the racer ahead. *I've fallen too far behind.* Racing on, he resigned himself to the fact that fourth place was respectable, just trying to put in the best time he could on the outside chance he could get into a later heat based on a technicality or a lack of finishers. After passing the checkered flag at the finish line he maneuvered his way back into pit row. All his friends were there to greet him. They were cheering, patting him on the back. "Miklós! Way to go! You made it!" He wondered what the big deal was. *So I made it* he thought? "Well, I guess fourth isn't so bad. What's the big deal?" "Fourth? What? No, you got third!" Miklós' eyes got wide. "What?" he asked in a daze, having been disappointed with what he thought was a fourth place finish. He was still coming down from his adrenaline rush. The boy repeated himself yelling over the noise in pit row. "You were third, not fourth. Why'd you think you were fourth?" Miklós explained "I've been trying to catch third place for a couple of laps." "Well, you were third. You're going on to the next round. Good luck, buddy. Hope to race you there. Got to go, my heat's next!" Miklós couldn't believe it. *Third place*? In his mind he was playing catch-up most of the race. It turned out the bike that caught fire had belonged to the third place rider he had been pursuing.

Miklós got off his bike to rest and get a drink of water. He would soon need to prepare for the next round. Minutes later his family appeared to congratulate him. "Look who it is, Mister hot-shot racer" his father called from behind. Miklós turned around and smiled. "Hey, I made it!" He hugged his father with one arm, holding a cup of water in the other. "You're lucky that your mother didn't have a heart attack. She was frantic the whole time." József held up his hand to Miklós as if it were deformed. "She was squeezing so hard I don't know if I'll ever be able to use it again!" "Oh please!" she scolded, slapping him on the shoulder. She hugged Miklós then looked at him. "Look at you, you're filthy" she said, taking out a hanky and wiping his face. "Mama! Stop!" She dipped the hanky in his water and tried to clean him. It was no use trying to back away. She grabbed him by the shirt, making him hold still. His brother was amazed. "Wow Miklós! I've never seen you go that fast." He noticed Miklós' elbow injury. "Hey, your arm is bleeding!" Margit looked down upon hearing this and examined the wound. "What happened? It looks as though blood has been running out all over." Miklós made his admission. "I slid out on the first turn. Someone in the front lost control and a bunch of us went down with him. I scraped my elbow going down, nothing serious really. My bike was still running and I hopped back on." Margit shook her head. "See, I knew you'd get hurt somehow." "Oh mama, I've had much worse. It's no big deal really." Now she became even more anxious. He had at least one more race to go. József figured it was time to intervene. "Well, there are a few more heats before Miklós has to get out there again. Let's clean up that arm and get some lunch."

As they walked Margit leaned in to József, speaking in a subdued voice. "He's been in a crash already, and it was only his first race! Is he going to crash in every race? If he keeps that up he may not walk away from one of them." József shared her concern. "Well, if he is involved in another mishap we will definitely have to rethink this whole racing thing. I agree. The odds don't seem in his favor so far." Margit voiced some additional concerns. "I don't want him becoming a thrill seeker either. He needs to concentrate on school. And what if he gets hurt and laid up before school starts? He could miss a semester or even a whole year and lose his eligibility." József nodded. It was not worth risking his academic career.

After Miklós was cleaned and bandaged they grabbed a quick bite and headed back to pit row. One friend had advanced and would be in the next round's heat with Miklós. It would be the third heat of six in the second round. Again the top three from each would move on to the final heats scheduled to be run the next day. Miklós prepared his bike for the upcoming race. Upon inspection, he found the crash had caused minimal damage. Just scrapes to some of the metal and a torn handle bar grip.

Starting positions for the subsequent heats were based on the racer's time in the previous round. Due to the accident in Miklós' heat, the time lost had given him a disadvantageous starting position. That being said, had the crash not eliminated some of the other competitors he likely would not have been racing that round. Miklós was assigned the number eight spot in his heat. He would be playing catch-up from the start, and any racers advancing to subsequent rounds were likely to be among the most skilled in the field.

The five-minute warning was given. Racers walked their bikes to the starting line and started their engines. The sun shone at a lower angle toward the West. That could come into play. Some of the riders wore sunglasses. It hadn't occurred to Miklós he might need them, making a mental note to acquire a pair in the future.

The green flag dropped and they were neck and neck going down the straight, each rider jockeying for position. Going into the first turn it would come down to who blinked in a high-speed game of chicken. The further to the inside one pressed the better one's position for negotiating the turn. As the pack drew closer to the bend they crowded each other more and more to the inside. Things were going to be tight, everyone's adrenaline levels high.

Miklós felt someone behind rub tires. Focusing on those ahead, the bump was a reminder of just how tightly they were bunched. He decided to brake early and avoid being forced outside. The guy that bumped Miklós, not expecting the maneuver, braked too late. Flying past Miklós on the left, they clipped handle bars, momentarily forcing the two toward the outside. Already applying the brakes, Miklós was able to maintain control, but still ended up in an unfavorable position. Forced way right, toward the hay, the driver that clipped Miklós went down hard, face forward on his left, slipping on the pavement then rolling, his bike sliding outside and up against the bales. Miklós narrowly missed ramming the two riders to his right. By the time he regained control the leaders were exiting the curve and accelerating away. Miklós practically stopped to avoid running off the track. Working his way around the downed rider and bike he was now in pursuit from last place.

He accelerated hard to catch up. Not expecting another bike would be coming along from so far behind spectators had already moved into the street to watch the two packs go by, jumping out of the way upon hearing Miklós approach, the sound of his engine echoing off the buildings lining the village street. The crowd cheered him on as he roared by. They knew they had a race on their hands. Miklós took each turn as tight as he could by leaning in even more than before, pushing himself and his bike to the limit.

Coming out of the final turn into the main straightaway he spotted the second pack, half way down the stretch to the first turn. He was closing the gap, making up time riding alone. He goosed the accelerator and the front wheel lifted. Snap! Something slapped the bike's frame, the engine suddenly whining loudly at high rpm's. The front wheel came down and Miklós eased off the accelerator. He tried shifting down but nothing happened. Coasting off the track he looked down to find the chain missing. Looking back he saw it laying on the track. One of the race crew ran out to remove the potentially hazardous piece of debris before the rest of the field came by. The crowd's cheers turned to groans, realizing his predicament.

Damn! His chain had broken, taking him out of contention regardless of what happened, unable to finish the heat. His race weekend had come to an abrupt end. Miklós cut the engine and coasted back to pit row. He had not counted on this.

His family arrived to console him. "Looks like I'm going to need a ride home grandpapa" Miklós sulked. "Rendben" "*Alright*, and since you are my grandson I'll give you a discount rate" he quipped, trying to lighten the moment. Grandpa was enjoying the beer again. Miklós forced a smile across his disappointed face. Margit was outwardly sympathetic, but inwardly relieved. He had survived the experience with only an injured elbow and a wounded ego, and she with a few more gray hairs. His friend from the same heat advanced to the finals, placing sixth overall. Not bad for a field of around one hundred. "Mához egy évre" he stated "*This day next year* that will be me in the winner's circle!" The gang congratulated him on being the only one of them to finish in the finals.

9 Risks

The third year of high school found Miklós without the accompaniment of his cousin Tibi, now off to University, having departed the week before. Miklós roomed with Imre again, who was in the process of unpacking when Miklós arrived. "Hey! Miklós! So, how was your summer? Do anything exciting?" "I was in my first motorcycle race." Imre knew Miklós had a bike but was not aware he would be racing. That had been decided after school had ended. "Really? Sorry I missed it. I see you survived. So, how did you do?" "Not bad, but not great. I made it into the second heat but I threw my chain and couldn't finish." Imre consoled "Well there's always next year." Miklós returned the question. "How about you, do anything interesting?" "I coached some kids at a wrestling camp in my town and got paid for it." "Not bad, getting paid to teach wrestling." Imre paused before continuing "And I met a girl." Miklós stopped unpacking his duffle bag and turned toward his friend. "Oh really, and how's that working out?" "Good. She works in the local bakery. She didn't go on to high school. I can't stop thinking about her." He presented her picture to Miklós. "Pretty. Known her long?" "Yes, since we were young. She's the sister of my best friend growing up. We kind of lost track of each other the last few years, but I ran into her at a picnic up at Lake Balaton and we really hit it off. We've been seeing each other for the last couple of months. I'm already looking forward to midterm break." Miklós chuckled and shook his head. Having not yet known love himself, other than the occasional crush, he could not relate to what Imre was experiencing; first love.

Hanging out with his friends that summer Miklós had picked up the smoking habit. Imre noticed the cigarette packs lying on the bed as Miklós emptied his bag. "I see you have something new to spend your money on." "Huh? What do you mean?" "You're smoking now I see." Miklós looked down at the cigarettes. "Oh yeah, the guys I ride with got me into it. The smokes seem to help me relax." Imre had tried cigarettes that summer as well, but didn't care for them. "When's lunch, I'm starving." Miklós felt a little famished too. "Soon I suppose. They should be calling for us any time now. I'd better finish unpacking."

* * *

With the passing of Stalin that previous spring people began airing their political opinions more openly. The seeds of change often are sown on university campuses, and to a lesser degree, at high schools. With the upheaval that had taken place in their country's political and legal systems over the years, the youth of the country were ready to push change, naively optimistic about the future direction of the country. For this reason repressive regimes, when sensing discord, real or imagined, periodically purge their countries of academics. Free thought is dangerous to the stability of an authoritarian government.

Stalin had been succeeded by Nikita Khrushchev, who ultimately deepened The Cold War between the East and West, tightening the Soviet grip on Eastern Europe, and isolating it from the rest of the world. Travel in and out became highly restricted for both citizens and visitors. With the media under government control, dissemination of news and information was severely curtailed. Only that which served propaganda in a positive way was allowed distribution.

* * *

Regime change had brought new found optimism. Even some of the faculty was beginning to tread cautiously toward more free and open discussions. Nowhere was this more evident than in philosophy and political science, a mandatory course each year, with the express purpose of influencing youth by contrasting the "virtues" of Marxism with the "evils" of Capitalism. A few teachers, embracing free thought, introduced materials normally considered counter to the curriculum's purpose. Encouraged, they wished to restore academia to its rightful place. It might take some time before the bureaucrats caught on, perhaps being too late to halt the momentum once they did.

Nowhere was this trend of openness more evident

than at university. At midterm break Miklós and family gathered at Tibi's house one evening for dinner. The boys each grabbed a glass of wine and went outside, sitting on the porch steps to have a smoke, Tibi also having taken up the habit. "Miklós, university is unbelievable. There are so many interesting people with different ideas. The laboratories and athletic facilities are beyond anything you've ever seen. The auditorium has wonderful acoustics, and I get to perform on a grand piano with the orchestra. And the girls! There are so many more. Some are really beautiful, and they're all really smart. Some of our female professors though – yikes! I think they could best you in wrestling. They must have been in the army." Miklós laughed. University sounded interesting. He could not wait for his turn. "Vacsora van felkészül!" "*Dinner's ready!*" came the call from the dining room. They flicked away their cigarettes and went in to eat.

At dinner the conversation centered on Tibi's life at Eötvös Loránd University, located in Budapest. It differed from the mining engineering school that Miklós wished to attend, offering more degrees and specialties, including law and medicine. In its distant past it had been named the University of Budapest, but in 1921 was changed to Pázmány Péter University. In 1950 it was renamed again to honor the physicist Loránd Eötvös.

With newfound confidence students at university were becoming more politically involved. There had been popular support for the newly elected premier of Hungary, Imre Nagy. A controversial figure in communism, he had been banished from the party at one time due to unfavorable comments toward the government, but was later reinstated after publicly recanting. He was elected by the Hungarian communist party to the position of premier in 1953 on a platform of worker support. Implementing a more liberal form of communism, he opposed the hard line system imposed up to that time. To consolidate support for this new approach the political coalitions that had been established with the minor parties in the early days of Hungarian communism were abolished in 1954.

* * *

The close of school found Miklós one year from graduation. That summer he once again descended into the mine, spending the days underground more often than not. New tunnels were being dug at rates higher than ever to support increased demand, requiring additional equipment and infrastructure. Miklós was assigned to a crew erecting tunnel bracing and trestles.

Equipment, technology, and demand were driving the mine deeper. Miklós' crew was descending, on average, to about 360 meters (approximately 1200 feet). Since a single lift could not be constructed to support such depths the trip required transferring from one to another through a series of tunnels, sometimes taking upward of an hour or more to reach an assigned work area.

Working in close proximity to the tunneling machinery was dangerous, but erection of tunnel bracing was being expedited to support recently cleared sections.

Equipment vibration caused frequent collapses of loose rock and coal. Hard hats and safety glasses often spared workers serious injury. Given the threat of cave-ins, a series of escape tunnels were constructed throughout the mine intertwined with the main tunnels. These passageways were extremely small, sometimes with only enough space for someone to crawl through. After a serious cave in these escape passages could become a miner's only hope. Vertical shafts equipped with crude wooden ladders, a part of this lattice work, provided an ascent path from one level to another. Miklós would learn first hand the importance of these secondary passages.

Blasting was employed to accelerate the extraction of coal from a seam or to remove sections of rock impeding progress. After the charges were set detonation was performed remotely, with workers moving up to another level for safety until the all clear was given. Fully evacuating the mine was considered too time consuming due to the limited lift capacity. Normally these operations went without incident; but not always.

One particular day Miklós and crew were moved two levels above to await a blast. Tensions ran high in anticipation, especially among new hires and those having survived a cave in. Miklós had experienced subterranean blasts before, always without a hitch, but never at such depth. The warning horn sounded, indicating detonation was imminent, bringing a cessation to most mining activity in preparation. Finally the blast was heard, then felt, an earth shaking rumble reverberating through their tunnel. At first only small bits of material loosed from the walls and ceiling. For about thirty seconds the crew sat quiet, motionless in a small chamber, listening for the tell-tale signs of danger. Then it happened. The crackling of splitting timbers could be heard giving way to the immense weight from above. *Boom!* A large section of tunnel near the lift shaft collapsed with a thud, shaking the ground again. The men ducked in unison, curling up and covering their heads, pelted with pebbles and clods of earth. Minutes later they began to stir, coughing on the thick coal dust stirred up by the collapse, cautiously taking note of the situation. The sounds of danger had ceased for the moment. Electricity to their section of tunnel had been cut off, leaving the miners in total darkness. By the light of their helmet lanterns they discovered the primary exit to the surface choked off by dirt and rock.

As a precaution, the chamber they had retreated to preceding the blast connected to the entry point of an escape route. Forced now to evacuate, the crew chief began preparing the men. Entering single file, they walked hunched over, the tunnel barely four feet tall and just wide enough for one man at a time. Minutes later the lead man came upon loosed debris that made passage nearly impossible. "Állj! Várakozás itt" he called out to the men behind. "*Stop! Wait here.*" A seasoned veteran of the mine he knew his way around. With barely enough room to squeeze through the opening he got down on the floor and began wriggling on his belly, propelling himself by his forearms, the only light that from his dimly lit helmet. Several meters from his starting point he encountered a large rock blocking the way. His light shone past the space between the tunnel walls and the obstruction, just able to make out the cavity on the other side. It appeared there was an opening just on the other side. Pushing firmly on the rock he could not immediately move it, lacking the leverage needed in such a confined space. Using his hands to dig and push the loose dirt from around the base he eventually shoved it out the other side, rolling to the bottom of the pile. Sliding through the opening he could again crouch on his feet. A ladder shone down the tunnel about 10 meters ahead by his helmet light indicated a vertical passage out.

Turning back he crawled up through the dirt again, shining his light back the way he had come, calling out "Rendben, kövess engem." "*Alright, follow me.*" The men resumed their escape, following head first after the lead man. As the first few reached him, he turned his attention toward the ladder leading up the shaft. Approaching, a pair of legs suddenly appeared from above, descending. "Hey there, what's going on?" Startled, the man coming down the ladder turned to look, not expecting to encounter anyone else. Seeing the other miner's lamps emerging through the small opening he responded "The tunnel above is blocked. We came down here to find another way out." This was unfortunate news. "We're trapped as well. The main tunnel down here collapsed." Continuing on with this narrow passageway was their only choice. "How many of you are there?" "Just three, the others are climbing down now." "We're fourteen. Everyone's alright. I'm waiting for them to come through. There's some debris partially blocking the way." The others making their way down came into view. Assessing the situation, there was but one option. One of the men that had just come down turned to the others and said "We'll scout ahead while the others catch up."

Fifteen minutes later they came upon the next vertical shaft. The two leading the group climbed the ladder, thirty feet or so, to assess the situation. Once up they could see a distant light shining from the direction the lift should be. "It looks clear" one of them called down. "Felmászik." "*Climb up.*" The light was a welcome sign. It meant power was available in this tunnel. The men stretched as they climbed out of the confining space of the escape passage, relieved to have found a way out.

Soon everyone had ascended and been accounted for. The group began walking toward the light. Closer, they heard the hum of the lift as a search and rescue crew was making its way down. Continuing on, the crews met up about fifty yards from the lift and reported their situation. Good news. They were the last of the unaccounted miners. That meant there were no known casualties. Once everyone was safely out the next shift would begin the task of cleanup.

József waited nervously at the surface for news regarding the missing crew. The call came over the intercom that everyone was safe and sound. A collective sigh of relief spread among the men above. Obviously something had gone wrong with the blast. No matter how much they refined their technique there always remained the danger of cave-ins. No one could explain why it sometimes happened. They just knew that the structure of the ground below was often unpredictable. Fortunately, Miklós did not experience any more life threatening situations at work that summer. The mine was, however, not the only place

Iron Cross, Iron Curtain, Iron Will

Miklós would encounter danger.

* * *

Miklós and friends looked forward to the coming competition, considering themselves veteran racers, confident they could improve their performance over the prior year. As during that previous summer, they practiced whenever possible, spending time fine tuning both their bikes and skills.

The arrival of race weekend found the boys making pilgrimage to the fair grounds. With the popularity of racing on the rise, prize money for the top three finishers had increased, as had the number of entrants, and consequently the entry fees. The boys surmised that meant more inexperienced riders. Hopefully one from their group would take home some money.

On race day Miklós had drawn the number 48, a bit of bad luck. That meant he would be racing in the fourth heat in the number eight spot. Starting in such a disadvantageous position required turning things up a notch to gain position into the first turn.

Through the first three heats, two of Miklós' friends managed to advance. One of them had even placed first, assuring a good starting position in the subsequent round. Receiving the five minute warning Miklós donned his gloves, the heat's competitors walking their bikes to the start/finish line. His father, brother, and grandfather had accompanied him in pit row during preparations, now making their way to the grandstand amongst the other spectators. Margit had decided to opt out. Based on her experience the previous year she felt the stress too much to bear again.

The racers started their engines, inching to the line. Miklós stared at the starter's flag unblinking, ready to rev the engine and pop the clutch. The flag dropped and they were off. It was a clean start. Miklós leaned as far forward as he dared in an effort to keep the front wheel grounded. Maintaining control at the start was essential to gaining advantage and maneuvering for position. Flattening his body reduced air drag as well. The strategy worked. He shot ahead of the pack, his lead less than a bike's length. He fought hard for the inside, cutting off several riders on the final portion of the straightaway, positioning himself for the first turn.

Conceding the inside, he entered wider than desired, managing to hold second. Leaning hard left through the curve his knee grazed the ground, the grip of his tires against the road pushed to the limit. Shifting down and gunning the engine out of the turn his front wheel was now even with the lead rider as the course straightened out. The crowds lining the streets cheered loudly seeing everyone in the heat still giving chase. He sensed the rider behind trying to make a move. Into the second turn Miklós hugged the inside on the right, warding off the challenger to the rear. For the moment his strategy was to stick behind the leader, waiting for an opportunity to overtake.

Turn three found the racers entering the first half of an S-curve. Four riders comprised the lead pack now, separating from the rest of the field. The rider in fourth challenged for third on the outside. If successful it would give him the advantage in the latter half of the serpentine. Miklós held fast to the inside, maintaining position, then began drifting to the outside in preparation for the next turn. Unaware of the two behind jockeying for third, Miklós nearly foiled the fourth place rider's plans to overtake. Neck and neck, the two trailing riders were forced to go left into the curve together, fourth overtaking third on the inside. Coming out of the curve they broke into the next stretch, everyone accelerating hard, trying to gain advantage. They shifted down, slowing without braking into turn four, a long gradual curve that allowed them to maintain a fair bit of speed before entering the main straightaway in front of the grandstand. All four hugged the inside tight, maintaining speeds that pushed the limits of both driver and machine. Sensing an opportunity, Miklós accelerated earlier than the others as they swung around the curve. He made a move, passing on the right, outside the leader coming out of the final turn. Shifting down and accelerating, he was even now. The lead rider spied Miklós out of the corner of his eye, responding to the challenge, both of them lying in a streamlined posture, shifting up as their engines began to redline. Miklós was glad he had put on a new chain days earlier, allowing sufficient time for stretching and break-in. He did not want a repeat of the previous year's unfortunate mechanical failure.

Approaching turn one, they were even, with Miklós forced to the outside. Taking a chance, he maintained a more aggressive speed than before, fearing that backing off could eliminate what might be his one opportunity to overtake. He was hell-bent on grabbing the lead. Downshifting into the turn (the most dangerous aspect of motorcycle racing) his rear wheel suddenly began bouncing, the bike bucking wildly. He had made a classic mistake; the RPM of the motor must match the speed of the wheel or the transfer of energy will go elsewhere, typically into the rest of the bike. Realizing his mistake he braked hard, locking the wheels, vainly attempting to lay the bike down on its left side, hoping to skid into the hay bales. The rear wheel began sliding out from under him as intended, but then caught traction. The bike's slide stopped abruptly, flipping upright. Miklós was instantly thrown off. Squeezing the brakes and pulling back on the handle bars he hadn't released his grip in time. This, coupled with his forward momentum, flipped the motorcycle into the air, slamming into his back just as he made contact with the ground on all fours. His hands hit first, the leather gloves grabbing the pavement, causing his arms to buckle under the force. Knees skidding along behind, his jeans shredded from the friction of the asphalt, tearing his flesh. He rolled on his right shoulder, scraping his ear and scalp. The bike bounced off him, cart wheeling into the bales. Miklós was rolling and sliding along at forty miles an hour, finally stopping after disappearing from sight, buried somewhere in the hay.

Volunteers and spectators rushed to his aid, digging through the pile to reach him. He was conscious but in shock. One of the rescuers called for a stretcher. Miklós' was bleeding from every part of his body that had engaged the pavement. The gloves spared his hands, keeping the skin from being torn away. "Hold still buddy, we're going to get you out of here." Miklós tried to sit up in his semiconscious state but the man held him down. "Don't move. There's help on the way." Miklós' shoulder was throbbing and the right side of his head felt numb. Two men arrived with a stretcher, hoisting him onto it, scurrying away to an ambulance stationed nearby. Around the time Miklós' was being loaded, his family members noticed him absent from the racers emerging from turn four.

The ambulance sped off, siren blaring. Miklós faded in and out of consciousness. The medic splashed cold water on Miklós' face by wringing out a cloth in an effort keep him awake. Sitting up slightly he attempted to take stock of his injuries. The medic eased him back down. "You're going to have to lie still and take it easy. We'll be at the hospital soon." Pain began setting in as the shock wore off.

Arriving, he was unloaded and rushed in. The medics yelled out the patient's condition to the nurse on duty. She called for a doctor then began working on him right away. The medics would remain until help arrived on the floor. The nurse took vital signs as the medics tore open the clothing around the injuries. She then prepared to flush the wounds. Miklós seemed focused on the sharp pains emanating from his shoulder and neck area until the nurse began flushing out his cuts. The stinging sensation shifted his attention toward her. Another nurse rushed to join the group aiding in his treatment. All clothing except underwear had been cut away by the time the doctor arrived. The nurse called out vital signs as the doctor began his exam, probing Miklós' abdomen looking for signs of internal injuries. Finding none he moved to the head and extremities.

The right knee showed obvious signs of trauma. Grabbing Miklós' shoulder and turning his head to examine the wound there caused him to scream out. Once the wounds had been sufficiently cleaned he ordered X-rays for the right side of the body, including the skull.

Miklós was wheeled to the X-ray machine with the medics helping position him. It was a long process taking several minutes between exposures. Once finished, he was wheeled to an examination room to await the doctor. After thirty excruciating minutes waiting for the X-rays to develop the doctor arrived to assess them. "Hmm, looks like you have a cracked knee cap" he said without turning his gaze. Continuing, "A broken collar bone too. This appears to be a large fracture. I'd say you must have taken quite a spill." He had two sprained wrists, and his scalp required several stitches just behind the ear. The open wounds were disinfected and bandaged and the doctor ordered Miklós put in traction. "Nurse, please administer enough morphine to numb Miklós. He's going to get moved around a lot as we set his shoulder and elevate his leg."

Family members attending the race arrived at the hospital as Miklós was being placed in traction. They had sought his whereabouts upon finding him absent from pit row after the race. Several anxious minutes elapsed before discovering he had been rushed off. Once he was set up they were allowed to see him, although deep in slumber, the morphine and sedatives working as the doctor had prescribed. It pained them to see Miklós like that. "He'll be sleeping for a while" the nurse said as she walked in to check on him. You may want to come back later when he's awake. It could be several hours yet." "What's the extent of his injuries" József asked. The nurse gave the prognosis while looking Miklós over. "He arrived with a mild concussion, a broken right collar bone, and a cracked right knee cap. He has a nasty cut behind the right ear. The doctor had to put several stitches in his scalp there. Both his wrists appear to be sprained." When finished checking the flow of his intravenous drip she turned to them. "He should come out of this alright. I imagine he's quite lucky it wasn't worse." After a few minutes József decided they should leave and give Margit the news. This would not be easy. The three climbed into grandpa's truck and headed for home.

When they walked in the house Margit was zipping around the kitchen preparing dinner, figuring the guys would have lunch at the fair. She heard them come in and glanced over. "You're home early. I wasn't expecting you so soon. Did you eat? It'll be a while until supper. How'd Miklós do?" No response. She looked up from her task at hand. "What is it? What's wrong?" József had a grim look on his face as he walked over to her. "Miklós had an accident. He's in the hospital. He has some cuts and broken bones but should be alright. He's sedated at the moment. He was asleep when we saw him." "Oh my God, he's in the hospital?" She dried her hands on her apron and pulled it off over her head. "He can't be alright if he's that broken up. That damned motorcycle! I knew something like this would happen. We never should have let him race. What were we thinking?" Stopping everything she was doing in the kitchen, "Let's go. I want to see him." She was on the edge of panic, mixed with anger, trying to remain composed. She grabbed her things as they all hurried out the door.

Miklós awakened moments before their arrival, still groggy from being medicated. His right leg and arm were elevated in slings supported by rods suspended over his bed. His wrists were bound tightly in cloth bandages. Layers of gauze covered both knees and the shaved scalp area containing stitches. His mother went to his side and began to tear up. "How do you feel? You look like you're in a lot of pain." "Not too bad at the moment. The nurse has been giving me something for the pain." She shook her head wanting to cry, deciding to leave the room. His father walked over to speak to him. "Your mother and I had a discussion on the way over. We've decided as long as you're living under our roof you won't be racing anymore. In fact we want you to quit riding altogether. Either the bike goes or you go." Miklós stared up at him through the fog of medication, sensing the seriousness in his father's tone. There was nothing he could say. Under the circumstances it was impossible to argue against his parent's ultimatum.

He spent four days in hospital before being released by the doctor. "I think you're well enough to go home now but you'll need to stay in bed. Based on the X-rays you should be alright if you don't move too much. It looks like you have a couple of pebbles and some grit embedded in your knee. They'll likely remain in your body for some time, possibly the rest of your life." He would convalesce at home in bed until the start of school.

School – what to do about school? He would have to manage carrying his things on and off the train somehow. No longer would Tibi be available to help, for he would be off at university. Péter, his friend that lived a few houses down, would likely help him. Playmates growing up, and wrestling teammates for many years, they still socialized regularly. Péter would be attending senior year as well.

Péter's family was of German (Deutsche) descent, similar to Miklós heritage, except one parent was Austrian rather than Hungarian. They had immigrated to Hungary many years earlier, long before the war. His parents spoke German in the home, Péter having been raised to speak it fluently. They had been presented with the same dilemma as the Falvai's when the German army rolled into town; how to prevent being discovered and repatriated? In order to blend in they had changed their last name to one of Hungarian origin as well. When German soldiers took up residence his family had also hidden their past. Fluency, however, had obvious advantages for eavesdropping on soldiers' conversations.

Miklós struggled with his crutch and broken collar bone, an especially difficult task when negotiating the porch steps, but managed. The day after coming home he had his brother help him out to the barn to inspect his bike. His father had gone back to retrieve it after visiting him in the hospital. József figured they could make the necessary repairs and get some money back out of it. As Miklós looked it over, the motorcycle did not appear in as bad of shape as he feared. Disappointed things had turned out this way he would miss riding. His racing days were over. Perhaps some day he might acquire another bike, but from now on riding would be purely for pleasure. "Miklós, I heard mama and papa talking about you getting rid of the motorcycle on the way to the hospital. I didn't think they would actually make you do it, but mama was really upset." Miklós sighed. "Yes, I should have known better than to take the risks I did. Oh well, I'm going to miss it. Sorry I ruined it for you. They'll not allow you one after what happened to me." "Oh, that's alright" József replied, "I don't think I would have wanted one anyway. I think I would rather have a car." "Good choice" Miklós said. "Take it from me. Stick with four wheels." Miklós was in no shape to work on the bike. That would have to wait until midterm break.

Péter came to visit Miklós after hearing of his mishap. They sat on the front porch for a while, talking and smoking, Péter offering to help Miklós get to school. Over the next several days Miklós managed to pack for the return, his mother helping occasionally when seeing him struggle. Still upset with him over the accident she was slowly getting over it. "How are you going to manage getting around campus?" she asked. "I'll manage. There's never more than one flight of stairs to negotiate." "Well, I hope you don't fall down the stairs. That's all you need on top of everything else!"

* * *

Back at school Miklós negotiated the stairs, but had to settle for the bottom bunk. Climbing into the top was not a practical option. Péter managed to carry their bags back to school. When Imre saw Miklós he was surprised. Suspecting what happened, he couldn't pass up an opportunity to harass him. "What happened, did your little brother beat you up?" "Ha-ha, you're such a comedian. No, for your information I wrecked my bike." Unable to contain laughter at his own joke Imre confessed "I figured as much. You know I enjoy giving you a hard time." Miklós was used to it. "Believe me, I know. You're never one to show any mercy. I'd hate to have *you* as a big brother." Miklós started unpacking. "So, anyway lover boy, how'd things go with the girlfriend this summer?" Imre's face lit up. "Great, we spent a lot of time together and enjoyed every minute of it. Her parents seem to like me well enough. They haven't chased me off yet anyway." Miklós chuckled "Well, that's always a good sign. At least you two don't have to sneak around."

Miklós managed to hobble around campus for several weeks, eventually well enough to abandon the crutch, and his collar bone was on the mend. The campus doctor, having run into Miklós that first week, made him check in regularly to monitor his progress. "Miklós, you seem to have a knack. This is the second time you've cheated death. First it was the ruptured appendix, now this." Miklós gave a small chuckle. "Well doc, if you're keeping score, I guess you could say it's actually three." "Oh? Dare I ask what the third was?" "A couple of summers ago there was an explosion at the mine as I was working in the machine shop." Miklós related the story. Finishing, the doctor stared at him for a moment. "I remember hearing about that. You were there? Miklós, we're going to have to start calling you 'the cat' with all these lives you seem to have. Let's see, I guess that means you only have six left." The doctor laughingly commented "My advice is that you use the rest wisely!" Miklós scratched his head and sheepishly replied "Well, I did have to crawl out of a cave-in this past summer. Would that count as one too?" The doctor rolled his eyes and shook his head. Gesturing toward Miklós, he held up his hand with outstretched fingers and corrected himself. "Make that five."

* * *

Following winter break students were to declare their intentions regarding university. Counseling on their options was provided, based on eligibility and availability. Miklós, familiar with the workings of the coal mine, applied to the college of mining engineering at Sopron University in Western Hungary, near the Austrian border (later becoming the University of West Hungary). The school concentrated not only in mining engineering, but metallurgy, mechanical engineering, and land survey engineering as well. He knew that receiving a degree in mining engineering from Sopron would provide him the opportunity of landing a well paying job at the mine. A career there would allow him to remain close to family.

Acceptance was tentative, subject to his final semester's grades, though entry was not guaranteed. With enrollment limited, one's high school curriculum and work experience were also considered. Miklós' academic track of math and science, combined with his experience at the coal mine, made him an ideal candidate. Letters of acceptance were sent to both home and school. His family could not have been more proud. He would be off to university in the fall, a cause for celebration at his midterm homecoming.

Everyone in the family came to welcome him at the train station. "There he is, the college boy!" his grandfather called out upon seeing him step off the train. They cheered and clapped as he walked toward them. "Köszönöm szépen, köszönöm." "*Thank you very much. Thank you.* Now please stop, you're all embarrassing me."

* * *

In 1953 the Nagy government had been elected by the party on a platform of worker support. By 1955 the Soviet Politburo decided it had put up long enough with his attempts to craft a "new course" for communism, removing him from office that April. He was succeeded by Matyos Rakosi, an outspoken critic. Nagy, however, had garnered widespread support across the country. The sacking of their popular premier by outsiders, the Soviets, created national resentment. That summer workers across the country began organized protests, threatening strikes and wondering when there might again be "support" for them. After all, hadn't communism been born in response to poor worker treatment?

Amidst all this Miklós pondered conditions at the mine. Looking to his forthcoming course of study at university, he was optimistic that as a mining engineer he could enhance safety and productivity through a combination of work experience and education by bringing a new perspective.

One evening over dinner, after another particularly

close call for Miklós, József was quietly contemplating the situation. Margit inquired if anything was the matter. "Dear, you seem subdued tonight. Is everything alright?" "Oh, just thinking about work. We've been having a lot of accidents lately and the men are starting to complain. I can't say that I blame them." Margit was aware of recent incidents, particularly those involving Miklós. "Is anyone addressing the concerns?" József shook his head. "I don't know what can be done. Complaints are running all the way up the chain. Our hands are tied by the bureau of mines. They're the ones with ultimate authority." Miklós understood his father's frustrations, the topic discussed often with Jani during their commute, adding "I've certainly noticed a change in attitude from years past. There's talk of slowing work in a show of protest. Doubtful it would help, but some seem prepared for desperate measures." "That's one of my fears" József responded. "If production slowed it might only serve to make things worse. On the other hand, something has to give before it all boils over."

* * *

At the fair that year Miklós resigned himself to once again being a spectator. Although he missed the excitement, he did feel relaxed, able to enjoy the fair in a manner typical of most. His father had found a buyer for his motorcycle that spring after making necessary repairs, selling it for most of what Miklós had paid. Every now and then Miklós was reminded of the previous year's accident by the scars left behind. He and Tibi would be cheering on their friends from the sidelines that year.

One noticeable change at the fair that year was the political activity openly taking place. Although not technically sanctioned by the government, certain political parties were making their voices heard, attempting to resurrect the multiparty system. Some carried placards, wearing the uniform of their party. Others passed out flyers seeking members and support, even going so far as setting up tables to recruit and disseminate information. Occasionally, authorities made an obligatory appearance to disperse these "nuisance" instigators, only to have them return hours later. Enforcement seemed lax. Perhaps the police sympathized, or with the passing of Stalin things had become less rigidly controlled. Whatever the case, something was making people more emboldened to express their opinions.

"It's kind of interesting" Tibi mentioned in passing, "but it reminds me of what was happening on campus this year." Miklós was chewing a bratwurst sandwich, unable to respond with his mouth full. Tibi did, however, have his attention. "A lot of outsiders have been recruiting for various political parties or causes. Some students are joining up, but most would rather improve the system we already have." Tibi continued as Miklós chewed and listened, "Some even speak up during philosophy class, debating on the country's direction, what the government is doing right or wrong, that sort of thing." Miklós responded "I've even noticed it in high school. Not that we had political recruitment going on, or anything like that. But some of the students - even some of the faculty - were being more open in their discussions of politics and economics." Miklós waxed philosophical "I certainly would like to see change for the better. Maybe grandmamma and grandpapa could even get their farms back." Tibi nodded in agreement. "Yes, that would be nice. They haven't seemed the same since."

* * *

The following week Miklós again waited at the train station, this time bound for Sopron University, about a 65 mile ride west by rail. His family had once again come to bid farewell. The crowd was not as it had been at the high school sendoff, for not all in his graduating class would be attending university, and fewer yet were bound for Sopron. It was, nevertheless, a popular choice for higher education in the region, with mining, agriculture and forestry among the area's biggest employers. Sopron was composed of a mostly male student population due to its association with male dominated heavy industries of the time. The university in Budapest tended to attract most of the female students, having a broader choice of specialties.

A couple dozen schoolmates, including neighbor and friend Péter, would also attend Sopron. Miklós' and Péter sat together for the duration of the trip. Péter had chosen to pursue a major in mining engineering as well, having worked alongside Miklós the last couple of summers.

The ride took hours, winding through the countryside and villages of western Hungary, most of the students never having ventured that far west. "Milyen gyönyörű" Péter mentioned as they passed through the wine region of Sopron, "*How beautiful*, I've never been out here before." "Neither have I" Miklós replied gazing out the window. "I've never seen so many grapes on the vine." Being the latter half of the growing season the vines appeared heavily laden. Smiling, he said "Although, I must admit to having sampled some of the area's harvest."

The region carries a reputation for its significant wine production, producing both red and white, unlike most regions of the country famous only for whites. Sopron is well known for wines like Pinot Noir, Blue Frankish, Tramini, and Green Veltelini.

The city of Sopron lies on a plain surrounded by low, forested hills, not far from the border with Austria (Österreich in German, spoken by 85% of its population). The area surrounding Sopron had seen its share of occupiers since ancient times, transforming it through the centuries. During Roman occupation the town of Scarbantia emerged, Sopron's city square now located where its forum once stood. With the fall of the empire, ruin befell the city. The eventual migration of Hungary's ancestral settlers into the region saw the old Roman walls strengthened and a castle rising between the ninth and eleventh centuries. The medieval town grew, eventually named for a castle steward by the name of Suprun. In 1529, during the Ottoman occupation, the city was ravaged, though remained unoccupied. For this reason, many fled there from the countryside seeking refuge, the swelling population adding to the city's significance. In 1676 a fire swept through the city, destroying most of it. Over the coming decades the city was remade in its modern form, with buildings of Baroque architecture replacing those destroyed, though some medieval buildings remain today, having survived fire and the ages.

University campus was larger than that of their high school, a sprawling collection of buildings and green areas, many of the structures and sculptures centuries old. The school of mining and metallurgy, established in 1735 by royal decree, had a distinguished history. Throughout the remainder of the eighteenth century several other colleges came into being; mathematics, mineralogy, chemistry, physics, and mechanics.

Life at university was less regimented than high school. There were no uniform requirements and no marching. Rules governing mealtime and curfew existed, and the genders were still prohibited from visiting each other's dormitories, but were otherwise allowed to commingle. Sleeping arrangements were made by the university prior to the student's arrival. Just as in high school, no one knew who their roommate's would be. Class attendance was mandatory except in cases of approved absences, such as illness, death in the family, or university athletic events. After all, they were "students of the state", their presence on campus made possible by the "largesse" of the government. As such, students were expected to fulfill their end of the contract.

Freshman year students took the mandatory prerequisites; math, science, Russian language, and philosophy. Miklós was becoming fairly fluent in Russian, having studied it many years by then. Excelling in chemistry and math, he brought home straight A's that first semester.

* * *

Relatively isolated from the rest of the country, the nation's political transformation was transpiring relatively unnoticed as compared to larger cities like Budapest. News of protests and unrest filtered in from time to time. Like other cities with universities, there existed a Student Revolutionary Committee. Sopron's had been meeting in secret for some time. Contact with other committees was made periodically, keeping the local chapter up to date. Expatriates urging regime change were in communication now. Sopron lacked a contingent of Soviet troops, allowing committee members to travel freely without raising suspicion. The area's lack of discourse and protest had kept the city off the Soviet radar. Troops were instead concentrated where it felt dissension most likely.

During second semester Miklós' had a professor of philosophy named Hideg that extolled the "virtues" of socialism and disparaged the "evils" of capitalism. A hard-line believer that kept debate to a minimum, most students quickly developed a dislike for him. Entertaining alternative approaches to strict socialist doctrine was discouraged. The implication was that multiparty systems and capitalism were a thing of the past, and it was best if students disregarded such notions. Socialism was the wave of the future, and once the workers of the world realized the advantages its inertia would be unstoppable. With some of the changes taking place the last few years, and the current wave of optimism, many students begged to differ, willing to argue the contrary.

Miklós was one such student. For their class paper the students were to compare and contrast capitalism versus socialism. The professor, no doubt, expected the papers to be weighted in favor of Soviet style communism. Apparently, many either did not get the message, or refused to accept his notions, arriving at conclusions contrary to those delivered during lecture.

The collectivization of industries had caused production to fall. Miklós was keenly aware of results this approach had brought to farming. Following the government's confiscation of his grandparent's farms yields dropped significantly, though bureaucratic goals had assumed production gains through an increased labor force. The decreases were often blamed on weather or allocation of resources. No one dared admit the truth, for that would contradict party dogma. When forced to work for a government where everyone is rewarded the same regardless of effort, it is human nature to simply put forth the minimum necessary. Removing reward created disincentive, a fundamental flaw of the socialist approach. Assuming every citizen would naturally gravitate toward working for the betterment of the state was a gross error in judgment. To believe one can change nature is arrogant, *human nature* included.

Many in the class produced term papers outlining these very ideals. Miklós had approached it from the natural resources angle, having intimate knowledge of the outcome befallen his area's farms and mines. The premise was soundly rejected by the professor. No matter what "short-term glitches" the system revealed, these were merely bumps in the road on the journey toward "worker utopia". Miklós' paper received a grade of 'D'. He was stunned, as were most his classmates upon seeing their grades. Even those writing of a more progressive socialist system, as opposed to a hard-line communist one, received no better than a 'C'.

Handing back the graded papers the professor lectured on his disappointment. "A few of you have produced work that has done the people, and me, proud. You grasp what it is to be a citizen of our great state. There are, however, those that have not. Obviously some of you have missed the point." He stood there in his grey suit, scanning the classroom with his beady little eyes through round, wire rimmed glasses, waiting to pounce on the first that retorted. Some glanced at each other uneasily. Picking up on the professor's tone no one spoke up, fearing his wrath would further jeopardize their grade. Miklós was stewing now. Like so many others, he wanted to debate but thought better of it. He would wait until after class. Arguing in front of everyone else would only make matters worse. The professor continued, seeing that he had sufficiently berated those targeted by his speech. "Based on the damage capitalism has wreaked upon the world I have but to assume you are blind, or simply incapable of grasping the basic concepts I have lectured on for the better part of this semester." He waved his hand at them in a dismissive gesture. "Now please leave - class dismissed!"

Nearly all the students gathered their things and headed for the door. A few remained, hoping to discuss their grade, Miklós among them. Never before had any of them received such a poor mark. After all, they had to be among the best students in the country to get this far. Miklós hurried to be first in line. "Mr.

Hideg, please, I beg you to reconsider. I believe my paper is based on a solid foundation of fact. I wrote of my grandparent's experience. I have witnessed what happens with collectivization." "No Miklós, I have read your paper and your accounts are most likely fiction. Negative propaganda if you will." Miklós was staring at him now, awestruck. *Does he think me a liar*? "What? You think I made this up?" he said, raising his voice now, shaking the paper he had worked so hard on in his hand. "My grandparents had their farms confiscated by the government, only to allow them to fall well short of their production potential, and then into disrepair. They have not been the same since." With another dismissive wave of his hand Hideg continued "Then I suggest that is the fault of your grandparents. Even if production is down in the short term it could be due to other extenuating circumstances. The system will eventually catch up to the conditions, and when it does, you will see the glorious bounty the state will provide to all the people." Miklós was incredulous. He wanted to say more, and almost did. Instead he bit his tongue, crumpling the paper in his hand then holding it up in a fist toward the professor. Hideg looked up at him "Yes Miklós is there something you would like to add?" Miklós began to tremble. He wanted to jump at the man and grab him by the throat. As a long time wrestling team member he could do a lot of damage before they finally pulled him off. His better judgment won out and he stormed out the door cursing.

The others, having witnessed the exchange, decided it best to leave well enough alone. They could see the professor would not be swayed. They took their lumps and departed, some already pondering what it might take to pull their grade up. Exiting into the hallway one of the students yelled "Hey! Wait up!" He jogged to catch up with a fuming Miklós who had already pulled out a cigarette, puffing away furiously. Coming up alongside him the student said "Let me get one of those. I don't normally smoke but I sure could use one right about now." Miklós handed over the pack and matches. The boy lit one, took a drag, and coughed on the strong, filter-less cigarette. East European tobacco was not among the smoothest in the world. "Miklós, I'd like to talk to you about something. I think you might be interested." Miklós looked at him sideways and kept walking, not saying a word. He was not in any mood to talk, feeling more like kicking the butt of a certain communist a-hole. As they walked down the hall together the student turned left for an exit. He looked back at Miklós as he got to the door, motioning with his head to follow "Hey, this way. Come on." Miklós stopped and looked at him, the paper still clutched in his fist, his cigarette clinging between two fingers of the same hand. After a moment's hesitation he decided to follow. *What the hell, why not?*

They continued walking in silence, puffing away. Miklós lit another and offered the pack to his classmate. The student declined with a wave of his hand. Once away from the buildings the young man veered off the path toward some trees. Miklós hesitated, looked around then followed. A minute later the boy stopped, gesturing for another cigarette. Taking a drag he said "Good, I don't think anyone can hear us." Miklós looked at him curiously, wondering what this was all about. "I saw the way you reacted to your grade. I think you might be interested in talking to some people I know. There are some among us seeking change." Miklós could tell the guy was purposely being vague in order to protect someone. "Really, what sort of change are we talking about?" "Real change, where socialism does not have to be this harsh system of repression and fear." Miklós had his doubts. "I don't know. I'm not very political, and would rather not get involved." Holding up his still crumpled paper "It looks like I'm getting myself in trouble enough on my own." His classmate chuckled "I understand. Are you happy with the status quo, or maybe not ready for change?" "No, it's not that I'm against what you are doing. I just don't think it's for me, at least not right now." "Well, think about it. Let me know when you're ready, anytime you want." "Alright, I will." The young man smiled and they began to walk back. Looking around he said "And remember - we never had this conversation." Miklós shot him a glance and nodded.

Once back on the walkway they went their separate ways. Miklós did not have another class for the rest of that day, planning on going to the library to study for midterm exams. Now he was also facing the potential of a poor grade in philosophy. Up until then he had an A-average in the class. The term paper was, however, a significant percentage of the grade. Miklós was still stewing when he arrived at the library.

In the main chamber he came upon Péter at one of the tables studying. Miklós pulled up a chair and sat down across from him. "So, Miklós" Péter asked in a hushed tone "how did you do on the term paper?" Miklós slid the crumpled paper across the table to Péter, who

Iron Cross, Iron Curtain, Iron Will

then flattened it out to read the grade. "A 'D'? He gave you a 'D'? Oh my. You've never made a 'D' in your life. What happened?" Miklós leaned toward him over the table. "Old man Hideg doesn't think I grasp the full meaning and potential of communism, that I'm missing the point. Apparently over half the class doesn't get it either. Not many people had a grade better than mine!" Péter shook his head, looking down at the paper still in his hand. He slid it back over to Miklós. "So what are you going to do now?" Miklós looked at him and said "I should go kick that son of a bitch's ass, that's what I should do!" almost forgetting he was in the library, raising his voice sufficiently to attract a few looks from other students. Péter quietly chuckled. "Well you know, that always is an alternative, but I would advise against going around and beating up on the faculty." Miklós lowered his head and gestured in disgusted agreement. "Harrumph! Igen, azt hiszem igazad van." "*Yes, I guess you're right.* Now I have to figure out how to bring my grade up." Miklós righted his posture and continued sarcastically, sitting up straight with his hands folded on the table "I guess I have to play along and pretend to be a good little communist - for the glory of the state of course!" This made Péter laugh some more. Shaking his head "Oh Miklós, what are we to do with you?"

Miklós suddenly remembered the conversation he had on the way to the library with his classmate. "Oh, teljesen elfelejtettem." "*Oh, I clean forgot.* On the way over here this guy from class pulled me aside to talk. Given my reaction to the grade he said that I might be interested in talking with some friends of his." Péter looked at Miklós quizzically. "About what? Beating up your professor?" "No, no, nothing like that. He said something about making real change in the system, like a friendlier socialism. He was vague, as though protecting someone or something." "What did you tell him?" "I told him I was already in enough trouble and not interested." Péter nodded, then leaned forward a bit, lowering his voice further, almost to a whisper "I think I might know who he's talking about." "Ki az?" "*Who is it?*" Péter looked side to side, and satisfied no one was listening said "The Student Revolutionary Committee. I overheard someone talking about it one day, how there were some new ideas being discussed. I bet that's who the guy was talking about." Miklós nodded. "Hmm, could be. Anyway, I told him I wasn't ready for anything like that." Having their fill of the topic they spent the rest of the afternoon studying.

10 The Will

Summer found the young men once again working for the mine. Péter had been riding to work in the truck with the others since the previous summer. It was not so bad when József and Miklós rode motorcycles, for then it was just Péter and Jani. Now that Miklós no longer had a motorcycle, all four of them would have to cram into the front when József had a flat or it rained. At least they had replaced the old truck. On its last legs, it was now used around the mine mostly for short hauls.

Miklós was working underground again. He had gotten used to it, not as apprehensive anymore. The risk of cave-ins still weighed on his mind. You never really let your guard down, and that summer had its share of close calls. More than once Miklós found himself using the escape passages after a primary tunnel caved in or a subterranean industrial accident.

Production demands were outpacing the mine's capability to operate safely. Workers were beginning to protest the hazardous conditions, brought about by lax controls and extended work hours. Accidents and incidents, caused by fatigue or poor judgment, were beginning to take their toll. New employees were more prone than ever to mistakes, hastily trained in order to meet someone's quota.

Discontent was running high, and though never officially going on strike, work stoppages and slow-downs were staged occasionally in protest. In fact, over the last several years, there had been protests not only at the mine, but in other industrial towns as well. Csepel and Diosgyor had seen marches in the streets. Workers protested in Ozd, to the northeast, near the Czechoslovakian border. The Czechs had been expressing their own discontent, rioting in Prague and Plzen. Much of the Eastern Bloc was experiencing discord with their Soviet dominated governments. Things were coming to a head. Strikes and riots in East Germany were put down as early as 1953. An uprising in Tblisi, capitol of the Soviet controlled state of Georgia, had been forcibly suppressed in May of 1956. Then in June workers of Poznan Poland made their voices heard through work stoppages and marches. Many within Hungary rallied in support of the Polish workers. Emboldened by the news of others rising up against the suppressive regimes throughout the region, Hungarian workers and students began marching and rallying more frequently and openly.

* * *

At university that fall students fell back into their

routines. Miklós and Péter began concentrating in mining engineering courses. Having just completed a summer in the mine, it looked as though they would be involved in some aspect of mining year round, both in work and study. Their routine did not last long. Change was coming. News of protests and marches filtered in with greater frequency. The politics of change became the topic of conversation outside studies. The universities in and around the capitol city of Budapest were seeing students and workers calling for the reinstatement of Nagy as premier.

On October 23rd, 1956, a student demonstration marched through the streets of Budapest in a show of support for Polish workers, and calling for political and economic reforms. Ernő Gerő, the premier of Hungary at that time, went on the radio denouncing the peaceful demonstrators. Workers organizations, having previously been in contact with student delegations, were outraged by the denunciation. Following Gerő's announcement, many workers from area factories decided to join the march. The crowd swelled, gathering around the radio station. It was here they insisted the student's demands be broadcast. Among them; reinstatement of Nagy as premier, withdrawal of Soviet troops, freedom of the press, and academic freedom. Unbeknownst to them, hundreds of Államvédelmi Hatóság (State Protection Authority), or ÁVH, were present in the broadcast building. These were the Hungarian secret police, known as the politikai rendőr, or *political police*. Created as an extension of the Soviet secret police, their mission was to suppress political opposition and enforce doctrine. A handful of demonstrators forcibly entered the building, with the more outspoken taken into custody, having been caught off guard.

As the crowds swelled, chants for change and the release of the detainees grew louder. Tempers flared. The police attempted to disperse the crowd with tear gas. Some of the demonstrators attempted a vain rescue of those being held inside. Gun shots suddenly rang out, the ÁVH opening fire on the crowd. People ducked or scattered for cover, bystanders included. It was not immediately clear if there were casualties, or if these were merely warning shots. Either way, the police had achieved their goal by dispersing the crowd, but the spark of revolution had been struck. The more militant of the demonstrators gathered next day, inciting riots and tearing down symbols of Soviet occupation. Joining them were not just ordinary students and workers, but members of the Hungarian regular police and military as well.

In the following days, word of the fighting in Budapest spread throughout the country. One town in particular, Magyarovar, drew a large crowd of citizens to the streets in sympathy, pouring out of homes and factories in a symbolic gathering of solidarity to the protesters in Budapest. They marched, carrying flags and singing Himnusz, or *Hymn*, the Hungarian National Anthem. "Isten, áldd meg a magyart ..." "*God, bless the Hungarians ...*" They marched unarmed and peaceful, save for tearing down symbols of Soviet domination, such as the red star. The town, like most in the region, had not witnessed a demonstration since abolishment of political freedoms in 1945. The march eventually made its way to the town's ÁVH headquarters. By then thousands were involved, mingling and calling out for the removal of the large red star adorning the building's facade.

Inside, whether in fear or anger, or perhaps just following orders, the ÁVH commander gave the order to open fire. Here again shots rang out, this time not for the purpose of warning, but to inflict damage. Machine guns, hidden from view, opened fire on the protestors from behind the building's windows. Men, women, and children were equal targets. Workers, students, and housewives that had gathered in the name of freedom were now paying dearly for their peaceful act of defiance. ÁVH officers intensified their attack by tossing hand grenades. Screams of the injured could be heard between bursts of gunfire and explosions. As the crowd turned and ran the wounded, limping and crawling, were again targeted through the smoke as they attempted escape. When it was over, dozens were dead, hundreds wounded. Many died for lack of medical treatment, unable to move, those having escaped afraid for their own lives if they dared attempt a rescue in the line of fire. The pained cries of the injured and dying eventually succumbed as they bled out on the street, the merciless attack of the police finishing them off. The violence had lasted but a few minutes.

The crowd, shocked and angry, sought a way to fight back after retreating into side streets for cover. Some students and former soldiers called for others to follow, leading those willing to get in the fight towards the town's military barracks. The townspeople found a sympathetic ear with the soldiers, all of whom were

Hungarian. The armory was opened and weapons distributed to those ready to root out the ÁVH from their headquarters. The now heavily armed crowd, loosely organized, returned to the scene of the slaughter. A fierce battle ensued. One officer was killed, and another captured and hung, with the remaining two suffering injuries severe enough to warrant hospitalization, one of them expiring during the night. Come morning the lone ÁVH survivor turned out to be the commander that had issued the order to shoot.

A crowd gathered outside the hospital demanding his head. The revolutionary committee had thus far kept the crowd at bay. The people had no quarrel with the council per se, but their patience was wearing thin. The following day the committee capitulated and the commander was carried out of the hospital on a stretcher, bandaged but conscious, suddenly aware of the fate that awaited him. The somber look of a condemned man written across his face, the panicked realization of what was happening gripping him in fear. His pleas for mercy fell on deaf ears. No one could have heard him anyway, the demands and insults of the mob drowning out his voice.

As he was carried out the crowd climbed the fence of the hospital grounds, forcing open the gates. Reaching him, the stretcher was dropped to the ground, the mob kicking and stomping out of him what life remained. His body was dragged and then hung by the feet for a time on Lenin Street for all to witness. Soon after, the crowd dispersed to bury and mourn their losses, tending the best they could to those still struggling to hang on.

The government went on a propaganda offensive in an attempt to quell rumors of what really happened. Radio broadcasts and newspaper articles insisted this was part of an organized effort by fascists to overthrow the government. The truth of the incident could be contained for only a short while, however. With so many witnesses word spread rapidly.

No troops were immediately sent since order had been restored and the revolutionary committee was still in charge. Committee members had kept the authorities informed, insisting everything was under control. Having contacted the members through official channels, they were eventually convinced that military aid was unnecessary. After all, they had a local military garrison if the need arose, didn't they?

* * *

"They are killing us" a voice called out repeatedly as Miklós and Péter walked across campus to class. The young man whose voice they heard was running through the common, obviously in a hurry. Other students took up chase behind him, curious as to what the fuss was about. "Who was that?" Miklós asked. "I don't know" Péter replied. "Looks familiar, but I'm not sure." By the time the two reached the building housing their classroom people were streaming out. Everyone was chatting excitedly. Miklós and Péter looked at each other confused, wondering why so many were exiting. A classmate Miklós recognized came scurrying out. Grabbing him by the arm, "Hey László, what's going on?" "The revolution, it is happening!" he responded excitedly, though tempering his reaction with a look of concern and unknowing. "Radio Free Europe has been broadcasting all morning about what's happening in Budapest and the surrounding towns." László paused and looked around. "Everyone is heading over to the union building to meet with the Student Revolutionary Committee for more information. Come on. Nobody's going to class anyway." Miklós let go of László and looked at Péter, who shrugged and said "Let's see what's going on."

Arriving at the student union it seemed over half the student population was already there. Someone standing at the top of the steps was giving a speech. "... have been fired upon. Citizens in Budapest have taken up arms. They are calling for the removal of Soviet troops from our soil and the return of Nagy". The speaker paused as some in the crowd began cheering. Miklós recognized the student giving the speech. "That's the guy that tried to recruit me" he told Péter. The speech continued "We have been in communication with Student Revolutionary Committees on other campuses. Word was received moments ago that some towns have been taken over by the local committees. Come join us in taking back our country. We shall march to the center of Sopron and begin by taking back our town!" More cheers erupted and the chanting began. "Everyone ..." The sentence was cut off. The speaker paused, listening to another student that had grabbed his attention, talking into his ear and handing him a sheet of paper. "We have just gotten word that the central committee has just reinstated Nagy as premier!" Hats, books, papers - everything - went flying into the air as the crowd erupted in cheers and applause.

Radio Free Europe had been broadcasting news and information around the clock, sketchy as it was. The government run press could not be trusted. It was difficult to tell what was really happening. The day after the demonstration in Budapest, Radio Free broadcasts stated that the Central Committee of the Hungarian Communist Party was meeting in the capitol to discuss the situation. Within hours official government radio stations began broadcasting that Imre Nagy had in fact been reappointed by the committee as premier. That very announcement was what had interrupted the speaker on the stairs of the student union.

Students fell in as a large procession and marched off campus into town. Reaching City Hall they met little resistance. No Soviet troops were stationed in Sopron, and apparently whatever ÁVH had been present either had gone into hiding or been summoned to another city to deal with the uprising. Within hours students and faculty were in control of the town. Days later they were running all municipal operations.

The following day, October 25th, Soviet tanks fired on protestors in Budapest's Parliament Square. A dozen or so were killed and hundreds wounded. The Hungarian Central Committee was quickly losing control of the situation. A major shuffling of top government officials was put in motion to try and bring an end to the crisis, attempting to appease both the protesters and the Soviets, and bring a cessation to hostilities. More importantly, they were trying to save their own skins.

Nagy went on Rádió Kossuth, the Hungarian national radio (named for a 19th century Hungarian freedom fighter and politician), announcing the changes, and promising a return to democracy. Not the elimination of socialism, but the realization of what the vision of socialism was meant to be. In the end it was the worker that should benefit from such a system. The speech struck a chord with the citizenry, making him the popular choice of the people. Within the week Nagy and his supporters took control of the communist party. Momentum continued to build as the press not only openly supported the shift in power, but called for the withdrawal of Soviet troops. Buoyed by the news, worker's councils and committees supporting the new government quickly formed in towns all across the country.

Political events continued unfolding in the days that followed. With the worst of the fighting having subsided, and no major moves by the Soviet military, Nagy announced he was freeing the outspoken Cardinal József Mindszenty, imprisoned since 1949, along with several other jailed political figures. In addition, he would be returning the country to a multiparty system of government.

The students and faculty in Sopron, emboldened not only by their own victory at wresting control of the town, but also by the appointment and subsequent broadcasts of Nagy, prepared an effort to distribute supplies from relief organizations finding their way across the Austrian border. The student committee recruited volunteers to drive any vehicles available, moving supplies for stockpile and distribution in Sopron. Budapest was especially in need due to the heavy toll fighting brought upon its residents.

Logistics soon became an issue. There was a shortage of large vehicles to move the supplies in sufficient quantity where needed. The Soviet army was still ever-present on Hungarian soil and the SRC dare not try moving anything by rail. Most railways could easily fall under Soviet control, making it likely shipments would be halted or diverted. As frustration mounted at the slow pace of distribution, Miklós came up with an idea. "Péter, let's go home and try to get to the mine. I'm sure they would let us use a truck." Péter agreed. They should be able to borrow a large flatbed and drive it back to Sopron. "Good idea. I hear the trains are running again now that the fighting has subsided. We can hop one back home and then hitch a ride with your dad to the mine tomorrow." Miklós was both pleased and relieved by Péter's response. "Alright, let's do it. But first let's tell the others what we're up to then go grab some things and head for the station." After explaining their plan, members of the Student Revolutionary Committee lauded their efforts, wishing there were others with opportunity to do the same.

The two caught the next train out, which happened to be the last of the day. They traveled well into the night, arriving in Csékút during the still, dark early morning hours, lacking a means of getting home. Just as they resigned themselves to walking the sound of a truck dumping coal at the depot broke the quiet of the night. "Listen, someone's making a delivery" Péter said. "I bet we can hitch a ride." The two sprinted off toward the sound in the coal yard. Arriving at the front of the truck, Miklós called out "Hey, driver, can we get a lift into town?" The driver popped his head around from the controls he was manipulating at the rear to dump his load and replied "Ki az?" "*Who is it*? You sound familiar?" Miklós recognized the voice at once. "Hey, Bela, is that you?" "Igen." "*Yes*. Miklós?" The boys looked at each other in the dark and chuckled. "I'll be! They have you working the graveyard shift?" "Yes, with things shut down the last couple of days they have us working around the clock to catch up." They greeted each other and shook hands. "So you guys need a lift? What in the world are you doing here this time of the morning?" "Well, now that you mention it, we actually want to get to the mine. They need trucks back at school to distribute supplies to Budapest. We're trying to get home so we can hitch a ride in the morning with my dad." Bela nodded. Miklós knew how Bela felt about communism, often speaking his mind regarding working conditions. Miklós was not the least bit nervous telling of their plan. "Sure, I'll give you a lift. I'm about done here anyway. I'll detour past your house before heading home. I need a few hours sleep before returning to work."

After being dropped off Péter headed a few doors down to his place as Miklós snuck into his own. Entering quietly so as to not wake anyone he nosed around for food, not having eaten since the previous morning in Sopron.

Margit awoke to someone rattling around in the kitchen. Seeing József sound asleep next to her she assumed it to be her youngest son. *That's odd, what's he doing up at this hour?* She arose to have a look. Coming into the kitchen she was startled by who it was. "Miklós? What on Earth are you doing here?" "Hi mama!" She shuffled over in her robe to give him a hug and a kiss. "Péter and I caught a train home yesterday morning. Had a couple of delays for whatever reason or we would have been home sooner. The SRC has taken over Sopron and we need trucks to get relief supplies from the border into Budapest. Péter and I volunteered a truck from the mine to help out." "What about class? Aren't you falling behind in your studies?" "No, class has been suspended for the time being with everything going on. I don't know what they're going to do as far as semester grades. I suppose things should get back to normal in a week or two." This would come to pass as a seriously flawed prediction.

By now Miklós' father was awake and came to investigate for himself what the matter in the kitchen was. "What are you doing here? Did they finally kick you out?" József said with a grin as he went to hug his son. "Actually, no, not yet anyway" Miklós quipped. "I came home to borrow a truck." "Mi célból?" József asked, "*What for?*" "We need to move relief supplies from Sopron to Budapest. There aren't enough large trucks up to the task so Péter and I volunteered to come back and see if we can borrow one from the mine." József scratched his head. He was not so sure about this. However, he did feel relatively helpless over what had transpired the last week, and felt this may be a way to contribute in some small measure. He was, after all, in charge of the equipment. "I suppose we could loan you boys a truck for a short while. It is government property, and with the events of the last few days I figure you'd be helping the new government anyway." Miklós smiled. He knew his father would come through. "You two can ride with us in the morning." "I was counting on it papa. Won't Jani be surprised." "That he will, my son; that he will." Margit decided since they were all up she would make them something to eat. The sun would be coming up within the hour. "Well, you two sit down and talk and I'll make some breakfast. Your brother will be getting up before you leave, he'll want to see you."

Young József awoke to the smell of cooking, coming into the kitchen squinting, his face alight upon seeing Miklós. They hugged and sat down at the table. Miklós and father discussed what would be needed for the "mission". "You're going to have to take enough diesel and oil along. A couple of inner tubes wouldn't hurt either. I wouldn't be surprised if you had at least one flat along the way. And pack ample food, a couple of day's worth. Do you have a map?" Miklós shook his head. "No. Why? We know the way." "I don't trust Moscow. I wouldn't be surprised if Russian soldiers start setting up checkpoints. I haven't seen any yet, but you never know. Alternate routes may become necessary, and a plan would help with course changes. Remind me to grab one when we get to the mine. The delivery drivers use them on their runs. By the way, how did you get home?" "Péter and I took the train and ran into Bela at the depot. He gave us a ride from the station." "Bela, huh? Oh yeah, that's right. He's driving graveyard this week. Pulled some doubles trying to help us get caught up."

As the two young men had been riding the train home Nagy declared Hungary a neutral state, formally withdrawing from the Warsaw Pact nations and raising the ire of the Soviet leadership. Since the crisis began the Soviet Politburo had been in session, keeping apprised of events. So far, they had allowed their military officers to assess situations as they arose and use force as they saw necessary to maintain the status quo. No orders had been issued to move on the government. Not yet, anyway.

* * *

Just as sure as the sun would rise, so also would Jani arrive to pick up József. "Miklós? Hey, what are you doing here? Aren't you supposed to be in school?" "Hello, Jani! Yes, I was there, but that's on hold for a little while. Stop at Péter's on the way, would you? We need to pick him up." "What's going on?" Jani asked. Miklós looked at József, who just shrugged and said "Tell him." Miklós turned back to Jani. "We're borrowing a truck. Relief supplies are coming into Sopron and they're coordinating distribution from campus. There's a shortage of trucks so Péter and I volunteered one from the mine." Jani looked at Miklós then back at the road. They stopped at Péter's, and Miklós hopped out to knock. Jani gave József a blank stare. József looked at him and said "Well, I've got to do something. My son and his friend are showing us up!" Jani grinned and nodded. "You know, I kind of envy them. I wouldn't mind going along. Have a family to think about, though." "I know. I feel the same way. I figured this would be our little way of helping out." Jani nodded in agreement. "Oh, to be young again, having that piss and vinegar of youth!" They envied the boys a little, if only to recapture those feelings of adventure and defiance, riding off into the sunset toward events unknown. Given their resentment of communism, they were all too happy to assist anyway they could.

At the mine József immediately set about securing a truck for the boys. He instructed some men he trusted to discreetly gather fuel cans before dispatching them to be filled. Returning to the depot with fuel they grabbed a couple of spare tires for the truck. A few of the younger workers, catching wind of the plan, wished to go along. The two youngest told József of their desire to join the boys and received his blessing. As word spread additional volunteers appeared, far more than could be accommodated. Miklós and Péter picked another two acquaintances they trusted from grade school, and the six prepared for the ride back to Sopron. "Wait" József called as they headed out the door, handing Miklós the map he had promised. "You forgot this." "Oh, I'm glad you remembered. I got distracted." They hugged, patting each other on the back. "You be careful young man. We're proud of what you are doing, all of us. Come back safe, you hear?" Miklós nodded, giving his father another hug, then left to join the others.

Fuel and supplies were fastened down to the large diesel's flatbed. They would drive in shifts to negotiate the roughly eighty miles from the mine to Sopron, most of it along dirt roads. A cover story was created should they be questioned by authorities, claiming to be university students away on work-study at the mine, now returning to campus. Stops would be made periodically to ask locals if roadblocks or checkpoints were present. Péter took the first shift as Miklós studied the map, plotting alternate routes if needed. Three rode in the cab, with three in back sitting between boxes and gas cans, covering themselves with blankets and tarps to ward off the cold.

Half way into the trip they got a flat. While jacking up the truck a farmer happened by on a tractor. The boys looked up as he cut the motor. "Jó napot." "*Good afternoon*. Need any help there?" "Oh, szervusz." "Oh, *hello*. No thank you sir, I think we have it under control." The farmer looked at them curiously, recognizing neither the boys nor the truck. "Where are you from?" he inquired. Miklós replied with their cover story. "We go to university in Sopron. We're returning from our work-study at the mine outside of Csékút." "I see" the farmer responded, seemingly satisfied with the explanation. "I guess you still have a ways to go." "Igen" answered Péter. "We're about half way." Péter thought this would be a good time to ask what might lie ahead. "Say, what's the best way to Sopron from here?" The farmer thought about it for a moment. "Well, you definitely want to stay on this road. Eventually you will get to a paved portion through town. I hear that things have been a little slow lately at the bridge in Sárvár crossing the Rába" (a tributary of the Danube). "Some sort of checkpoint set up. I suppose it has something to do with all the trouble going on lately." The boys glanced at each other, attempting to mask their apprehension. "Really, a delay you say?" Péter responded, thinking of a clever way to ask for an alternate route. "Well, we really are in a hurry to get back tonight, hopefully in time for supper. If we're late, we don't get to eat. Might there be another way?" The farmer thought for a moment. "Well, if you head toward Szemenye, you can cross the river there without delay as far as I know. Don't know how much time it will save you, but it may be a worth a try." "Well, it seems we did need your help after all! Köszönöm. *Thank you.*" "Rendelkezésedre áll. Sok szerencsét!" "*You're welcome. Good luck!*" The farmer started his tractor, waved, and continued on. Getting a flat, it seemed, turned out to be a bit of good fortune.

Once the farmer was safely out of sight Miklós retrieved the map as the others finished up. The wheel was almost back on and they needed to get going. It appeared the detour might add about thirty kilometers (18 miles), but would probably be worth avoiding a checkpoint, deciding to go by way of Szemenye. The wheel fixed, they turned around and headed in the direction of their new route. Making it through Szemenye without a hitch they got back on track heading north.

* * *

In Sopron the truck was parked among other vehicles waiting to be loaded. A light snow fell as the young men made their way toward the group organizing supply lines. Coming within earshot they heard some sort of ruckus. A man in a grey suit with his back to Miklós and his friends was yelling at the students and workers, gesturing with his arms and hands every now and then. "Mi a fenét csinálsz?" "*What the hell are you doing?* Are you out of your minds? This is treason. Do you realize that?" People were doing their best to ignore the man, glancing at him every now and then as though irritated by his presence. The boys halted several paces behind, listening to his rants. "You have no authority to do this. Before long the true authorities will be here, and you'll soon see that your illusion of control has been nothing but a farce. Stop fooling yourselves!" Miklós' eyes suddenly got wide with recognition, balling his hands into fists. "Hideg!" he snorted. Péter turned to look at Miklós, "Uh-oh" he said to himself. Miklós stepped up behind the professor, tapping him on the shoulder. The other boys had no idea what was going on. The man whirled around, recognizing Miklós at once. "Oh, it's you. I should've have know you'd be involved in this!"

Bam! With a right jab Miklós punched him square in the nose. Hideg stumbled backwards a couple of steps, stunned, glasses splayed across his face and blood beginning to trickle from the nose. Putting hands to face, he attempted to straighten his glasses with one, covering his nose with the other, eyes welling up with tears of pain. Everyone around stopped what they were doing, watching, waiting for what might happen next. "Kurva anyját!" Hideg said, looking at the blood on his hand. "*Son of a bitch*!" Looking back at Miklós "Why you arrogant little bastard!" Hideg continued to bark in defiance. Returning his hand to his face with a handkerchief, he attempted to stem the flow of blood. "You just ended your academic career" he muttered from under a muffling hand gripping his nose. Miklós stepped forward, punching Hideg in the gut, knocking the wind out of him. He dropped to his knees hunched over, arms crossing his stomach. Miklós stood over him for a moment contemplating whether or not to proceed kicking the man all the way down the street.

Suddenly hearing those around him applauding and cheering he looked up, taking his eyes off Hideg. They were delighted that someone had finally shut him up. It took a moment for Miklós to get his bearings as he came out of his adrenaline induced trance. He nodded and smiled, then pumped his fists in the air as though a victorious prize fighter. Many in the crowd had secretly longed to do what Miklós just had, sharing a common dislike for this particular staff member. His friends came over and patted him on the back, laughing, then proceeded to join the others loading supplies aboard the awaiting vehicles.

Hideg eventually got up, regaining his composure, and crept away, tail tucked between his legs. It appeared not many of the faculty supported his view, at least not openly, for now it was known many of them had been secretly collaborating with the Student Revolutionary Committee.

Miklós and his friends would depart for Budapest the following day, not having gotten much sleep the past few. The city was in urgent need of supplies. Work stoppages and Soviet interference in the outlying areas had hampered relief efforts. The campus cafeteria was serving food extended hours to support those involved in distributing aid. Miklós and his friends decided to get a hot meal before turning in for the night, hoping for an early start. Not being students, their friends bunked with Miklós and Péter in the dorm.

Through the night supplies continued to trickle over the Austrian border. So far the Soviet and Hungarian militaries had done little to interfere with delivery. Although the situation seemed to be calming down there was still no word on a Soviet withdrawal. Nagy had called upon the United Nations and the West to recognize Hungary as a neutral state, but a unified position had not yet come forth.

* * *

Miklós and friends arose with the sun. They grabbed a quick breakfast then provisioned a few days worth of food. An early winter's chill hung in the air. It would be a long, cold ride to Budapest. They prepared the truck then set about examining the map to plot their route, deciding to avoid the main highways and larger towns in order to bypass checkpoints. Relief supplies were finally loaded later that afternoon. Soon after, they were on the road for Budapest.

Unbeknownst to all involved, János Kádár, one of Nagy's ministers, made a power play, breaking ranks and forming a counter government in collusion with fellow hardliners. Sensing Soviet frustration with the situation, he requested to Bulganin - the Soviet Prime Minister at the time, and staunch ally of Nikita Khrushchev - to forcefully put down the revolution. As Miklós and his companions drove toward Budapest that night, the Soviet military began targeted bombing strikes on resistance fighters in the capitol. By the early morning hours Soviet tanks and infantry began moving on the city. Fierce fighting broke out, and the confrontation had now become all out war.

Taking turns, the boys drove through the night, catching sleep when they could, unaware of the situation unfolding at their destination. Along the way they passed small Hungarian military units posted on the side of the road. Fortunately, they were never halted or questioned. As the sun began to rise they stopped in a clearing along the roadside to rest, cook breakfast, and fuel the truck for the final leg into the capitol. As one of the young men was relieving himself on a tree he noted a distant rumble. "Did you guys hear that?" "Hear what?" "It sounded like thunder." "Thunder is rare this time of year." A couple of them were clanking around utensils in preparation for the meal. "Shush, there it is again!" They all froze to listen. A faint *boom-boom* could be heard by everyone that time. Glancing at each other in silence, continuing to listen, none of them were ready to admit what they had just heard. Again, *boom*. Finally Miklós spoke up "That sounds like bombs or artillery, not small arms fire. I remember hearing that as a kid during the war." Indeed. They were hearing the Soviet assault on Budapest.

"We better eat quickly and get moving" one of them said. "Get in, drop the stuff off, and get out." Everyone agreed. They were certainly more apprehensive about the situation now. They had not anticipated encountering fighting. Hurrying down to the stream, they made a fire, quickly cooking and eating. Finishing, they washed up, packed the gear, and continued on.

Nearing the city they came upon a band of men appearing to be a mixture of revolutionaries and Hungarian infantry. Approaching the group, one of the soldiers stepped into the road raising his hand, gesturing for them to stop. The young man driving rolled down his window and spoke to the soldier "Szervusz. Mi folyik itt?" "*Hello. What is going on here?*" "The Russians have mounted an offensive against us. We're waiting here in case they try to flank us." The driver informed the armed men of their mission. "We have a truckload of supplies here to help the relief effort." The men now gathering around were quite appreciative to hear this. "Köszönöm." "*Thank you.* That's great! We are running low on food and water." Miklós yelled from the window on his side "Where should we unload?" Another man directed them to pull over to a nearby building. "Over there" he said pointing. "There are too many barricades and the truck would never get through. The supplies will have to be carried in by hand from here. We'll get some others to help."

The boys parked the truck as instructed. Shutting down the engine they heard the sporadic rapport of gunfire in the distance. Not far away it seemed. It was a scary situation, the boys anxious to just unload and leave. "About a kilometer from here we've set up a distribution point" one of the men said, a rifle slung over his shoulder. Every one of the men around them carried some sort of rifle. The boys were not accustomed to seeing civilians walking around with firearms. Before long, a half dozen or so others gathered to join them. They headed off in the direction of the gunfire to drop off the supplies. Miklós and his friends were completely out of their element. None of them had ever been in this part of the city, and never this close to combat, even during the war. They kept a brave face making their way, each one concealing his fear. The situation seemed surreal, walking down once bustling city streets now devoid of its inhabitants. Tall abandoned buildings that seemed to touch the cold, overcast sky rose above the detritus of war strewn along the streets between them. The smell of smoke and gunpowder hung in the air. *What the hell are we doing here?*

Reaching the drop off point it seemed the fighting was just around the corner. The gunfire had become louder, echoing down the streets off the building facades. *Boom!* A thunderous sound echoed suddenly from somewhere close by. They could hear the debris thrown by the explosion rattling off walls and onto some unseen street. The boys stopped in their tracks. "The Russians have brought armor" one of those accompanying them commented. "They began bombing us from the air last night, and now they are assaulting us with tanks. We've captured a couple of them, though. We'll have them on the run before long." His bravado did nothing to reassure the young men.

After dropping off what they had carried the revolutionary soldiers insisted the boys join in the fight. "There are people in trouble over there, pinned down. You need to go help save them. Go on, your countrymen need you. Here, take a gun and some ammo." One of them shoved a rifle into Miklós' hands. The boys looked at the each other apprehensively, not sure what to do. Two of the men, rifles across their chests, moved to block the way back. It was difficult to tell if this was an attempt at intimidation, or merely a bluff. None of them were brave enough to risk calling the bluff, if indeed it were one. Others began handing out rifles and boxes of ammunition. They were quickly shown how to load and fire the guns. Screams of the wounded and the holler of orders sounded in the distance. "Now go, go!" They scrambled over a pile of debris, stone and mortar having once been a wall separating two alleys. And just like that they were in the midst of it, a firefight between Hungarian Freedom Fighters and the Soviet military.

They gathered among some revolutionaries preparing to mount a counter strike, attempting to push back a Soviet contingent down the block. Counting the boys they numbered roughly two dozen. The group began making its way down the street toward the sounds of an intense firefight. *Boom*! A tank shell shook the ground. Everyone ducked instinctively. *Boom*! Yet another explosion was heard. They rounded a street corner, coming upon a smoldering Soviet tank. A Hungarian resistance fighter had managed to open the hatch and drop a grenade in, taking out the crew and disabling it. They slipped by the burning armor under the cover of its thick black smoke. Bullets began whizzing overhead, ricocheting off buildings. Everyone scattered toward a group of burned out vehicles, ducking behind for cover. Bullets ripped into the metal, punctuating the air with the clang of lead hitting steel. Once getting their bearings on the enemy they opened fire, joining those already in the fight. With additional firepower now bearing down on them the Soviet soldiers retreated down the avenue minutes later. The leader of the group Miklós and his friends had joined broke in a run to pursue them. "Kövess engem!" "*Follow me*!" he shouted. They rolled out, joining the pursuit. Fellow combatants on the flanks emerged from their positions of cover to join the chase.

The Russians fell back, every now and then stopping to

fire off a few rounds, causing their pursuers to duck for cover, slowing the pursuit. A few blocks later they rounded a corner, stumbling into the soldier's fallback position. A barricade of rubble and destroyed vehicles lay across a large intersection. The freedom fighters stopped to fire on the soldiers fleeing over the heap of debris. Just as the Russians disappeared from sight, a large caliber machine gun mounted somewhere in the pile loosed its fury. The pursuers retreated for cover in any direction they could, their smaller caliber weapons no match for the heavy automatic fire. After a futile few minutes of return fire it seemed merely a waste of ammunition. One of the freedom fighters tossed couple of grenades taken from a dead soldier. Exploding close to the machine gun shooting halted momentarily, allowing precious seconds for the men to make a hasty retreat and regroup.

Half a dozen were lost in the pursuit and ensuing firefight. As they retreated, the more organized among them took up positions in various storefronts on both sides of the street, the others following the leader, continuing on for cover behind various objects dispersed along the way. They were mounting an attempt to trap any pursuing soldiers. Within minutes a couple dozen Soviet regulars proceeded cautiously down the street, sensing the possibility of ambush. The shooting had abruptly halted and the freedom fighters were nowhere in sight. As the soldiers crept past the blown out storefronts, resistance members hid among the shadows, waiting for them to pass. From inside, the crunch of glass and mortar under the soldier's boots could be heard. Once by, they would strike from behind as the others confronted them head on.

Listening patiently but nervously, those hiding stayed put until the sound of footsteps faded. After a few minutes they crept to the windows, checking that it was clear. Exiting the buildings they quietly followed their enemy. Pockets of distant fighting in other parts of the city could be heard echoing off buildings, difficult to gauge the direction of origin.

The sound of gunfire rang out just around the corner. The men that had gone ahead, hiding behind some rubble, opened fire on the Russians as they came into view. Some crawled for what little cover was available, while others attempted a hasty retreat back the way they had come, only to find themselves staring down the fiery barrels of those that had laid in wait and followed. Within minutes the Hungarians had managed to reduce the group of soldiers to a mere handful. Suddenly an explosion blew off a large portion of a building face, throwing some freedom fighters into the street, covering others with debris. A Soviet tank had snuck up on them during the firefight. Additional soldiers were coming up from the rear, using the mechanized armor for cover. Those still standing after the blast scrambled into a narrow alley to elude the artillery now aimed at them. Somehow the boys had managed to survive up to this point. None of them was familiar with Budapest, having only a vague idea of their location. With all the running around the city that day they were turned around and disoriented, especially with the sun beginning to set. The buildings' shadows accelerated the city's descent into darkness, all power to the city out. Attempting to make a break for it posed too great a risk, not knowing which way to turn for safe passage. They could easily be captured, or more likely killed, by Soviet soldiers. Their only hope of survival, really, was to stick with the group. Following the leader into a nearby building, they were instructed to disperse among the floors and take up positions by the windows until told otherwise. "If you see a Russian, kill him!" was the order.

Three stories tall, it was a plain structure consisting of small apartments, the former residents now refugees of war. Bullets rained on the building. Soviet infantry was advancing without the tank, the narrow alleyway preventing its passage. Taking up positions around blown-out windows the freedom fighters returned fire, shooting and ducking, sometimes just firing with the gun over their heads without sighting a target. Several times the Russians tried mounting an offensive, but the men in the building held their ground, exchanging gunfire for several hours, resulting in a standoff. They were surrounded, the Soviets seemingly on all sides. No one could get in, and no one could get out. "What the hell have we got ourselves into?" Péter yelled to Miklós at one point between shots. "I don't know" he replied. "I certainly didn't bargain for this. Just kill all the bastards you can so we can get the hell out of here!" The fighting dragged on into the night. Casualties mounted as Soviet bullets occasionally found their mark, some wounds proving lethal, others debilitating, the resistance fighter's numbers declining as the hours passed.

The stalemate continued through the next morning and into the afternoon. Fortunately the tank had been unable to get a bead on their position. Trapped in the building, they soon ran out of food and water. Any attempt to flee meant almost certain death. Overnight, in a matter of hours really, these young men had aged beyond their years. Experiencing death and misery up close, they were fighting for their lives in the midst of a battle for freedom none of them had anticipated. They helped the wounded as best they could, but as time passed, some expired, helpless to save them without first aid. As darkness approached, the situation grew dim, those remaining in the fight having only enough ammunition to hold off the assault for perhaps a few more hours. After that, if still alive, there would be some serious decisions to make.

"Péter, what do you think? Should we make a break when it gets dark?" Miklós asked. The friends had gathered in the same apartment now. Miraculously, they were all still alive, though some were nursing wounds. Roughly half of the others entering the building had become a casualty one way or the other. "Miklós, I don't know. Damn. It's looking bleak. I've only got two boxes of ammo left." This was only forty eight rounds. "Me too, more or less" summed up the replies from the rest of them. Shooting had stopped for the moment, allowing time to regroup. "I think the best we can hope for is reinforcements. Where the hell are they anyway? It's not like we came all that far to get here. They must hear the fighting. They should be practically right around the corner!" All agreed. *Where was everyone else?*

The sun set behind the buildings as night fell once again. Shots rang periodically as opportunity presented itself, but the intense firefight that had persisted throughout the previous day subsided. The stalemate had taken its toll, and now it seemed merely a waiting game for the Russians. Even without reinforcements their numbers were sufficient to eventually starve out those in the building.

Miklós and Péter sat on the floor, leaning up against a wall, fatigue beginning to set in. They were fading from a lack of food, water, and sleep. The temperature dropped again that evening and they struggled against the cold, no windows left in their frames, and no source of heat. Miklós was staring blankly at the wall across the room, the vapor of his breath visible by the moonlight shining through the nearby opening. Péter looked over at him. "What are you thinking?" Miklós was startled from his trance. "Oh, I was just thinking about my parents" he said, sitting up. "They may never know what happened to us. We could end up buried in this building." Péter nodded. "I was thinking about my family too - and about never having been married, or raising a family of my own. You know - that sort of thing." Miklós looked back at him and nodded in the darkness. They sat there for a while alone in their thoughts, waiting and wondering, resigning themselves to the inevitable. After a few minutes Miklós said "I'll tell you what, though. I'm not going down without a fight. I'm going to take as many of those bastards with me as I can!" Péter smiled. "I'm right behind you brother!" They put their rifles down, shook hands and hugged. They may have been low on ammo, but were high on defiant spirit.

Minutes later a hail of bullets could be heard outside the building. Everyone still able to fight sprang to look, cautiously trying to catch a glimpse. The Russians surrounding the building appeared pinned down, prevented from returning fire. Those inside opened up as well, shooting at soldiers retreating for cover. Shouts in Hungarian were heard from the alley alongside the building. "Gyerünk!" "*Come on*! Get out of there." Reinforcements had finally arrived, breaking the ring of soldiers surrounding the building, pushing them back in order to mount a rescue of those trapped inside. They had not been forgotten after all. The boys clambered down the stairs and out the alley from where the calls had been heard, running back the way they had come, ducking as bullets zipped by them ricocheting off buildings, stumbling over debris, occasionally tripping and falling as they ran down the dark streets.

Arriving back at the pile of rubble where their brush with death had begun they climbed back over to where they had dropped off supplies two days earlier. Handing their rifles back to the men on the other side they made a break for it. "Isten veled és sok szerencsét!!" "*Goodbye and good luck*! We're getting out of here!" The young men had somehow managed to make it out alive. They ran to where the truck had been left. Miraculously, it was still there! They could not believe their luck. It was a wonder it had not been taken or somehow damaged or destroyed in the fighting. They climbed aboard, started it, and took off as fast as they could, heading home for Csékút. Miklós had managed to cheat death once again. *Four lives left*.

The sun rose as they made their way. Arriving back in town hours later, they stopped at Péter's house. All but one of the young men got off the truck. From another town, the mine was actually closer to his home than Csékút. The others walked home, and Miklós went in the house with Péter. His parents were not home at the moment. After washing up the young men went to the kitchen famished, desperate for something to eat. Before having a chance to get food out there was a knock at the back door. The two looked at each other, wondering who it could be. Figuring one of the others from the truck had come back for some reason Péter cracked the door and peered out. Surprised to see who it was, he turned to Miklós "It's your brother!" "Mit?" "*What?*" Péter opened the door and let him in, looking around outside and then closing it quickly behind him. "Miklós don't come home. There are soldiers out front in a truck waiting for you. They want to take you in. Somehow they found out what you were doing in Budapest. They think you were fighting with the revolutionaries!" Miklós heart sank. Apparently someone had alerted the authorities to their activities. The tide seemed to be turning in favor of the Soviet backed hardliners. "How long have they been there?" "Since last night. They've questioned mamma and papa already." Miklós and Péter stared at each other in silence for a few moments. They had been through a lot together, especially the past week. Thinking they had made it home free, a cruel fate now awaited Miklós at home.

"Let's eat something. We can't think on an empty stomach" Péter said, breaking the silence. "They're not here anyway. We'll come up with a plan in the meantime." The three sat down to eat and plot their next move. In the end, Miklós decided he would wait until after sunset before slipping home to speak with his parents. He needed to get a better handle on the situation. Soon thereafter Miklós' dispatched his brother to inform their parents of his intentions.

As night fell, Miklós sneaked out Péter's back door. "Légy óvatos" Péter whispered. "*Be careful.*" Miklós ran crouching between houses under the cover of darkness, stopping behind trees and hedges to assess the situation as he crept closer. Nearing the back of his house, he was able to hear the soldiers talking, the smell of their cigarette smoke drifting his way. *I could really use one of those about now* he thought to himself. He snuck up to the back door and tried the knob. *Locked.* Peering through a window he spied his parents in the kitchen. It appeared no one else was inside with them. Creeping up the back porch he tapped lightly on the door. No answer. Again he knocked, this time a little louder. The door opened. Miklós waved from his crouched position and slid inside. His mother almost could not control herself. "Miklós!" she whispered loudly. "Where have you been? What's going on? We sent József to find you." "Igen" he said hugging her. He came by Péter's to warn me." "Oh, thank goodness. How are you doing?" "Köszönöm jól." "*Fine thanks.* We're lucky to be alive, though. We got caught up in the fighting in Budapest. I didn't think we were going to make it out alive." His father hugged him and said "Soldiers have been waiting outside for you, did you see them?" "Yes, that's why I snuck in the back. Lucky for me they're not too bright!" His father continued "They're here to take you in. You're not going to be able to stay here I'm afraid, not for a while anyway." Miklós knew what he had to do. "Sounds like

I'm a wanted man. I don't think I'll be able to come back at all. I'm going to try and leave the country. Make my way to the United States. I'm sure our cousins would take me in." Margit's heart sank. "The United States? You've never even been out of the country. How would you get there?" Miklós shrugged. "I don't know. What I do know is I can't stay here. They'll throw me in jail, or maybe even execute me!" There was nothing in Hungary for him now. Miklós reached into a cupboard for some items to make a sandwich. He was exhausted, not having slept much for days, but he had to keep going. He figured he ought to eat. No telling when his next meal would come. "I'll make my way across the Austrian border. That's the only way I'll have a chance. Anywhere else will be in control of the communists."

He made some sandwiches, quickly eating one, and stuffing another couple in his jacket pockets, then said goodbye to his family. Everyone was crying. Margit could not bear the thought. "Mama, let go. I've got to leave while I still have a chance." "I know. Be careful dear" she sobbed. "You write as soon as you can. I'll do nothing but worry until I hear from you again." She kissed him several more times before letting go. His father hugged him and asked "How are you going to get to the border?" "I guess I'll see if I can grab a train without being noticed. That is if they are running. Otherwise, I don't know what I'll do. Walk if I have to." "Légy óvatos fiú." "*Be careful son.*" Miklós looked into his father's eyes. "I will papa." "Én ígér." "*I promise.*" With that he slipped out the back door into the darkness, not knowing when he would ever see his family again. As fate would have it, this was the last time Miklós would see his father.

He snuck back to Péter's, knocking at the back door. Péter slipped outside onto the porch with him. Miklós spoke in a hushed tone "They're still waiting in front of the house. There's nothing here for me anymore. I'm going to try and go to America. Want to come?" Péter responded "I need to leave too. My parents came home and said they were looking for me earlier as well. I don't know how they found out about us, but I'd sure like to get my hands on whoever told them." Miklós agreed. "Me too! So are you in? You want to go to the United States? I've got some cousins there that would take us in for a while." "Thanks, but no. I've an uncle in Holland I can stay with. I'll try and make my way there. You're welcome to come with me. I know he'd let you stay there a while." Miklós nodded. "Thanks. I'll think about it. In the meantime we've got to figure out how to get across the border. You think the trains are running?" Péter shrugged and repeated to Miklós what his father had told him. "Papa came home. He told me people have been leaving for a couple of days now, afraid of what might happen. The trains haven't been running on a regular schedule. Turns out anybody that can figure out how to run a locomotive has been stealing one. They take whoever wants to go within a few kilometers of the border. Lots of people looking to get out have been riding them. Most times the trains are just left abandoned. Somebody from the rail service has to go and bring them back." Miklós was hopeful they might catch one. "Maybe one will come through soon. Do you think they would slow down for us if we flagged them down?" "I don't know, and I've never stolen a train before." Miklós laughed under his breath. "Neither have I! All I really know is that it's going to be cold tonight and would prefer not spending it outside." Péter nodded agreement. It was becoming extremely cold. "Well, only one way to find out. I've got some money. How about you?" Miklós pulled out a wad of bills from his pocket. "Every bit that I have left." Péter nodded once. "Good. Let's get going."

* * *

Back in Sopron they were having their own troubles. While Miklós and Péter were fighting for their lives in Budapest, the Student Revolutionary Council caught wind that Soviet tanks were on the move toward their city. Essentially still in control, they were determined to defend themselves. Many of the students and faculty had already been through compulsory military training and knew how to operate the weapons stored in the local armory. They raided the weapons store, hoping to use antitank guns to fend off an attack. Unfortunately, the military had been one step ahead. The guns, it turned out, were inoperable. The firing pins had been removed, apparently stored separately in a secret location. The paranoia of the Soviet military had paid off by preventing the use of the weapons. Not so for the students and faculty complicit in the town's insurrection.

Fear swept through campus. Most had no choice but to make a hasty escape. Unable to defend themselves against mechanized armor and artillery, they had to shift the use of the vehicles from supply distribution to evacuation. In the long run the choice proved prudent. No doubt the Soviet military would have crushed the rebellion in Sopron, just as they eventually did throughout Hungary that following week. Many, if not most, of those participating in the uprising would likely have perished.

About two thirds of the students and around half the faculty made their way toward Austria. The close proximity to the border allowed them to leave before the military arrived. However, the crossing would still be dangerous and difficult. No way to tell what steps had been taken to seal the border. And these students would not get to say goodbye to their parents as Miklós and Péter had. They would leave without their families knowing their fate. Faculty members with wives and children had to quickly make their way home and gather family. Everyone was hopeful that Western Countries, led by the United States, would get into the fray and help drive out the Soviets perhaps making their exodus short lived. In the end, this would not be the case.

* * *

Miklós and Péter walked quickly to the train station under the cover of darkness, taking side streets and alleys where possible to avoid being spotted, continually keeping an eye for anyone watching or following. Everyone seemed to be staying inside. The young men wondered if they were violating a curfew the streets were so quiet. Approaching the station they hid behind a hedge for a look, gauging for the presence of authorities. The area appeared deserted but they sprinted between buildings and trees for cover anyway until getting to the station. It was closed. With no trains operating they ran to the rail yard seeking a truck that might take them to the border. "Nothing, and we can't wait around for a train that may never come" Péter said. Running through the yard they darted between freight cars and stacks of cargo, searching in vain for some means of transportation. "Look!" Miklós pointed. Péter saw it too. A railway hand car was sitting off to the side of the tracks. This seemed their only alternative. They ran for the little car looking it over. "What do you think? Doesn't look too heavy" Miklós said. Péter tried lifting one end. "I think we can move it. I would expect a couple of guys probably lifted it off the tracks, so we should be able to put it back on." Each grabbing an end they managed to lift it a few inches off the ground. Heavier than it looked, they struggled to get one side over the first rail before having to set it down. It took a couple of young, strong backs to move the thing. They took a breather and then lifted it over the second rail. After a few minutes of lifting, pulling, and tugging they managed to set it on the tracks. Sitting down on the handcar to rest, they looked and listened to see if anyone had been around to take notice of their small commotion.

Before long they decided it best to move in case a train came through or a railway worker happened by. They pushed the little handcar in the desired direction, leaning on one end with their hands and pushing with their legs faster and faster, reaching a steady jog. Rolling along they hopped aboard and started pumping the handles up and down, making their way through the darkness down the tree lined railway. Their escape had begun.

* * *

They soon got the hang of it, settling into a rhythm and increasing their speed. Traveling along the rails the only sounds were the hum of the wheels and their breathing, punctuated every few seconds by the clack of the track. After a few minutes of breezing through the winter-night's chill their hands and face began to numb. Soon, however, the physical demands of propelling the handcar quickly warmed them, and they found themselves having to unbutton their jackets. Having escaped the authorities waiting for them at home, Miklós had cheated death yet again. *Three lives left.*

Hours later they came upon another rail yard, allowing the handcart to coast, catching their breath and their bearings, looking out for anyone that may be watching. Squinting in the dark Miklós noticed a faint light in the distance. "What's that ahead?" he asked, gesturing in their direction of travel. Péter stood and turned to look, having been mostly blind to the direction of travel. They could make out the silhouette of a figure standing next to the tracks, a lantern hanging from his hand. Closer, they could see a man in overalls next to a rail switch, his free hand on the lever. "Állj!" the voice bellowed. "*Stop!*" The young men, unsure how to react, just stood there on the cart, staring at the ghostly figure as they rolled along, neither braking nor accelerating. The man by the tracks suddenly pulled the lever, the squeak and clang of the switch diverting the boys onto a side track. Now heading straight toward the rear of a freight car Péter screamed "Fékez!" "*Hit the brakes!*" Miklós grabbed hold of the lever, squeezed and yanked back abruptly, so much so that the momentum shift caught Péter off guard and he barely grabbed hold of the push handle in time to keep from being thrown clear of the cart. An ear piercing screech was sent aloud as the brake caught grip, sparks illuminating the underside of the carriage near the frozen wheel as it scraped along the rail. They stopped within a few meters of the freight car. The railway worker walked up between the rails behind them, his lantern swinging back and forth with each step. The two stepped off the cart as he approached. The gentleman stopped and stood a short distance away, raising his lantern in hopes of getting a better look. "I don't care where you guys are going, but you can't take that cart. It's government property. I can guess where you boys are headed, and it doesn't make any difference to me either way. Go if you like, I won't turn you in, but you have to leave the cart." The young men looked at each other and thought it best not to resist. It appeared they could take the man at his word, just an average Joe trying to make his way in the world, avoiding trouble and doing his job the only way he knew how. No use causing a ruckus and bringing attention to themselves.

They continued on foot sticking to the tracks, not having come across authorities patrolling the railway thus far. The roads could be crawling with soldiers, and the tracks steered clear of towns for the most part, except for the occasional rail yard. They had yet to see a train.

Walking into the next day, they stopped occasionally for water at streams running under trestles. Knowing the track would eventually lead them near the Austrian border they stayed the course, hiking over hills and flatlands, making their way closer to the border, finally spotting the mountains of Austria in the distance. It appeared they had chosen the correct route. Hunger nagged at them, but they dare not stop in any town along the way. Their only food had been the sandwiches stuffed in their pockets, and by that afternoon those were gone.

Walking over a hill they happened upon an abandoned train. Approaching cautiously they listened for anyone still onboard. Satisfied the train was unoccupied they searched it hoping to find food, or perhaps some warmer clothing, but found nothing useful. Disappointed, they continued on their way, quickening their pace, figuring the border was close given where the locomotive had stopped.

Around a bend, out of the trees, they came upon a clearing. Atop a hill they could make out the Austrian border just on the other side of the river a couple of kilometers away. A steel-truss bridge spanned the water, connecting the two countries. That would be their goal. "Look over that way" Péter said pointing in the distance. Military vehicles, some of them armored, could be seen moving along the roadway. Thinking it best not to stand in the open Miklós suggested "Quick, over there before someone spots us." They ducked and ran for a small stand of trees, hiding behind the trunks, peering around them to study the area. They could make out the sounds of some military vehicles now, undoubtedly the loud roar of the armor's large diesel engines. "What do you think?" Péter whispered, as though there might be someone around to hear. "It doesn't look good" Miklós responded. "They would spot us in a minute trying to get to the bridge." It appeared a mixture of both Hungarian and Soviet military were present. Péter noticed something else. "Look along the ridge. I see machine gun nests being set up." About a kilometer or so away soldiers were setting up emplacements, stacking sandbags and mounting heavy automatic weapons and mortars. Set a ways back from the border, they were likely preparing for what was thought to be an impending invasion by the West coming to aid the revolutionaries. "We've got to move closer to the bridge" Miklós spoke a few moments later after studying the scene. "I don't see anyone near it. They seem to be holding positions back from the border." Péter nodded, agreeing with Miklós' assessment. He could not see anyone in the immediate vicinity of the bridge either, nor the river for that matter. He eyed a truck towing artillery toward the machine gun emplacements. "It looks to me like they're getting ready for an invasion. That could work to our advantage. They may be more interested in someone getting in than getting out." Miklós came around to the tree on Péter's side. "Do you think help might be on the way?" Péter shrugged "I don't know, but I wouldn't want to be here when they open fire." Miklós agreed. Best if they made their way down toward the river. "I think we might be able to sneak along the tree line into that corn field. We can probably hide in there until dark." They decided this to be their best course of action.

The sun was making its way west as they sprinted between elongated shadows, staying inside the tree line when necessary. Finally they ran along the edge of the field, crouching behind the tall grass of the clearing before dashing into the corn. It was late in the season and fortunately this field had not been harvested yet, left for feed or seed. The leaves rustled loudly against their bodies as they ran between rows, trying to make their way sufficiently deep into the field where no one would spot them. Hopefully no soldiers were within earshot, or close enough to observe stalks moving as they skipped between the closely spaced plants, brown and brittle with the cold dryness of late fall.

They stopped twenty meters in, squatting down to catch their breath. "What do you think?" Péter asked, still panting, "Are we safe here?" "I think so" Miklós replied, his breathing labored as well. They decided to sit there and rest. The sun would set soon, allowing them to continue under cover of darkness. For a while they listened intently, trying to determine if there was any military movement nearby.

The shadows growing longer, Miklós spoke softly "Well, the sun is beginning to set. I hope ..." "Shush!" Péter put a finger to his lips. There was some rustling in the grass, the two turning their attention toward the sound. The silhouette of someone coming into the corn could be seen, not far from where they entered. Sitting in silence they tried to determine if it was civilian or military. Minutes later another came, and then another. The last two were definitely civilian, allowing them to relax for the moment. They were hearing others rustling through the stalks as they had. "Well, it looks like we weren't the only ones trying to leave this way" Péter whispered. "I'm surprised really" Miklós whispered back. "With all the trains that have been heading toward the border I would have expected to come across a lot more people."

* * *

Night fell. Staying put, even after the final glow of the sun flickered from the sky, they waited to be certain of total darkness. Finally they stood, retracing their steps from concealment. Soon, others were heard doing the same. More and more it seemed, the rustling growing louder, seemingly coming from all directions. Emerging from their cover they were surprised to witness dozens of others doing the same, leaving the shelter of the corn to join the exodus moving toward the border. They had unknowingly hid themselves among many doing the same.

Hundreds now walked across the open pasture, coming from other nearby fields, making their way toward freedom. Everyone avoided the roads, leery of military patrols that might happen by. The boys began to quicken their pace, less than a kilometer from the bridge now, looking about, stumbling now and then in the dark. No one spoke - the only sound that of hundreds of footsteps shuffling through the grass.

Suddenly several loud, hollow, thumps were heard from behind, as though mortar rounds had been fired. Everyone froze in their tracks, startled, snapping their heads back in the direction of the sound. A few seconds passed and then *flash*, the sky became brilliantly illuminated, momentarily blinding those walking toward the border, their eyes adjusted to the darkness. Sounding like fireworks, *pop-pop-pop*, more points of light appeared. The military had fired flares over them, illuminating the entire area, their ignition heard overhead. People were screaming, terrified by the sudden transition from darkness, calling out to one another. The boys covered their eyes, attempting several times to open them, squinting, trying to get their bearings as their eyes adjusted to the bright light. Miklós looked at the ground. It was so bright he imagined he could pick up a needle if one had been lying there. People stumbled, some falling, disoriented by the dizzying light of the flares drifting slowly overhead, suspended by small parachutes.

Shots rang out, the military opening fire on the would-be refugees, trapping them in the open between guns and the border. Still bewildered and unsure they were heading in the right direction Miklós and Péter ran. Agonizing screams called out as bullets struck random targets. Mass confusion ensued, some retreating for the cover of the stalks, others scrambling toward the border, family members separated in the chaos. Parents and children alike were falling victim to the indiscriminate rounds raining down upon them. The young men's eyes finally adjusted to the light. Running for their lives they stopped when happening upon children screaming or crying over a parent, tugging on them in hysterics "Mama, papa, please get up, please, please!" Many were unable to move due to the crippling nature of their injuries. Some had already expired. As the two continued encountering victims in their path they stopped to assist as best they could, helping the wounded and abandoned to the nearby shelter of trees as bullets continued to crater the earth around them. Soon the boys had done all they could without jeopardizing their own lives. Making a dash for the river, the bridge was well within sight now, illuminated by a flare still drifting overhead. Bullets continued whizzing by as they ran for their lives and freedom. It was close now; close enough to make out the rivets in the steel trusses. They sprinted toward the bridge, the crossing only steps away.

Poof, everything went dark, the lone, remaining flare lighting the way burning out. Night blindness ensued, their eyes having adjusted to the light. They were running in pitch blackness now, having only a vague idea of which direction the bridge might be. For a moment they continued running together blindly, but then quickly drifted apart, neither knowing where the other was. Miklós suddenly had the unexpected sensation of going downhill and began stumbling forward. Trying to right himself his momentum was too great. *Splash*, the sudden sting of ice cold water engulfed his body, falling face first into the partially frozen river. Momentarily submerged he panicked and inhaled a mouthful of water. Struggling to the surface he choked it out, gasping for breath between fits of coughing. Once regular breathing returned he found the shooting had stopped, the soldiers ceasing fire as the last flare went out. His eyes had adjusted now and he could see the far bank. He knew that to be Austria and freedom. Fear and adrenaline drove him to swim across, swimming like never before, swimming for his life. With single minded determination he pushed himself to the other side. Once there he would be free. Then he would have to search for his friend, whereabouts unknown.

He struggled against chunks of ice drifting down the river, the coldness of the water numbing the nicks and bruises he received from their rough edges. Making it to the edge he dragged himself out, slogging through the water and mud. He collapsed on the grassy slope, catching his breath. Once feeling he could move again he sat up, only to find his waterlogged clothes beginning to stiffen in the freezing temperature of the night air. He would need to do something quickly or risk hyperthermia.

Just then someone came sliding down the hill. It was Péter. As he got close he could see Miklós was soaked and began laughing. "What happened, did you go swimming?" Miklós glared at him. "You say that one more time, and I'm going to throw *you* in!" "Nagyon sajnálom" he continued chuckling. "*I'm sorry*, I couldn't help myself. I thought you were right behind me running across the bridge. I was worried when I didn't see you, and was just so glad to find you down here I just couldn't help myself." Péter's relief at finding Miklós had triggered his reaction, the laughter a reflex manifestation caused by his rush of emotion. With all they had been through the last week it was as though some survival instinct had triggered a much needed moment of levity. "We need to get out of here, though, and find you some dry clothes before you freeze to death."

From the looks of things they were the only ones that had made it across, so far anyway. They continued on the road for a while, walking briskly in the cold night air. Miklós shivered but was able to make his way. They stopped at the first house they came to. Knocking, the owner, a farmer answered moments later. In his night clothes he cautiously peered out the crack in the door.

"Wer ist es?" he asked in German with a stern voice. "*Who is it?*" Fortunately Péter spoke fluently. "Ich bin Péter, und das ist Miklós" he replied. "*I am Péter, and this is Miklós*. We have just tonight escaped from Hungary. My friend here has fallen into the river and his clothes are soaked. Might you be able to help us?" The man inched the opening a little wider, holding his lantern up, eyeing the scruffy looking figures up and down. They had not bathed or shaved in a week, except for Miklós' dunk in the river, who was dancing back and forth trying to keep warm, the ice on his clothes visible. "Sie sprechen *Deutsch*?" "*You speak German?*" "Ja, even though I am from Hungary my family speaks Deutsch." The man nodded and stepped out onto the porch. "Alright, I'll help you. Tell him to go around to the barn. I'll go in and get him a change of clothes, then bring his back to me to dry." Péter translated for Miklós. Miklós nodded but asked Péter to translate something for him. "Ask him if he has any rum. I don't want to catch my death of cold, and that might help." Péter turned to the man and asked "Würden Sie vielleicht irgendwelchen Rum für meinen Freund bitte haben? Er will nicht seinen Tod der Kälte fangen." "*Would you possibly have any rum for my friend, please? He doesn't want to catch his death of cold.*" The man gave Miklós a look and nodded. He gestured for Péter to follow him in and Miklós went around to the barn and waited. Before long, Péter came out with some dry clothes for Miklós. "A little big, but I feel better already. It felt I was about to freeze to death." "I'll bring your wet things in. Be right back!" Soon Péter returned with the promised rum, along with some sausage, cheese, and bread. They slept in the barn that night, using the hay for both mattress and blanket.

Iron Cross, Iron Curtain, Iron Will

Sleeping soundly but fitfully, their dreams were filled with images of the carnage and violence they had witnessed that week. The acts of cruelty that humans are capable of perpetrating on each other would haunt their thoughts for some time.

* * *

Morning found the farmer out at the barn early to rouse them, the boys still sound asleep with the exhaustion of recent days. Squinting in the bright morning light, still disoriented, they looked about the interior, examining their surroundings. The barn had been dark when they went to sleep, their memories of the previous night still groggy from both exhaustion and the rum. The farmer had dried Miklós clothes near his wood burning stove overnight, feeling warm and comfortable now in his hands. He quickly changed, thanking the farmer profusely and returning the loaned clothes. "Nagyon szépen köszönöm" Miklós said, shaking the man's hand. "*Thank you ever so much. You saved my life!*" The farmer could read the gesture of gratitude in Miklós' face and actions. Péter spoke, "Mein Freund sagt herzlichen Dank, Sie sparten wahrscheinlich sein Leben." "*My friend says thank you so much, you probably saved his life. Mine too, for that matter.*" The man nodded and shook both their hands. "Well, I don't feel sick" Miklós said. "Last night I thought I was going to die. I guess we made it after all." *Two lives left.*

Péter asked the farmer "Would you know where all the refugees are going? We have relatives in other countries and would like to make our way." "Vienna" he replied. "That's where everyone is heading. If you go down the road about half a kilometer you'll come to a main highway. You can probably hitch a ride there. Coal and log haulers go back and forth all day. I'm sure one of them would give you a ride in that direction." Péter translated for Miklós. Just then the farmer's wife appeared with a pot of coffee. She wanted to meet the boys, having heard all about them from her husband, feeling bad there wasn't more they could do, but the two indicated the couple had done enough already. She handed them a loaf of bread for the journey. Finishing their coffee the young men thanked them kindly again and began walking toward the highway, breaking off pieces of the bread, thankful to have something for breakfast.

Along the highway they began hitchhiking. It was a cold morning, the wind blowing steady. In their haste to leave Csékút they had not dressed appropriately for the weather. Before long a coal truck stopped. "Wo werden Sie angeführt?" the driver yelled to them. "*Where are you headed?*" "Vienna" Péter replied. "We just came over the border from Hungary and we're trying to make our way to the refugee camp." "Well, I'm going in that direction but not all the way. Climb up on top of the load. We don't have room in the cab for you." "Danke!" the boys yelled back to the men. "*Thank you!*" They made their way to the back of the truck and climbed up into the load of coal. Once the driver saw they were safely aboard he put the rig in gear and merged back onto the highway.

Barreling down the road their thin clothes provided little insulation against the wind chill of highway speeds. They curled up as tightly as they could, the wintry rush of air penetrating deep into their skin. They began to wonder if they would survive the ride, feeling so cold, neither of them having ever been chilled so deeply before.

After what seemed like a couple of hours the driver stopped the truck at an intersection and yelled out to the two in the back. The boys were stiff from the cold, their muscles cramped from being clenched tightly for so long. The two of them managed to climb down, walking up to the cab to speak with the men. "This is where you have to get off. A couple of kilometers down that road you'll find a refugee camp. Good luck!" "Thanks again guys. We really appreciate it." They waved goodbye to each other and the boys stuck their hands in their pockets, walking down the road in the direction instructed. Just as the driver had said they soon came upon the camp.

There was a cement wall perimeter with guards at the entrance. Refugees were allowed to enter, but once in, leaving was *verboten*. Reports had surfaced that Hungarian revolutionaries wrested control of prisons and jails from authorities in some regions. Many freedom fighters, feeling their judicial system unjust, emptied the prisons of inmates regardless of whether or not they had been incarcerated for political reasons. Criminals of every sort including killers, robbers, and rapists had found their way to the border, mingling among the other refugees. The Austrian government was justifiably cautious. With incidents having already occurred in the camp soon after accepting the new arrivals, the authorities now had the long, arduous task of screening out those that would not be allowed among the general refugee population. They certainly could not allow the new arrivals to come and go as they pleased given the situation. Of the estimated two hundred thousand Hungarians that fled during those weeks, Austria was now dealing with around one hundred thousand of them.

***

The short, but violent, Hungarian Revolution of 1956 had occurred almost spontaneously. In reaction to pent up frustrations with the Soviet controlled communist government the people had risen up. The conflict lasted from October 23rd until November 4th, 1956. Roughly 20,000 Hungarians and 3500 Soviets died in the confrontation. The conflict was unique in that communists, joined by democratic socialists, had risen up against other communists. The working class desired consideration on an equal footing with their occupiers, demanding a say in who would govern them. Even after the violence had ended, work stoppages and strikes continued in hopes of bargaining with the government. The actions proved fruitless however, and by early December the strike organizers were arrested and the worker's organizations dissolved that following month.

Prime Minister Imre Nagy and those closest to him found sanctuary in the Yugoslav embassy. Yugoslavia was an independent communist country, not directly under the sphere of Soviet influence. Despite a written declaration of safe passage for Nagy and his group by the Kádár government, they were arrested by Soviet authorities after leaving the embassy on November 22nd. For a time Nagy was held in Romania. Later, he was returned to Hungary, tried and sentenced to death in secret, eventually executed in June 1958. His trial and subsequent execution were not revealed until after the fact. Khrushchev wished to make an example for anyone like minded.

* * *

Miklós and Péter were allowed entry. An abandoned military base set up by the Russians during World War II, it was used for a short while during the offensive into Germany. Unprepared for the massive influx of Hungarian refugees, the Austrian government was struggling to contain and accommodate them. Facilities such as this one were utilized for quick conversion into refugee camps. The country's infrastructure strained under the effort to distribute aid. Some of it was finally arriving from international sources, but the world had been caught off guard.

The young men were showered, examined quickly by medical personnel looking for contagious diseases, assigned quarters, and then given directions to the makeshift kitchen and dining hall. Miklós was thankful he had not contracted an illness after his plunge into the river. He probably would have been quarantined, becoming separated from Péter.

Following the crowd into the dining hall the boys queued up. It was loud, but not unpleasantly so. People reuniting, shaking hands, hugging and talking, surprised yet relieved to have found each other. Children were scampering around playing and giggling. The long tables were mostly occupied with those already eating. Parents were trying to coax their kids to sit still and eat. Some talked and shared stories. A few just sat there, staring into space, catatonic, appearing to be victims of exhaustion or some horrible experience. All were homeless now, some waiting to make their way to relatives in another country, others wondering where they might seek asylum. Minutes later the young men were given a tray of food, then managed to find a couple of seats. They ate ravenously, the first civilized meal in days, served warm, enjoying it while sitting at a table and chairs under a roof.

A little girl seated between her family and Miklós kept staring up at him. She appeared to be about four or five years old. Every time Miklós looked her way he found she was looking up at him smiling. He pretended not to notice her, but after a while she was just too cute to ignore. He paused from eating and finally smiled back. "Szervusz, mit van te név?" he asked. "*Hello, what's your name?*" "Mariska" she said in her little girl voice, smiling even broader and giggling. Péter smiled at them. "She seems quite taken by you. Good thing you showered!" "Ha-ha" Miklós shot back sarcastically. He leaned over to her and said "Don't listen to my friend Péter over here. He likes to pick on me, even when I'm freezing to death in a river!" She had no idea what Miklós was talking about but giggled at him anyway. Miklós took a coin from his pocket and showed it to her, holding it between two fingers, preparing to perform a simple magic trick that his father had taught him. With a wave of his other hand, the coin had disappeared from his now open hands. Her eyes got big, amazed by the coin's disappearance. Concentrating, her eyes darted back and forth between his open hands, searching vainly for the vanishing object. He reached back behind her ear and magically made the coin reappear. She gasped smiling, taking the coin from him as he placed it in her hand.

Striking up a conversation with Mariska's parents the young men found that the group of families they were sitting amongst had already spent several days in the camp. Introductions were made all around. As the conversation continued it became clear they would likely be residing inside the perimeter walls for some time. There had yet to be anyone sent by the government that could facilitate emigration procedures.

Continuing to chat, they explained their backgrounds, exchanging tales of how they came to be there. Everyone had a story to tell. The boys related the adventure they had been through the last couple of weeks. Afterward, Mariska's father introduced everyone. "I'm Áron Kálmán, and this is my wife Sára. I see you've met my precocious little daughter Mariska." He went down the line introducing the other parents and children. "Pleased to meet you. I'm Miklós and this is Péter." The three young Jewish families followed with their tale of escaping together on one of those "borrowed" trains from a suburb of Budapest. They had four children between them. Áron asked "Have you been assigned quarters yet?" The boys looked at each other. "Igen" "*Yes*, but I suppose we ought to go check it out soon. The last sleep we got was under some hay in a barn. Building twelve I believe we're in." Mariska's father continued "Oh, that's right next door to us. Well, you should come over and visit with us for a while. Our three families share quarters. It would be better than hanging around in a building full of strangers without any heat." That last statement caught the boy's attention. "There's no heat?" "No, none of the other quarters have stoves except for ours." The boys looked at each other and nodded. "Well, thank you. After spending the last week out in the cold it would be nice to spend an evening somewhere heated." "Good. It's settled then. If you're done eating why don't you come back with us?"

"That's your building next door" Sára said pointing. The boys sized it up. All the structures looked nearly identical. "We'll have a look and get acquainted" Miklós said. "We'll be over soon." The two entered their barracks. Sure enough, no stove or fireplace. They found their assigned bunks and talked with a couple of the guys living there. There was already a chill inside. Hopefully their bedding would be sufficiently warm.

After introductions with their cabin mates the two went next door. It was definitely cozier there with a fire going. Áron pointed out "We have to be careful how quickly we burn our coal and wood. They provide us only so much a day and we need to make sure it lasts until given more. We try to save as much as we can for night when it really gets cold." He bent down, opening the stove, and threw another log onto the coals.

The boys stayed a couple of hours chatting. Eventually a couple of the children complained to their parents of being hungry. "I'm sorry dear" one of the parents explained "but we only get two meals a day. We should be grateful for even that, shouldn't we?" The children nodded and went back to what they were doing. The two young men felt sad at seeing the children hungry. They could relate, recalling their pangs of hunger at that age during the war, food often scarce.

As they all got to know each other better that night, the families invited Miklós and Péter to move in with them. "Really, you would have us move in with you?" "Sure, you seem like a couple of good guys. We have enough room, and the children have really taken a liking to the two of you. What do you say?" "Sure, we would be glad to. Thank you so much. That is so generous of you. That means a lot, sharing your heat and your space with us." "You'll have to go back and collect the bedding out of your quarters, though. We don't have anymore here." Miklós and Péter had no problem doing that. It was fortunate they would be staying in a heated room, for their lack of winter clothing and the sparse linens would have made sleeping difficult.

After bringing their bedding over, they set up in an unused corner containing a couple of empty bed frames. Eventually everyone grew tired and wandered off to sleep. "Thank you again. It was so nice of you to invite us." "It was our pleasure. Good to have met the both of you." Everyone bid goodnight. The boys slept more soundly than they had in weeks.

* * *

Rising the following morning the pair returned to the mess hall for breakfast. Finishing, they sat there quietly, contemplating what to do next. Very little separated the dining hall from the kitchen and Péter turned to watch the men preparing food. After observing for a few minutes something caught his eye, but wasn't quite sure what he had seen. The more he thought about it, the more he convinced himself. "Hey Miklós, see those kitchen preps?" "Yes. What about them?" "That big guy there, emptying the sacks of potatoes. I just saw him slip one into his shirt pocket, real quick, like he was doing your coin trick or something." Miklós looked at the large burly man. "So, I wouldn't begrudge him anything. It's not like we're starving." "Oh, I know" Péter continued, "but I was just thinking. What if we got jobs working in the kitchen?" He turned back to look at Miklós across the table. Miklós looked at Péter, realizing what he was getting at and nodded. "I think I like your idea. Let's go find out who we need to talk to." They got up and sought out whoever was in charge of staffing.

By that afternoon the boys were working in the kitchen, the overburdened personnel glad to have a couple more able bodied men helping. The camp's population was swelling with the steady stream of refugee arrivals, straining the worker's ability to feed the burgeoning population. Miklós and Péter were assigned various mundane tasks. They unloaded trucks, brought food in from the warehouse, peeled and boiled potatoes. Most importantly, though, they had access to food. It was very tiring and labor intensive, but they were warm and well fed. Staying active with meaningful work gave them a sense of purpose. They were young, strong, and brave, sometimes foolishly so. As much hardship as they had experienced, it was unimaginable what parents must be going through. Then there were the widows, orphans, and the elderly, alone and scared, all relying on the generosity and goodwill of others to navigate the nightmare.

At one point Miklós was sent to retrieve more fuel for the cooking stoves, rolling a wheelbarrow to a building located behind the kitchen. Entering the structure he found piles of coal and stacks of firewood. Loading up, he recalled Áron explaining their limited access to heating fuel the night before. *I don't think anyone would notice a little missing*. Walking out the front door with it would be too obvious, and stuffing a few lumps of coal in his pockets would make little difference in heating the cabin. There was light coming from the rear of the room. He peered out the doorway, and seeing no one around, scrambled up a pile of coal. *Bingo*! He found a dust coated window at the bottom on the other side. He slid down the other side to the wall and undid the latch. The frame was stuck, but a couple of hard, upward bangs with the heel of his hand made it budge. Leaving it open a crack he slid back over to the wheelbarrow and resumed his delivery.

Entering the kitchen one of the cooks yelled at him "Hey Miklós hurry up, would you? What's taking so long? We can't feed the people if we don't feed the fire!" Miklós hurried his load over and promptly started shoveling coal into the stoves. "Sorry, I made a wrong turn." "Well, go fill the wheelbarrow again so we don't get so close to running out." Miklós headed back for more, passing Péter along the way carrying a burlap sack of potatoes on his shoulder. "Hey, put one of those sacks aside for later" Miklós relayed in a hushed tone. "What are you going to do with a whole sack of potatoes?" Miklós shook his head. "No. Just the sack!" Péter turned as they passed and began walking backwards. "What for?" "Trust me" Miklós grinned. "You'll be glad you did!" Péter nodded and smiled, knowing Miklós was up to something clever.

***

That evening, after the kitchen shut down the boys loaded up their front shirttails with some extra food to take back to the cabin. "Péter, where's that potato sack?" "Outside, around back. Why?" "Can anybody see it?" Péter shrugged "I don't think so." "Good. We'll come back later and get it." Péter was curious "What are you going to do with it?" "I'll tell you later. I don't want to say right now." They walked through the darkened alleyways between buildings, back to the cabin. Knocking on the door Sára answered. "Oh, good evening. We saw you working in the kitchen today. How was it?" "Jó, jó." "*Good*, good, everything went well. We brought some leftovers for the children." "Oh my! Come in, come in." The boys entered and set the food down. "We felt so bad for them last night we brought them a little snack." "Oh, that's so kind of you." The children ran over to see the gifts the young men had brought. Mariska was beaming at Miklós again. "Well, you were so kind to us. It's one of the benefits of working in the kitchen. I have another surprise for you. Come on Péter. Let's get that sack."

They headed back toward the coal shack. "Where are we going?" Péter inquired. Miklós explained "When I went to get coal for the stoves I found a window in the back and unlocked it. That's what the sack is for." Péter smiled. "I knew you were up to something." They retrieved the sack and snuck around back. Miklós slid the window up, allowing enough room for him to reach in. "Hold the bag open" he told Péter. Miklós proceeded to stuff it full of coal. Finished, he pushed the window closed and they headed back to the cabin. Arriving, surprised expressions were heard from all the parents. They could not believe it. "Where did you get this?" Miklós shrugged. "Don't worry. It'll be our little secret." Péter added "My mischievous friend has a way of seizing opportunities." Setting the sack of coal by the stove the boys went to clean up. "I expect you'll have it toasty warm in here for us when we return!"

* * *

In the weeks that followed, the young men continued supplying everyone with a little extra food and heat, helping make life a little less burdensome, a little more pleasant. Unfortunately, the pace of processing immigration applications was painfully slow. The system was overwhelmed, not simply from an Austrian perspective, but all other diplomatic channels as well. No system in the world was equipped to handle that many requests and screenings in a timely manner.

Miklós grew restless. Living in the camp was wearing on him. He decided it time to take matters into his own hands and visit the United States consulate in Vienna. Submitting an application for emigration directly would surely speed the process, wouldn't it? Talking to someone there he could make a case for himself. He had his aunt and uncle as potential sponsors in the U.S. after all. Problem was, with the camp guarded, no one could leave. He would have to devise a plan allowing him to slip out without being noticed. And who else, except his buddy Péter, would be able to help him pull it off?

"Péter, this place is driving me crazy. I need to sneak

out and make my way to Vienna. At the rate they're processing people we could be in here a year, maybe more." Péter was skeptical. "You'll have to slip past the guards. You know they won't let you out." "That's where you come in" Miklós grinned. Péter was afraid to ask "What do you have in mind?" "I need you to create a diversion. One that will get the guard's attention long enough for me to sneak out the front gate." "What if they don't all respond? There may still be someone at their post." Miklós had already considered this. "That may happen, but doubtful. It's not like they're expecting an armed insurrection or anything like that. No one's going to be storming the gate. Besides, if someone does stay put we'll just have to come up with a plan B." "What's this *we* stuff?" Péter had to agree with the logic, though. "So what's your plan?" Miklós suggested "Get yourself caught up on the wall, you know hang from it somehow as though you got stuck trying to get out, and start calling for help. They'll come to investigate the ruckus, and while dealing with you I walk out." Péter thought the plan had merit, but still wasn't sure, agreeing to scope things out, perhaps giving it a try the next day. They usually worked the kitchen afternoon and evening shifts, so no one would be expecting them early in the day.

* * *

Next morning they walked the perimeter walls near the camp entrance, concrete and block, about ten feet high. "How about up there?" Miklós pointed. "If you throw a rope over the light post embedded in the cement, climb part ways, and dangle from it screaming, that should get their attention. Just make sure you're high enough to be out of their reach so I have time to make my escape." Péter laughed and shook his head. "I got to hand it to you Miklós; you come up with some crazy ideas! So where are we going to get enough rope?" Miklós looked around, and seeing the coast was clear, pulled a length from under his jacket. Péter laughed, shaking his head again. "You are one resourceful son of a bitch, I will say that! You already had this planned out, didn't you?" Miklós smiled and shrugged. "Guilty! What do you say cowboy, think you can rope the light post?" "I'm sure I can. I better not get in trouble. I don't want to lose my job in the kitchen over this." Miklós brushed off the statement. "Oh, come on, it's not like prison where they're going to put you in solitary confinement." Péter took a deep breath and looked at the rope. "Rendben" "*Alright*, go get in place near the gate. When the coast is clear I'm going to start, so you better be ready!" Miklós smiled and nodded. "Thanks buddy. I owe you one!" "You owe me more than one!"

Miklós strolled toward the gate, counting three guards. He didn't want to get too close, fearing it may arouse suspicion. Casually leaning on the corner of a barrack he glanced back at Péter and nodded. Péter looked around, and seeing nobody watching, attempted to loop the rope over the light post. It took a few tries but he got it. Pulling himself near the top of the wall he waited for Miklós to move closer to the gate. Once he was within about ten meters Péter began yelling. "Segít! Segít! Engem lesegít!" "*Help! Help! Help me down!*" He was kicking and swaying against the wall, screaming like a child. Miklós shook his head, laughing under his breath. It was almost comical. Péter appeared a poor actor, but it seemed to be working. He had captured the attention of two guards, now walking slowly inside the perimeter a few steps, assessing the situation. "Was ist es?" one of them yelled to the other. "*What is it?*" "He Sie, kommen Sie von dort herunter!" "*Hey you, get down from there!*" Turning to the other guard "There's some crazy guy hanging from a rope. Seems he's gotten himself hung up trying to get over the wall." "I guess we better go get him. Hey Hans come and help us get this clown down." The third guard peeked out of the shack and put down whatever he had been reading. The plan was working. Miklós had been standing off to the side where they hadn't taken notice of him. The guards walked over to Péter, who was still acting like a monkey. "Hey du verrücktes Kind, was denkst du tust?" "*Hey you crazy kid, what do you think you are doing?* Get down here!" Péter understood everything they were saying but didn't let on, trying not to laugh. He carried on in Hungarian "Segít! Segít!" He glanced over to see Miklós sneaking out and smiled. Miklós broke into a jog down the road. The guards were looking up at Péter, scratching their heads. After giving Miklós a minute or so to put distance between him and the camp, Péter climbed down. He was amused by the guards all yelling at him at the same time in German, one of them smacking him in the back of the head. "Nagyon sajnálom, nagyon sajnálom!" Péter apologized in Hungarian, trying not to laugh. "*I'm sorry, I'm sorry!*" He started running back to his quarters, one of the guards giving him a boot in the rear end. Péter reached behind and grabbed a hold of his butt cheeks without turning around to conceal his laughter.

Miklós reached the highway and began hitchhiking toward Vienna. Eventually a trucker heading toward the city stopped to give him a ride. "Wohin gehen Sie?" "*Where are you going?*" This much Miklós understood. "Nach Wien, das amerikanischen Konsulat." "*To Vienna, the American consulate.* Ich spreche nicht viel." "*I don't speak much.*" The driver looked him over. "Magyar?" Miklós nodded and replied "Ja." There had been a lot of guys like Miklós along the highway that week.

Miklós stared out the window at the countryside rolling by. It was not unlike home. Home - he wondered how his family was doing, and the rest of the country for that matter. News out of Hungary was spotty, the borders having been closed. Péter would pick up German language newspapers tossed aside by the camp's Austrian workers, translating the news. As expected, most of the articles were occupied with reporting on the exodus. Western governments, diplomats, and the United Nations had all issued strong statements condemning the Soviets, but little action was forthcoming. The revolution had been suppressed before outside forces could mount any meaningful support.

Miklós was a man without a country, technically an illegal alien in Austria as he rode down the highway without visa or passport, a fugitive from the refugee camp. Returning to Hungary would never be an option. Péter's uncle in Holland may not be able or willing to sponsor him, and for that matter, who knew how many refugees the Dutch would accommodate. Austria had more than its share of asylum seekers. His focus would now be on making it to America. It was his only logical hope for refuge. Otherwise, he may end up in immigration limbo for who knew how long.

Nearing his turnoff the trucker stopped, giving Miklós directions as best he could. Miklós thanked him and climbed down, waved, and made his way through the city streets toward the embassy. Before long he found the avenue of the American consulate. As the building came into view his heart sank. There were hundreds of people lined up outside, the queue winding past the building, then down several city blocks. "Excuse me, do you speak Hungarian?" he inquired of a man standing in line. "Igen." "Where is the end of the line?" "I'm not sure. You'd have to walk down the street and find out. I've been in line since yesterday morning." "Yesterday morning? You're kidding?" "Nem", "*No*, it's taking forever just to move a few steps. They just don't have enough people to handle all of us." This was bad news, indeed. Miklós had not counted on so many waiting in line. *My god, I'm not going to do this.* He couldn't wait in line for days by himself. That would be impossible. The sheer magnitude of the situation was overwhelming, his efforts abruptly halted by the throngs of people facing the same situation.

He decided to go around the building, seeking another entry. Walking in the street he made his way along the line of people on the sidewalk, looking into their faces, nervous and weary, standing in the cold, desperately hoping for a chance at freedom. Like him, they belonged nowhere, and to no one. *What a mess* he thought to himself. *How did it ever come to this*?

He discovered a walkway leading to steps and a back

door. There was no handle to open it, likely an exit only. Seeing no other way in, he sat down on the steps, dejected, contemplating what to do next. Setting his head in his hands, he felt as though he could cry, but was too tired and depressed for even that. It was one thing to be out on your own, another entirely to be nowhere on your own. Holding none of the local currency he was relying on the generosity of strangers that spoke a different language. His only source of food and shelter was a refugee camp that, in many ways, restricted his freedom more than what he had just fled. His only possessions were the clothes on his back and the shoes on his feet. Heck of a place to be at eighteen years old.

Minutes later the door opened and a young man stepped out. He looked at Miklós sitting there and began speaking to him in German. "Hallo kann ich Ihnen helfen?" "*Hello, may I help you?*" Miklós turned, startled by the voice. "Oh, Hallo. Ich weiß viel nicht." "*I don't know much.*" Thinking he recognized Miklós' accent, the man began speaking to him in Hungarian. "Vagy Magyar?" "*Are you Hungarian?*" Miklós' face lit up. "Hé, igen, én vagyok!" "*Hey, yes, I am!*" The friendly stranger asked "Where are you going?" Miklós stood to face him, "I'm trying to get to the United States. I've got an aunt and uncle there, but I can't wait over here outside in line because ..." Miklós thought up something quick, not wanting to let on that he was not about to wait in line for days. "...back at our refugee camp I have a brother that's really sick, and I need to go back and take care of him, keep his health up." Feeling sympathetic to Miklós plight, the man said "Never mind, let's go on inside. I'll take you and get the necessary papers. Then we'll make a telephone call."

The young man, seemingly not much older than Miklós, took a set of keys from his pocket and unlocked the door he had just come out. He let Miklós in and secured the door behind them. Walking down the corridor they struck up a conversation about themselves and their backgrounds. They introduced each other shaking hands "I'm Dániel." "Miklós, pleased to meet you, and again, thank you so much." Miklós told of how he had come to Austria, and of the camp, and of the nice families that had invited him and his "brother" to stay with them. Hearing the family names the young man exclaimed "Kálmán!? Not Áron Kálmán?" Miklós said "*Igen*, yes and his wife Sára!" "You've got to be kidding. That's amazing! What a coincidence. Áron and Sára are my aunt and uncle!" "Whoa, no kidding, they are the nicest people. And Mariska - what a sweetheart. All the families are really wonderful. We would have been living without heat if it wasn't for them." Dániel smiled. "Well, I'll be. What a small world. After all that you've been through, somehow landing here on the back step, and you're staying with my cousins." They were both laughing and shaking their heads. They could hardly believe the circumstances.

Through a window Miklós eyed the line outside winding through the main entrance, thankful for his good fortune at bypassing the excruciatingly long wait. They made their way into a large room with rows of desks and took a seat at Dániel's. The situation was nothing short of controlled pandemonium. Phones were ringing, interviews being conducted, children crying or running around, workers shuffling paperwork across the room from one desk to another. Miklós had never experienced such a bustle of activity outside the mine. "Am I keeping you from something?" Miklós asked. With a wave of his hand Dániel said "Oh, that's alright. I was just heading out on my lunch break to grab a bite when I happened upon you. Don't worry, I'll get something later." He began asking Miklós a series of questions, filling in some forms with the responses. Toward the end of the interview he asked "You mentioned an aunt and uncle in America. Would you know how to get in touch with them?" Miklós shrugged "We only send letters back and forth. I wouldn't have to wait for a letter from them, would I?" "Nem, *no* it's just that if you have a sponsor that agrees to take you in, it makes the process simpler and quicker. We'll make a call and see if we can get a hold of them." Dániel picked up his phone and began dialing. "What city did you say they live in?" "Detroit. Detroit, Michigan I believe it's called." Dániel nodded and wrote it down on a form while waiting for an answer on the other end. Apparently someone finally came on, and he began explaining who he was and who he was trying to get a hold of. He read the names Miklós had given him off one of the forms. "Thank you" he finally said to the operator that was about to connect him. "Hello, yes, this is Dániel ..." he began explaining in English, identifying himself and the reason for the call. Dániel smiled and nodded at Miklós. After a while he began asking questions over the phone and filling in another form. Eventually he handed the phone to Miklós. "Szervusz?" "*Hello*?" It was Miklós' uncle. Miklós began explaining his situation, but after a minute or so Dániel had to cut him short. There were only so many phone lines at the consulate, and someone else would need this one soon.

Dániel wrote on a piece of paper and handed it to Miklós. "Take this with you and bring it back when the time comes. You can come directly to the back door and knock. When somebody answers show them this and they will let you in to see me. I've already been processing the others in your cabin, so I'll pass word on that when the time comes you can travel back here with them." Miklós rose and walked around the desk to hug the guy. "Köszönöm, köszönöm szépen!" "*Thank you, thank you so much*! I don't know how to repay you." "Rendelkezésedre áll." "*You are welcome to it.* Any friend of Áron and Sára's is a friend of mine. Say hello to them for me, will you?" "You bet. And thank you again." As Miklós turned to walk away Dániel yelled "Oh, by the way, aren't you forgetting someone?" Miklós stopped and turned back to Dániel. "Forgetting someone?" "Yes, your poor sick brother. Don't you want to take him with you?" Miklós felt awkward and embarrassed, caught off guard having forgotten his fib. "Oh, yes, I almost forgot about him." Dániel threw his head back in a hearty laugh. "Oh don't worry about it. You're a lousy liar!" Miklós smiled, feeling relieved. He was had. "Well, I don't really have a brother. Sorry I lied, but I was desperate. There is someone you could help though", thinking of Péter. Dániel nodded and motioned for Miklós to sit back down. "Alright, let's get their paperwork started, too." Reaching into the drawer for another packet of forms, Dániel asked "And your friend's name?"

After providing the information he knew about Péter,

Miklós left. He was on cloud nine, almost in disbelief at his good fortune. Some might say lucky. Though to be lucky in life, you have to create opportunities for luck to occur.

Miklós exited the building through the backdoor and headed toward the highway, hitchhiking back to the refugee camp. As he approached the front gate one of the guards came out of the shack, recognizing him from the kitchen. "Wo sind Sie gewesen?" he asked, not having seen anyone leave. "*Where have you been?*" Miklós shrugged, responding "I went for a stroll", and walked leisurely through the gate acting as though nothing were amiss. The guard just stood there with his hands on hips for a minute then went back in the shack to finish reading his paper, shaking his head and spouting off some choice words in German regarding Miklós.

Returning to the cabin Miklós could not wait to tell his story to everyone. "I hitchhiked to Vienna, and you're not going to believe who I met – your nephew Dániel!" "Dániel, you met him?" "Igen, igen …" he exclaimed, reliving the story from the time he and Péter came up with the diversion up until returning to camp. After listening to Miklós' tale Péter said "Miklós, you're the only guy I know that could ever possibly happen to, although, I can't think of anyone more deserving either." Péter put his hand on Miklós shoulder and started shaking him. "Congratulations buddy! You did it! You're going to America!"

* * *

Several days later Péter received word he was leaving

for Holland, his uncle agreeing to take him in. He would have to be ready that afternoon on short notice, his flight leaving that night. Péter looked at Miklós, "We've never flown before. I wonder what it's like." "I don't know, but I can't wait to find out." Later, as everyone gathered to bid Péter goodbye, he turned to Miklós, "You're like my brother. We've been through so much together. I'm going to miss you. I hope you get out of here soon." "I'll miss you too Péter. Don't worry about me. They put in a good word with Dániel. I should get processed soon. We'll meet again someday, I'm sure of it." They shook hands and patted each other on the back. Péter turned to board the bus. As the bus began rolling Péter waved out the window to Miklós, who waved back, finishing with a salute as the bus turned toward the gate.

Four more days passed before word made it back to the Kálmán's that Miklós' paperwork was ready. Again, Miklós had to sneak out, this time getting a couple of the guys from the kitchen to stage a mock fight near the gate, wrestling and chasing each other around. Miklós hitchhiked back to Vienna and knocked on the back door as instructed. "Ja, kann ich Ihnen helfen?" "*Yes, can I help you?*" Handing over the piece of paper from Dániel the gentleman scrutinized it before looking Miklós over. With a gesture of his hand, "Alright, come in." Finding his way to Dániel's desk he waited for a family being processed and then approached. "Miklós, it's so good to see you! Great news! Sit down, please, sit. Glad you made it back alright. How are things?" "Jó, *good*, really good. Péter has left for Holland already, a few days ago in fact. He was so happy. I'm sure he's there by now. They said my paperwork is ready?" Dániel nodded and retrieved Miklós' file.

The president of the United States, Dwight D. Eisenhower, had issued an executive order granting asylum to 15,000 refugees that had fled from Hungary into Austria. On December 10th, 1956, the US military set into motion Operation Safe Haven, the transporting of Hungarian refugees from Europe to the United States.

"Here you are. Everything you need is in here. Guard it with your life. This file is your pass to the United States." Miklós thumbed quickly through some of the pages. "When can I leave?" "Well, I'm not sure. The weather has really socked things in this winter and the military hasn't been able to make many flights out. There are a lot of people ahead of you. I'm afraid you're going to have to go back and stay in camp until your turn comes. We'll be sending transportation for the ride to the airbase as flights become available. Show them the paperwork when you get back to camp so they know your situation." Miklós thanked him profusely, shaking his hands and hugging him. "You'll have to come visit me in America!" "Well, one of these days I'll have to take your offer and look you up."

Miklós caught a ride back in a logging truck returning from a run to the saw mill. Coming back through the gate the same guard was on duty, this time with an incredulous look on his face. Hands on hips, shaking his head in disbelief he said "Sie wieder? Wer sind Sie, Houdini?" "*You again? Who are you, Houdini?*" Miklós smiled at him and said "No, but I'm a free man" holding up the folder containing his paperwork toward the guard, the consulate's seal visible. "Oh, so that's what you've been up to! I can't say that I blame you." Miklós didn't understand most of what the guard said, nor was he interested. There were more important things on his mind.

Back at the cabin he showed everyone his paperwork, though shared his disappointment with the weather's effect on the travel situation. "Oh, don't concern yourself with that." Áron said. "Your paperwork wasn't ready until now, anyway. And besides, we've already been in touch, making travel arrangements. Your name will be right behind ours." Miklós could hardly believe his ears. "Really? You're taking me with you. I'm on a plane?" "It appears so. You should be right behind us when they come." Miklós was so excited he could hardly contain himself, emotions getting the best of him. He was running around kissing and hugging everybody.

* * *

The next day a bus arrived to take those processed to the airbase. The driver began calling names; first Áron's, then Sára's, followed by Mariska. Miklós' name eventually rang out as promised. He was so excited he began jumping up and down, grabbing his few possessions and joining the others. Waiting to board it felt as though the line was taking forever.

They rode the very highway Miklós had hitchhiked, traveling to an airbase outside Vienna. The military had been providing the refugees quarters as they awaited their departure date. Many of the previous arrivals had been waiting weeks. Based on the conversation with the Kálmán's during their ride Miklós could hardly contain himself, commenting to a couple of young men in the waiting area "I'm sorry to hear you guys have been waiting so long. We'll likely be leaving today after the plane arrives." They scoffed, laughing at him. "No way, we've been stuck here over two weeks already. You're not going anywhere wise guy. Just sit tight and get comfortable." Miklós smiled, "Thanks for the information. Don't mind me. I'll go ahead and make myself at home." He stretched out on a couple of chairs, relaxing with his hands behind his head. The two looked at each other, picking up on Miklós' confidence. They were beginning to wonder if he knew something they didn't.

Soon after, the plane arrived, everyone rushing out and crowding against the fence in hopes of getting a spot aboard. Military personnel held the crowd back as those next on the roster were called. Sure enough, the Kálmán's were summoned with Miklós right behind. The guys telling him to sit tight went slack-jawed, disbelief written across their faces. Miklós shrugged and smiled at them in a sort of *I told you so* gesture.

This aircraft was assigned to the Military Air Transport Service (MATS), based out of McGuire Air Force Base, near Trenton, New Jersey, a part of the 1611th Air Transport Wing. Also taking part in Operation Safe Haven was the 1608th Air Transport Wing from Charleston, South Carolina, and the US Navy's Sea Transportation Services, taking passengers from Bremerhaven, Germany, to New York City. From the end of 1956 through midyear 1957, all told, more than 14,000 refugees would be transported from Europe to America aboard planes, and about 9,000 more by ship.

They boarded the large, four engine military transport. The infirmed, unable to use the seating, were secured on stretchers within an area that had the seats removed. The plane was filled to capacity. Soldiers took everyone's bags as they boarded, other military personnel aboard walking the aisle, showing everyone how to operate the seating restraints. Configured for military use, it was not a comfortable aircraft by any stretch, but it was better than the alternative. After all, it was a flight to freedom.

Waiting to depart Miklós sat thinking about his aunt and uncle and their children. They had never met, at least that he could recall. Apparently they had paid a return visit to Hungary a long time ago, before the war, but Miklós had no recollection, too young at the time for such memories. He had been shown photographs by his mother and grandmother, some taken on their visit, others from America. Miklós' impression of them was one of generosity. For many years his family had received gifts from them through his grandmother. Items not readily available in the East would arrive in time for Christmas, with instructions to give everyone something from the package. They trusted grandmamma to distribute the gifts appropriately. Knowing how hard life was in Hungary, they tried to share a little of their good fortune with family members.

Everything secured, the pilots started one engine, whining and sputtering to life, belching smoke; then a second, and a third, until all four were idling steady. Everyone aboard was excited, whooping it up, hooting and hollering, happily chatting amongst themselves. The plane began moving, taxiing toward the runway, the passengers quieting in anticipation of what was to come. Most had never flown before, anxiously waiting.

The plane stopped, waiting for clearance. Other than the drone of the engines, the only sounds were a couple of small children crying and a few hushed conversations. Most strained to see out a window in hopes of catching a glimpse outside. The engines revved up for takeoff. The brakes were released and they accelerated down the runway. Bouncing along, Miklós grabbed tight to whatever he could, not sure what to expect. Catholics were easy to spot, making the sign of the cross, clutching their rosary beads. As the nose lifted everyone experienced momentary weightlessness as the landing gear lost contact with the ground. They climbed fast, visibility nearing zero as they entered the low cloud ceiling. It was eerie seeing only gray wisps of moisture quickly blowing past.

Suddenly, breaking through the clouds, the world outside became brighter than anyone had ever seen. The "oohs" and "ahs" could be heard in response to the scene unfolding. Other than pictures perhaps, most had never seen cloud tops before. It appeared as though they had left Earth, in heaven as it were. Pictures could never fully capture the spectacular beauty.

Miklós smiled, straining to glimpse all he could through his window. The experience of flying was all he had imagined, and more. Nothing could have prepared him for what he was feeling. His instincts were correct. Flying was the most thrilling thing he had ever experienced.

Soon the clouds parted, revealing the earth below. At cruising altitude it was amazing to glimpse so much at once. Most things seemed unrecognizable, and those that were took on new perspective. Lakes, rivers, roadways and canals, farms, fields and forests seemed to take on a symmetry all their own. *Amazing* he thought, *so this is what it is like to fly!*

Many hours later they were over the Atlantic Ocean. Miklós had never been to the sea, Lake Balaton was the largest body of water he had ever experienced. While large, the lake vistas could not compare to what he was witnessing. It was mind boggling, the sheer scale of the view. He could just make out what appeared to be waves, or whitecaps, or whatever they were, but at that altitude it was difficult to judge. As he sat peering through the window scanning the horizon they encountered turbulence. Bouncing around Miklós felt butterflies in his stomach again. The plane began to climb, the pilots seeking smoother flying conditions.

What sounded like mechanical misfires began emanating from one of the engines. Miklós strained to look out the windows on either side. The crew quickly shut down the troubled engine, continuing to fly on three. They had not been over water very long, but nevertheless decided to carry on westward. People began discussing this unexpected event amongst each other, unsure of the situation. Seeing the crew unalarmed by the disabled engine the passengers began relaxing again. Obviously three were enough. It would take more than losing an engine to change everyone's demeanor. They were happy, heading for

America, and it didn't matter whether they got there on three or four engines. Although, when they lost a second engine it did become a cause for concern.

Several hundred miles out over the Atlantic they were beyond the point of return. Their flight path had taken them over the United Kingdom toward Iceland, a common route minimizing the distance from land during flight in case of emergency. Now it seemed the situation was urgent. Losing one more engine would certainly fit the definition. The crew altered course for a stop at the US Air Force base in Reykjavik, Iceland. Attempting the remainder of the flight with only half power was risky for such a large aircraft.

They landed safely, the plane touching down smoothly with the two remaining engines. After taxiing to a hangar everyone was unloaded with their belongings. Mechanics appraised the damage, announcing it would take several days to make the needed repairs. That meant their unscheduled stopover in Reykjavik would require quarters on base while waiting. It seemed that Miklós had cheated death yet again. *One life left.*

They were provided living arrangements; food, medical treatment, and toiletries. In many ways the conditions were better than back home. Most of them witnessed television for the first time. It was fascinating. Miklós had seen movies on big screens with projectors, but never behind glass in a box. Not speaking a word of English, he was lost on the dialogue. Those that understood translated the broadcasts as best they could while gathered around watching, especially news regarding Hungary. There were board games, like chess and checkers, and decks of cards to occupy their time. They were free to walk around outside as long as they refrained from restricted areas. The base personnel were friendly and cordial, making sure that their guests were comfortable.

The next day word came that there were only enough spare parts to fix one of the engines. Another would have to be shipped from the states. In all, it ended up being a four day stay. Once the aircraft was tested and ready they boarded again, taking off for their new home, the United States.

They landed at McGuire Air Force Base outside Trenton, New Jersey. After deplaning, they were interviewed and processed in a building set up to handle the incoming refugees. Again they were provided quarters while waiting to depart for their sponsors. Everything they needed was provided. The friendship and generosity shown by the military during their journey contradicted everything they had been told of the American people by their government. The propaganda, force fed to them in school appeared to be nothing but falsehoods.

* * *

The following day they completed processing and were issued refugee cards. Phone contact was made with the respective sponsors. Instructions were given as to where each refugee could be found upon arrival at their destination. Brief descriptions of the persons and their clothing were given to help with identification, along with an affixed name tag.

Afterward the refugees were briefed on plans by the

American government to make all males of service age granted asylum perform mandatory military service. Eventually they were to be drafted, serving a minimum of two years. Like most others in the group, Miklós did not speak a word of English, though they gladly agreed to serve in the US military, grateful to be given an opportunity at freedom.

After breakfast the next day those with arrangements in order were issued a one-way train ticket and provided a bag lunch. Everyone said their goodbyes and lined up to depart for the railway station not far from base. Miklós would be on his way to the Detroit area, already inhabited by a sizeable population of Hungarian descent. A Little Budapest of sorts. Miklós would be joined on the trip by many others, a high percentage of refugees having sponsors there.

His relatives resided in the Detroit suburb of Lincoln Park, with Miklós' train ride taking the better part of a day to reach. Two would greet him based solely on the description given over the telephone, and the name tag affixed to the shoulder of his clothing. After the train pulled in, the station swelled with Hungarian refugees, most unable to read or speak English. Sponsors searched for arrivals, arrivals searched for sponsors, calling out each other's names hoping to be found, craning their necks above the crowd to catch a glimpse of a responding voice.

Miklós worked his way through the crowd. There were some joyous reunions, but mostly introductions of relatives having never met. Finally, through an opening between people, Miklós thought he spotted his younger cousin Irene, whose pictures he vaguely remembered.

It had been a while since looking at the photographs. She was a young teenager now. Walking over he was almost certain it was her, calling out "Irene, Irene!" She looked in the direction of the voice, knowing it likely Miklós. He was relieved to see her respond to his calls. She couldn't locate him through the throngs of people. Finally Miklós stood before her. "Irene?" "Yes, I'm Irene, Miklós?" "Miklós, igen. Falvai Miklós!" She hugged him, tears beginning to stream down her face. "I'm so glad you made it. Mom and dad couldn't be here. They sent me with our neighbor, Frank, to come pick you up." Frank and Miklós were introduced shaking hands. Frank was a neighbor and good friend of Miklós' uncle, living just a few houses down from them. An older, retired gentleman, Frank had offered to drive Irene down to the train station to retrieve Miklós. She explained "Father could not come to get you himself, he's working. It seems he could not get the day off." Miklós understood nothing she said, but politely nodded acknowledgement every now and then to let her know he was listening. She was talking away about how glad she was to see him, and that he had a safe journey and so on. Suddenly she realized "Oh, my, gosh! I'm sorry, I forgot, you probably don't speak English." Miklós shrugged and shook his head. Caught up in the moment she had reverted to English, her native tongue. She began explaining things to him in Magyarok, speaking fluently, having grown up among the Detroit area Hungarian community.

Making their way to the parking lot Miklós could hardly believe his eyes. He had never seen so many automobiles. There were more cars in this one parking lot than he had seen throughout his entire life. "Does everyone in this country have a car?" he asked. Both Frank and Irene began laughing and shaking their heads. "No. Not everyone. Why do you ask?" "I've never seen so many cars." "Oh, well, I would say most families have a car. Not everyone, though. My family doesn't have one. We came here in Frank's."

On the drive Miklós was impressed by the size and attractiveness of all the homes, with manicured lawns and automobiles in the driveways. To him every house appeared a mansion. All the roadways and interchanges, traffic lights, and overpasses; he had never known anything like it. The beautiful cars rolling down the highway were an overwhelming sight. Sitting in the back seat looking out the windows he tried to take it all in. There were even billboards of beautiful people with beautiful cars. Mit egy ország! *What a country!*

Pulling into the driveway Miklós was surprised by all the people outside to greet him, and the house was practically full. Extended family and friends from the neighborhood had gathered for his arrival. Just about everyone his aunt and uncle knew was there.

Overwhelmed, his emotions began welling up. Upon seeing his aunt and uncle he could not hold it in anymore and began crying. They hugged and kissed, and hugged some more. Everyone wanted to hug him or shake his hand. Tears of joy were streaming down Miklós' face, a mixture of relief and happiness upon seeing everyone, knowing he had found a new home. He was safe now, reunited with people that truly cared, hardly believing it was real. He had been through so much, traveled so far, and struggled against impossible odds. Yet here he was, safe and sound, all of this happening in the span of a few months. In just a short period Miklós had experienced more sorrow and joy than most people would in a lifetime.

Soon he was bombarded with questions, everyone curious about his adventure, his family and friends in Hungary, and the situation in general. Eventually someone got around to asking him if he spoke any English. "Nem" he responded. "*No*, I only know three words; sheriff, cowboy, and Colt 45!" This cracked everybody up. Who would have guessed Miklós was a fan of the American Western? They carried on about this for several minutes. It turned out that American Westerns were among the most popular films in Hungarian movie houses as he was growing up. "Well, you'll get to see plenty of Westerns here" his uncle told him. His aunt quipped "Yes, but you're going to have to learn a little more English than cowboys and guns I'm afraid!"

The neighborhood was a close knit community of Hungarians, many having emigrated over the years, now with extended families of their own born as Americans. Friends and neighbors would gather several times a week, enjoying the company of those they had grown close to. Like most communities with a large immigrant population, where people of a like language tend to network with one another, so too did the Lincoln Park Magyars. They were dependent on each other for both physical and social support. Miklós' impending arrival had been the neighborhood news for the past week. Keenly aware of the situation regarding Hungary, everyone was, of course, both interested and sympathetic to his plight.

* * *

Miklós' aunt and uncle had never owned a car. That was why Frank had brought Irene to the station. Miklós' uncle would ride a bike or take the bus, never really comfortable driving. A holdover from the old country perhaps, being a bit older when he arrived in America. And living right in the capitol of automobile manufacturing no less!

His uncle worked two jobs to support the family and own a home. In the early morning hours he would get up and ride the bus to work. In the afternoon, after arriving home, he would visit with the family if time permitted, then prepare for his afternoon job, riding his bike there, and then back home in the dark. Before moving to Lincoln Park, Miklós' aunt and uncle had owned a small grocery store in downtown Detroit. Irene would manage the store while her husband was at his day job. At the end of the day, after work, his uncle would go to the store and restock after closing for the night. As the family grew it became more difficult for his aunt to continue working days, and they decided to sell the store and move to the suburbs.

A few days passed, and as Miklós settled in he began looking for a job. The trick would be finding an employer offering a position requiring little familiarity with English. Ideally something labor intensive, requiring minimal written or verbal communications. His relatives helped by reading the classifieds and inquiring with friends and neighbors. Eventually Miklós landed a position at a car parts factory. Demand for labor was steady, automobile manufacturing the dominant industry in the area.

He was to operate a metal stamping machine. Familiar with running shop machinery in the mines Miklós was stamping metal in no time. Fortunate, since he would otherwise have needed to be instructed extensively in English regarding its operation. Like most machinery of that scale in the day, it was loud and dangerous. While conditions in the factory may have been safer than at others around the world, it was not without risks. Accidents occurred on a regular basis, sometimes through carelessness, other times from mechanical failure or lack of safeguards.

The work was monotonous, placing sheets of steel on a table-like platform that was machined to create a specific shape out of the metal when the stamp came down. Several thousand pounds of pressure were applied to shape the metal in one swift, but efficient, motion. The operator would open the press, place the metal on the machine and align it, then activate the press. Once the panel was stamped, it was removed and stacked with others waiting for delivery to the automobile factory's assembly line. Minimum quotas required the workers keep a steady pace.

Occasionally the machines jammed, or a piece of metal would stick, requiring the operator to reach in and clear the problem, in some cases even servicing the machine. One day as all the machines in Miklós' area were humming along he heard someone cry out from behind. As Miklós raised his press and removed the piece of metal he had just stamped, he turned toward the voice. Other workers were already rushing to the injured man's aid. "Raise it up, raise it up!" one of them yelled. "Oh my god, get his arm out" hollered another. Miklós dropped the panel he was holding and went to help. Once the man's arm was freed they laid him gently on the floor. "Tie it off or he'll bleed out!" One of the men took off his own shirt to use as a tourniquet. Somehow the victim's arm had gotten caught under the press when it came down, crushing it with such force that is was now hanging bloodied and limp next to him. The floor supervisor was already on the phone calling for an ambulance. Blood was everywhere, the machine crushing his arm into something barely recognizable.

The ambulance arrived a short while later, the worker rushed to the hospital. The incident ended their shift. There would have to be an investigation into the cause, the machine cleaned and repaired, and the area prepared for the next shift. The accident had shaken Miklós. He had witnessed industrial accidents before, but never expected anything like that. It gave him pause about returning to work.

The following day word arrived the man's arm had been amputated. There was no way it could be saved. Not the first time such an incident had taken place. In fact, while talking over lunch with some Hungarian speaking coworkers Miklós discovered it happened more often than he knew. "So, how about what happened to Joe yesterday, huh? I heard him yelling and turned around to look, and there he was, caught in the machine. I don't know what happened, but it sure scared the hell out of me." One of them replied "Unfortunately it happens every now and then. More than it should. I'd say someone loses an arm or a hand operating the presses every few months. Usually they get tired or careless and stop paying attention." He paused for a moment, reflecting on Joe, then said "Poor guy. He has a wife and a couple of kids. He really enjoyed playing ball with his son." For the remainder of lunch they ate in relative silence, alone in their thoughts about what the family must be going through.

Turned out the coworker's statement was accurate. A month and a half later another worker lost an arm. Miklós had been there only two months and in that short time witnessed two workers losing limbs manning the presses. One incident might be explained away as just an accident. A second one so soon was indicative of a dangerous situation. Alarm bells went off in Miklós' head. He decided it time to find a different line of work.

Seeking employment elsewhere while still working at the parts manufacturer, he soon landed a position with a shipbuilder. A friend of the family had recommended Miklós apply after hearing of the stamping accidents, and many Hungarians already worked this particular shipyard. During the interview he explained of his experience working in the mines back in Hungary welding, machining, framing, and the like. There were no immediate openings for a welder, but he was hired on as a basic helper in the meantime, partly to see what kind of a worker he was, and also to assess his industrial skills. If things worked out he could have the next available welding position.

His first day Miklós' supervisor instructed him in Hungarian "Why don't you go ahead up on the deck and have a look around. You know, get familiar with things and introduce yourself. Somebody will find something for you to do." "Rendben, *alright*, which way should I go." Pointing, the super said "Cross the plank up there near the top of the scaffolding and make a right when you're aboard. Then climb up the first ladder you see." Miklós nodded and walked along the slipway to board the ship. It was a long ways up, the large vessel being constructed in dry dock.

Once up on deck he found himself amidst a buzz of activity. Workers rolling carts of steel, welding torches throwing sparks, pneumatic hammers pounding rivets. It was not unlike working in the mine. Most around him were speaking Hungarian. He began walking, observing the work taking place. Occasionally he stopped to watch what someone was doing, familiarizing himself with the task being performed. As he watched a worker grind a weld joint a man appeared from his periphery, planting himself right in front of Miklós, spreading his feet wide, putting his arms forward one in front of the other, crouching slightly into an aggressive position and said "Rendben Magyar, nekiront nekem!" "*Alright Hungarian, come and get me!*" Startled, Miklós stepped back, unaware of the man's intentions. A smirk formed on the man's face, becoming a wide grin. "Imre!" Miklós shouted in a sudden outburst of recognition. It was his old wrestling nemesis and roommate. "How in the world are you?" "Hey Miklós, I never thought I'd see your ugly mug again." They shook hands and hugged, patting each other on the back. Imre inquired "So when did you get here?" "A few months ago. I've been staying with my aunt and uncle. I came across the Austrian border with Péter. Remember him from school? I've been working at an auto parts plant on the stamping line, but after I saw a couple of guys lose an arm I decided it was time to get out." Imre nodded. "I don't blame you. Not like you can't get hurt here, but I guess most jobs available to us Hunky's will have some sort of risk." "So, how long have you been here?" Miklós asked. "Not much longer than you. Managed to catch a train to the border and sneak across with my wife." "Wife - you're married?" Miklós asked surprised. Imre responded "You know that girl I was seeing? I showed you her picture, remember? When things got crazy somebody told us of a way out, and she had relatives here in the states. So we took a chance, and here we are." Miklós shook his head. He could not believe his luck running into Imre. "Well, glad to see you. You're the first familiar face I've come across since getting here, other than my relatives of course." "It's great to see you too, Miklós. Come on. I'll show you around and introduce you to the crew."

***

A couple of months passed and Miklós was promoted to welding, something he felt comfortable with. The work was hard, and the hours long, but he earned a good wage. His coworkers were a great group, hardworking, patient, and helpful, always looking out for each other. Miklós enjoyed the work, the environment, and most of all, his newfound home.

Managing to write his family, he informed them of his situation, finally letting them know he had arrived safe and sound. He described the adventure he and Péter had through Hungary and Austria, the stopover in

Iceland, and his eventual arrival in Detroit. Not too many of the scary details, for mama had undoubtedly worried enough already. He described to his father the car he had bought, an old clunker he was constantly working on, cobbling it together with parts from the junkyard. He figured that would impress papa. Heck, he was the first in the family to ever own a car! Why not? He was living in Detroit, *The Motor City*, automotive capitol of the world.

It took another month before receiving a reply letter. Things in Hungary had finally settled down to where the postal system was up and running again and mail was allowed to flow across the border. Slow, but moving nevertheless. They were relieved to hear Miklós had made the journey safely, finding his way to his aunt and uncle, and gainfully employed in America. Their village, and the rest of Hungary, had begun to pick up the pieces and carry on. The *Iron Curtain* was, however, as impregnable as ever. Miklós wondered if he might never see his family again.

Almost daily he found himself down in the hull of the ships, welding rib joints and plating. The work needed to be exacting, for a mistake here would not only risk the structural integrity of the vessel, but could also facilitate small leaks. His superiors were satisfied with the work, noting he was indeed an experienced welder. Unfortunately, the job lasted a total of only seven months, during which Miklós worked on the construction of two ore transport ships. Lacking firm orders for additional vessels, the company had to turn the workers loose until more work became available. Bids had been placed on a couple of contracts and it would probably be two months or so before there was anymore work. When the time came they would be notified.

Miklós had befriended a coworker by the name of Bertók, also growing up a fan of American Westerns. Together they decided to see America. With no work to be had, the time was as good as any, deciding to try and make it to the west coast. Upon arrival they would search for work in hopes of staying a while. They acquired some maps, planned their routes between points of interest, and pooled their money. Miklós' car was in such bad shape he decided to sell it rather than risk driving all that way. His aunt and uncle helped plan the trip, explaining how to read the roadmaps and signs, how to use the bus system, and how to get in contact with them if anything happened. Just because they spoke little English didn't mean they couldn't do it. Coming halfway across the world without speaking the local tongues hadn't stopped them yet.

Well, not speaking the language was merely one impediment to their adventure: The other being their lack of knowledge regarding economics. They managed to get as far as Cheyenne, Wyoming, before running out of money. "Miklós" Bertók said upon their arrival at the bus station "I'm out of money. How much do you have left?" "Enough for lunch I think. Not much more. I guess we need to find work and save up some more if we're going to continue."

They walked down the street and happened upon a diner, stopping in for a cup of coffee and a bite to eat. Sitting at the counter a waitress came over. "How are you boys doing today?" she inquired. "Coffee?" "Yes please" they responded. As she was pouring she examined them with an inquisitive look. "Where are you boys from?" "Detroit, Michigan." "Oh, just passing through?" "Not today. We need work" Bertók tried to explain. The waitress was helpful, asking some of the others at the counter about job prospects in the area, reporting back to the young men where they might go to find work. They listened intently, understanding some of her words, the three often having to communicate with hand gestures and drawing on napkins.

They paid their tab and left, seeking out the opportunities passed along in the diner. It was winter, and as they walked down the street a cold Arctic wind chilled them, blowing down across the plains from Canada. During their time in America they had picked up enough English to ask basic questions, soon finding the local office of a livestock company that was hiring. "Where did you say you boys are from?" asked the hiring manager. "We are from Detroit" replied Miklós. "You don't sound like you're from Detroit. You sound more like you're European or somethin'." The two looked at each other and shrugged. The man stared ponderously at them for a moment. "Alright, well I guess you'll do. Strong backs are what we're looking for, anyhow. Follow me. I'll show you where to catch the next bus out to the ranch." To the boys he looked like a real cowboy, wearing his ten gallon hat, flannel shirt, blue jeans, leather boots, and a big leather belt with a shiny buckle. They were going to be paid to be cowboys. How great was that! The young men were led out to the back of the building where several other men were already waiting. "Follow these guys. The next bus should be by shortly."

The ride out to the ranch took roughly an hour. They had never seen such wide open spaces before, except in those old black and white movies. The main gate was flanked by barbed wire fencing as far as the eye could see. On this particular ranch the company raised cattle, horses, and sheep. The foreman, a large burly man sporting a moustache, also dressed like a cowboy. He assigned the two working cattle; feeding, watering, and watching over them. Occasionally they had to herd steers between pens when it came time for transport. Not exactly the romantic cowboy image they had in mind when at first they had ventured west.

"You boys can stay in here" the foreman said walking them into an old barn, an introduction to their new living arrangements. Pointing to a loft above "Up there is where you sleep. There are a couple of mattresses and some blankets. Chow time is at 6:00 am in the mess hut, and the outhouse is around back of it. Work starts at 6:30 sharp." He proceeded to show them the well, the feed and water troughs, the hay loft, and of course the shovels.

"You boys know how to ride?" the foreman inquired, tilting his head toward the horses. The boys nodded and went to examine the animals. Miklos grabbed a saddle and strapped it to one of the horses as Bertók did the same. Satisfied, the foreman gestured for them to follow. "I'll get you set up with a couple of rifles." He led them over to a small mobile home set up on blocks that was utilized as his office. He unlocked the gun safe and took out a couple of old Winchester rifles. "You boys know how to shoot?" Miklos had used a carbine during the battle in Budapest, but Bertók had not. They nodded anyway. The guns looked just like those from the movies. "You might need these to chase off predators and rustlers. They make their presence known from time to time." He handed each of them a rifle and a box of ammo. They headed out and he mounted his own horse to show them around.

Both had learned horseback riding in Hungary and were able to keep up with the foreman. They would be watching over roughly six hundred head of cattle in shifts, four hours on, and four hours off. Luckily during their stint on the ranch they never needed to fire the rifles. Just as well, since half the time they shivered so much they probably would not have been able to aim accurately anyway.

The meals were paltry, consisting of a small breakfast of eggs and toast, and a basic dinner, usually a steak and a potato. There were no facilities for hygiene to speak of, giving themselves the occasional sponge bath using ice cold well water in the middle of winter. With only cow chips as fuel, it wasn't worth trying to boil water. That, or slowly dismantle the barn to make fires. Sometimes it's just better to go without.

It was a barn in the most primitive sense. Large gaps between the wooden planks allowed the wind to blow through freely, and there were holes in the roof where snow would fall upon them as they slept. The barn doors were barely functional, with the horses penned just below the loft. Cleaning the stalls daily they got used to living with the smell after a while.

They labored in the sun and snow, day in and day out,

dumping the feed into the troughs that went in one end of the cows, and shoveling what was left of it that came out the other end. They did, however, get to do some of the more cowboy-like things, such as riding and herding strays.

After two weeks their first payday arrived. The foreman summoned them to his office to collect. He sat there with his adding machine performing some calculations. "Let's see, we have room and board", tap-tap-tap, "taxes", tap-tap, "and transportation fee" tap. He wrote some notes, finally counting out the money and handing it over. "Two dollars?" Bertók said incredulously. "What's this?" The foreman looked at them as though surprised by the reaction. "Well, you didn't think the food and accommodations were free, did'ja?" The two looked at each other. "No way" said Miklós. "We can't stay here for a dollar a week. Are you crazy?" Now the foreman was the one acting incredulous. "Well, if you don't like it, you can always leave." Believing a couple of foreigners wouldn't have any choice he thought he could call their bluff.

Well, they weren't bluffing. "We can't stay here for a dollar a week" Miklós told Bertók as they exited the office. Bertók responded "Yes, but how will we get back to Detroit? We can't travel back on a couple of dollars." Miklós knew there was only one thing they could do. "Let's head back to town and call my aunt. I'll try and get her to wire us some money for a ticket back." The boys returned to the barn, collected their few belongings, and caught the next bus from the ranch back to Cheyenne.

In town they located a wire transfer station and paid to

make a long distance call. Miklos explained their situation to his aunt and if only she would wire them some money for the bus ride home he would pay her back as soon as the shipyard job restarted. She agreed, sending the money within a couple of hours. They returned to the bus station, each of them purchasing a one-way ticket to Detroit. Their short-lived careers as cowboys had come to an end. They spent their last dollar getting a bite to eat in Lincoln, Nebraska.

* * *

The timing of their arrival back in Detroit could not have been better. Within days of their return they received a call from the shipyard. The contract for the two vessels was awarded to the company and the order placed sooner than expected. They reported back to work the following day.

Attending the briefings Miklós was frustrated by his inability to understand English. He decided then and there to make learning the language a priority. That night he talked it over with his relatives. They suggested he ought to try the University of Michigan. That would be the most likely place to find people that could help.

Miklós worked another eight months before heading off to the university for English lessons, long enough to save up for the trip and pay back his aunt and uncle. He packed some clothing and hopped a bus for Ann Arbor, about thirty five miles from Lincoln Park. A neighbor had provided a contact on campus to show him around, someone that spoke both Hungarian and

English.

If felt good to be back in a university setting, his own academic aspirations having ended abruptly. He needed to find a place to stay long term, though. He could not afford residing in a hotel for several months. With the help of his contact he located the student union postings for off-campus housing, soon renting a room from a retired professor.

Having neither the money nor the qualifications to formally enter the university and become matriculated he was undeterred. Ever resourceful, he sought out the wrestling coach. *Perhaps*, he thought, *I could swing a deal sparring and working for the wrestling team in exchange for English lessons*. His contact put him in touch with the coach. Translating the conversation, they discussed Miklós' situation, and the coach decided to make a few phone calls. "Well, they agreed" he said hanging up the phone. "Unusual as it is, the assistant dean thought if nothing else Miklós deserved a shot just for his perseverance. He can start being tutored tomorrow. Follow me and I'll show you around the gym." The coach gave them a tour and explained what Miklós' responsibilities would be then handed him a schedule.

The coach was pleasantly surprised with Miklós wrestling skills. It was good to have somebody from another country demonstrating a different style, providing his team another perspective on the sport. Likewise, Miklós enjoyed being able to wrestle again. Something he had not done for a while, realizing how much he missed it.

The English tutors were comprised mostly of students born to parents of Hungarian descent that were attending UM. Speaking Hungarian in the home growing up while attending American schools, they were fluent in both languages. This made Miklós a quick study, and he was soon speaking practical English.

After three months at university it was time to return to the shipyard. He was now the only one of his crew that comprehended English. Often an American engineer or manager would need to discuss something with the men, and it could be frustrating to explain or instruct without translation. From then on whenever the guys needed to speak to someone in English Miklós would get "Hey, Miklós, go ahead, talk to that guy and translate for us, you know English." He had become the crew's official translator.

* * *

A few months passed and men of age received notice that they were to be drafted into the US Army. Miklos had no desire to enter the army and become infantry, deciding instead to investigate whether there might be a different branch of the military more suited to him. Locating the area's Air Force recruiter Miklós sidestepped the army and volunteered. At least he might spend time around airplanes. Now that he could speak English relatively well, and was to become a US serviceman, he decided it was time to Americanize his name. He would join as Nicholas, or Nick for short.

Passing basic, he shipped out a couple of weeks later, assigned to a unit that performed refrigeration and air conditioning maintenance. His shop skills, especially welding and electrical, had made him a natural for the job. Transferred to a base in Virginia, Nick was trained in all aspects of the cooling industry, a vocation not often associated with the military. Although, it has been said an army runs on its stomach. Refrigeration certainly plays a major role in delivering and storing the necessary provisions for a modern military. He enjoyed the work, acquiring valuable skills along the way; additional skills that would be useful upon his discharge from the military.

Given the experiences of those first eighteen years, exciting as they might have been, the rest of his life in America, though comparatively mundane, was certainly preferred to the years spent in his tumultuous youth.

Epilogue

Within a few years Nick had decided to follow his passion for flight, and began taking flying lessons, hoping to someday make a living as a pilot. Eventually he earned his pilot's license for single engine aircraft, then multiengine, followed by flight engineer, and ultimately becoming a flight instructor for the very company he had taken lessons from.

Along the way Nick earned his citizenship, raised four children, and found a career with the FAA until retirement. His extraordinary journey to America provided him with what might, in the end, be ultimately considered an ordinary, yet welcome life.

* * *

After being freed from prison during the unrest in 1956 and the subsequent quelling of the uprising by the Soviet military, Cardinal József Mindszenty sought and was granted asylum in the US embassy in Budapest, where he remained as an outspoken critic of communism until he was granted passage out of Hungary in 1971. He spent his remaining years living in exile, passing away in 1975.

Around two thirds of the Sopron University student body, and about half of the faculty fled Hungary in 1956. A good many of them were granted asylum in Canada, joining the University of British Columbia Forestry department. In all, Canada accepted approximately 38,000 Hungarian refugees.

With the eventual fall of the Soviet Union and the *Iron Curtain*, Hungary became a free and democratic state. While it had been treated a little more liberally after 1956 than many of the other Soviet Bloc countries, it remained under communist control. By the 1980's, some aspects of capitalism were allowed to creep into the Hungarian system, and with the uprising in Poland, and the fall of the Berlin Wall, momentum pushed the East European countries toward freedom. They would, however, have a long and difficult road to economic sustainability in the years that followed.

When looking back on the experiences of Miklós, the governments, and the people that forced war and expatriation on him and his fellow citizens, one can't help but reflect upon what might have otherwise been. The forces that had created such hardship ultimately led those people to a better life in the West, where freedom prevailed for those that survived, creating the opportunity for this story to be told.

ABOUT THE AUTHOR

Originally from Virginia, I moved to Florida in High School, eventually settling in South Florida, where I currently reside, enjoying the climate and marine activities provided by the subtropical location. A software engineer by training, I have always been an avid reader, and always wanted to try my hand at writing.

For years people had urged my father to put his story to the written word, but he just never seemed to find the time. Given his incredible journey through the turmoil of mid-twentieth century eastern Europe, and his eventual flight to the United States, I decided to chronicle his early life as my first novel. His experiences certainly provided ample material to weave an amazing story.

Appendix A The Magyarok (Hungarian) Alphabet

A   Á   B   C   Cs   D   Dz   Dzs   E   É   F

G   Gy   H   I   Í   J   K   L   Ly   M   N

Ny   O   Ó   Ö   Ő   P   (Q)   R   S   Sz   T

Ty   U   Ú   Ü   Ű   V   (W)   (X)   (Y)   Z   Zs

Letter	Name	Pronunciation (approximate English)
A	a	f**a**ll, b**a**ll, m**o**d
Á	á	sm**i**le, f**i**nd
B	bé	**b**rick, kno**b**
C	cé	ba**ts**
Cs	csé	**ch**air
D	dé	**d**im, pa**d**
Dz	dzé	Hu**ds**on
Dzs	dzsé	**j**am, **G**eorge, ju**dg**e
E	e	p**e**n, k**e**pt
É	é	h**ey**, caf**é**
F	ef	**f**ine, **ph**one

G	gé	**g**ate, fo**g**
Gy	gyé	Not used in English. Similar to British **d**ue or **d**ew
H	há	**h**igh, **h**ot
I	i	**i**n, br**i**ck, th**i**n
Í	í	n**ee**d, b**ea**n
J	jé	**y**es, plain
K	ká	**k**ept, pee**k**
L	el	**l**and, pee**l**
Ly	ely	he**y**, fra**y**
M	em	**m**any, ti**m**e
N	en	ma**n**y, fi**n**d
Ny	eny	**n**ew, **nu**de
O	o	h**o**rse, b**o**ring
Ó	ó	n**o**, s**ew**, fl**ow**
Ö	ö	Like German Ö, not used in English but closest to b**u**rn.
Ő	ő	Not used in English; a longer, more closed variant of Ö.
P	pé	**p**edal, **p**ee**p**
(Q)	kú	Appears in foreign words.

R   er   Not used in English, pronounced like Spanish R.

S   es   fi**sh**, **sh**ine

T   té   **t**ap, fla**t**, s**t**ree**t**

Ty   tyé   Not used in English. Similar to **stew**ard or S**tu**art.

U   u   r**u**de, d**u**ke

Ú   ú   p**oo**l, d**o**

Ü   ü   Not used in English. Used like German Ü. A shorter ű.

Ű   ű   No corresponding sound in English.

V   vé   lo**v**e, **v**endor

(W)   dupla vé   Double v instead of double u. Only used for foreign words.

(X)   iksz   Only used for foreign words or names.

(Y)   ipszilon   Only used for foreign words or names.

Z   zé   de**s**ert, **z**ebra

Zs   zsé   mea**s**ure, **g**enre

The letters of the Hungarian alphabet are not unlike those of English. Many pronunciations are the same as those in most European languages. Hungarian contains several additional vowels, having a number of phonetic "letters" represented by more than one character. Several consonants are pronounced differently from most other languages.

Consonants:

Most Hungarian consonants approximate the English pronunciation with some notable exceptions. Most are forms of **c**, **s**, and **z**. The following consonants are pronounced differently than their English counterparts:

> **c** - Pronounced like English TS, as in *bats*.
> **j** - Pronounced like English Y, as in *yell*.
> **s** - Pronounced like English SH, as in *ship*.

Magyar contains several consonant pairs representing a single spoken sound. These digraphs, as they are called, are designated as members of the alphabet in Hungarian. Dictionaries index them as separate letters.

> **cs** - Pronounced like CH, as in ***ch**air*.
>
> **dz** - Pronounced like DS separately, such as in *Hu**ds**on*.
>
> **dsz** - Pronounced like J or soft G, as in ***j**ust* or gender.
>
> **gy** - Pronounced similar to DG, as in *ju**dg**e*, but toward the back of the mouth.
> **ly** - Pronounced like an L and Y simultaneously.
> **ny** - Pronounced like an N and Y simultaneously, as in Spanish **ñ** or Italian **gn**.

sz - Pronounced like S, as in *send*.

ty - Pronounced like a T and Y simultaneously, similar to *stew* or *Stuart*.

zs - Pronounced like ZH or hard SH, as in *genre* or *measure*.

Vowels:

Magyarok uses fourteen distinctive yet symmetrical vowels, each one signified by a fixed character, and used to pronounce a precise sound. All accents and dots are required since many Hungarian words are spelled exactly the same, except for the characters with these diacritical marks. The short vowels are **a e i o ö u ü**. The long vowels are **á é í ó ő ú ű**.

Appendix B Some Facts about Hungary

Map of Hungary. The town of Csékút was located near Ajka, in the west-central part of the country, north of Lake Balaton. Csékút was located at Longitude: 17° 34' 0" East, and Latitude: 47° 6' 0" North in west central Magyarország, or Hungary as it is known in the west. In 1961 the towns of Padrag, to the south, and Csékút were united as Padragkút. The town of Veszprém is located just southeast of Ajka. Sopron can be found to the northwest, near the border of Austria.

The capital, Budapest, is located in the north-central part of the country. It is actually named for the twin cities of Buda and Pest, separated by the Danube

River.

Lake Balaton is the largest lake in Central Europe and has always been the premier tourist retreat in the region. Fed by the Zala River at the western end it eventually flows into the Sió River on the eastern side. It is a relatively shallow lake for its size, ranging in depth from about ten feet (3.2 meters) to forty feet (12.2 meters), covering approximately 229 square miles (592 square kilometers), with 147 miles (236km) of shoreline.

Flag of Hungary.

A flag and propaganda poster of the Hungarian Arrow Cross Party.

Translation
  Despite all...!

Aircraft like those involved with dogfights over Hungary.

German Me109 fighters.

Soviet Pe-2 Dive Bombers.

Soviet MiG-3 fighters.

A very young Miklós.

Mother Margit, brother József, and father József.

Outside their home on József's motorcycle.

Iron Cross, Iron Curtain, Iron Will

US Air Force Douglas C-118 Liftmaster like the one that brought Miklós to America.

Miklós along the shore of Lake Michigan shortly after arriving in the United States.

Miklós with yours truly.

Made in the USA
Charleston, SC
24 November 2012